The Philosophy of Cognitive-Behavioural Therapy (CBT)

This exciting new edition of *The Philosophy of Cognitive-Behavioural Therapy (CBT)* demonstrates how techniques and concepts from Socratic philosophy, especially Stoicism, can be integrated into the practise of CBT and other forms of psychotherapy. What can we learn about psychological therapy from ancient philosophers? Psychotherapy and philosophy were not always separate disciplines. Here, Donald Robertson explores the relationship between ancient Greek philosophy and modern cognitive-behavioural psychotherapy.

The founders of CBT described Stoicism as providing the "philosophical origins" of their approach and many parallels can be found between Stoicism and CBT, in terms of both theory and practise. Starting with hypnotism and early twentieth century rational psychotherapy and continuing through early behaviour therapy, rational-emotive behaviour therapy (REBT), and cognitive-behavioural therapy (CBT), the links between Stoic philosophy and modern psychotherapy are identified and explained. This book is the first detailed account of the influence of Stoic philosophy upon modern psychotherapy. It provides a fascinating insight into the revival of interest in ancient Western philosophy as a guide to modern living. It includes many concepts and techniques, which can be readily applied in modern psychotherapy or self-help.

This new edition, covering the growth in third-wave CBT, including mindfulness and acceptance-based therapies, will appeal to any mental health practitioner working in this area, as well as students and scholars of these fields.

Donald Robertson is a cognitive-behavioural psychotherapist, writer, and trainer. He specializes in the treatment of anxiety and in the relationship between ancient philosophy and modern psychotherapy. He is the author of six books on philosophy and psychotherapy, including *The Practice of Cognitive-Behavioural Hypnotherapy: A Manual for Evidence-Based Clinical Hypnosis* (2013).

Praise for the First Edition:

"Robertson rightly reminds us of how much CBT owes its philosophical origins to the Stoics but, sadly, how often this debt is insufficiently acknowledged. He urges us to redirect our attention to the past to see how modern CBT still has much to learn from its ancient precursors. Highly recommended."

Michael Neenan, *Co-Director of the CBT Programme,*
Centre for Stress Management, Bromley, Kent, UK

"Many of us have felt the need for a book that covers the underlying philosophy of the cognitive-behavioural therapies in much greater depth. This book is a fascinating read and could be considered as either a prequel or a sequel to the standard textbook read by a trainee or experienced cognitive-behavioural or rational emotive practitioner who wants to understand these approaches to therapy within an historical framework."

Professor Stephen Palmer, *PhD, FARBT, FBACP,*
Director of the Centre for Stress Management, London, UK

"The author has uncovered a wealth of connections between modern cognitive-behavioural therapies and ancient Stoic philosophy. It should be read by anyone interested in understanding the historical roots of CBT or in learning about how ancient psychotherapeutic methods can add to the modern therapist's toolkit."

Tim LeBon, *UKCP registered psychotherapist and*
author of Wise Therapy

The Philosophy of Cognitive-Behavioural Therapy (CBT)

Stoic Philosophy as Rational and Cognitive Psychotherapy

Second Edition

Donald Robertson

Routledge
Taylor & Francis Group

LONDON AND NEW YORK

Second edition published 2020
by Routledge
2 Park Square, Milton Park, Abingdon, Oxon, OX14 4RN

and by Routledge
52 Vanderbilt Avenue, New York, NY 10017

Routledge is an imprint of the Taylor & Francis Group, an informa business

First edition published by Routledge 2010

British Library Cataloguing-in-Publication Data
A catalogue record for this book is available from the British Library

Library of Congress Cataloging-in-Publication Data
A catalog record for this book has been requested

ISBN: 978-0-367-21987-1 (hbk)
ISBN: 978-0-367-21914-7 (pbk)
ISBN: 978-0-429-26870-0 (ebk)

Typeset in Times New Roman
by Apex CoVantage, LLC

Contents

Note on translations

All quotations from Epictetus' *Discourses*, *Handbook*, and *Fragments* are taken from Robin Hard's translation unless otherwise specified (Epictetus, trans. 1995). All quotations from Marcus Aurelius' *The Meditations* are taken from Robin Hard's translation unless otherwise specified (Marcus Aurelius, trans. 2011). Quotations from Plato are taken from John M. Cooper's edited *Complete Works* (Plato, trans. 1997). Where necessary, certain translations have been quoted from other sources or modified, as indicated in the text.

Foreword to the first edition

Cognitive-behavioural therapies are at the cutting edge of modern psychological therapeutic interventions. They are evidence based and, therefore, are underpinned by much research. In the United Kingdom (UK), the National Institute for Health and Clinical Excellence (NICE) has recommended cognitive-behavioural therapy for depression and anxiety-related disorders such as panic attacks, obsessive- compulsive behaviour, body dysmorphic disorder, and post-traumatic stress disorder (e.g., NICE, 2004, 2005, 2006, 2009). It is no surprise that this interests stakeholders wishing to provide cost-effective psychological therapies to their customers, that is, the public, in order to improve well-being and reduce financial expenditure. In the UK, the government has taken the next logical step and funded cognitive-behavioural therapy training as part of the Improving Access to Psychological Therapies (IAPT) programme. Stressed, depressed, and anxious citizens cost countries billions of pounds, according to the research data, and, understandably, reducing absenteeism from work due to psychological illness is an attractive target to focus on. An effective IAPT programme can benefit both the country and the individual.

Cognitive-behavioural therapy has become one of the main approaches for dealing effectively with a wide range of psychological disorders, and this has led to a large increase in the training of health professionals in this approach, especially within the UK. Key handbooks available to trainees, based on Dr Aaron Temkin Beck's cognitive therapy (Beck, 1976) or Dr Albert Ellis' rational emotive behaviour therapy (REBT) (Ellis, 1958), only briefly, if at all, cover the historical roots of these therapies. Ellis, in his publications, is often more explicit about the early origins of REBT in comparison to the books on cognitive and cognitive-behavioural therapy.

Yet, for many of us, something is missing from most of the literature. What has been needed is a book that covers the underlying philosophy of the cognitive-behavioural therapies in much greater depth. This book, *The Philosophy of Cognitive-Behavioural Therapy (CBT)*, by Donald Robertson, provides us with the missing link between the theory and the philosophy. This book takes us on a historical journey through millennia and highlights the relevant philosophies and the ideas of the individual philosophers that can inform modern cognitive-behavioural therapies. This book also includes some therapeutic techniques that seem to be modern, yet were developed and written about many years ago. It is a fascinating read. *The Philosophy of Cognitive-Behavioural Therapy (CBT)* could be considered as either a prequel or a sequel to the standard textbook read by a trainee or experienced cognitive-behavioural or rational emotive practitioner who wants to understand these approaches to therapy within a historical framework.

Professor Stephen Palmer PhD FAREBT FBACP
Director of the Centre for Stress Management,
London, UK July 2010

References

Beck, A. T. (1976). *Cognitive Therapy and The Emotional Disorders*. New York: International Universities Press.

Ellis, A. (1958). Rational psychotherapy. *The Journal of General Psychology, 59*: 35–49.

NICE (2004). *Anxiety: Management of Anxiety (Panic Disorder, with or without Agoraphobia, and Generalised Anxiety Disorder) in Adults in Primary, Secondary and Community Care*. http://guidance.nice.org.uk/CG22/guidance/pdf/English.

NICE (2005). *Post-Traumatic Stress Disorder: The Management of PTSD in Adults and Children in Primary and Secondary Care*. http://guidance.nice.org.uk/CG26/guidance/pdf/English.

NICE (2006). *Obsessive – Compulsive Disorder: Core Interventions in the Treatment of Obsessive – Compulsive Disorder and Body Dysmorphic Disorder*. http://guidance.nice.org.uk/CG31/guidance/pdf/English.

NICE (2009). *Depression in Adults (update): Depression: The Treatment and Management of Depression in Adults National Clinical Practice Guideline 90*. www.nice.org.uk/nicemedia/live/12329/45896/45896.pdf.

Introduction

Philosophy and psychotherapy

> Philosophy does not promise to secure anything *external* for man . . . the subject-matter of the art of living is each person's own life.
>
> (Epictetus, Discourses, 1.15.2, my italics)

Why should modern psychotherapists be interested in philosophy, especially *ancient* philosophy? Why should *philosophers* be interested in psychotherapy? There exists a kind of mutual attraction between what are today two thoroughly distinct disciplines. Indeed, it was not always the case that they *were* distinct. Ancient philosophy was frequently concerned with what the French philosopher Michel Foucault has called the *technê tou biou*, or "art of living" (Foucault, 1986). As the Stoic philosopher, Seneca, writes:

> Philosophy teaches us to act, not to speak; it exacts of every man that he should live according to his own standards, that his life should not be out of harmony with his words, and that, further, his inner life should be of one hue and not out of harmony with all his activities. This, I say, is the highest duty and the highest proof of wisdom – that deed and word should be in accord, that a man should be equal to himself under all conditions, and always the same.
>
> (Seneca, *Moral Letters to Lucilius*, 20.2)

Philosophy, to a large extent, has always been about transforming the life of the philosopher, in a manner broadly resembling modern psychotherapy or self-help. As far back the Socrates of Plato's *Gorgias*, philosophy has been compared to the art of medicine for *psyche*, the mind or soul. In other words, what we now call "psychotherapy" was explicitly recognized as an aspect of philosophy in ancient Greece and Rome.

Some have pointed to this in order to criticize modern psychology. The behaviourist B. F. Skinner once complained:

> Greek physics and biology are now of historical interest only (no modern physicist would turn to Aristotle for help), but the dialogues of Plato are still

assigned to students and cited as if they threw light on human behavior. Aristotle could not have understood a page of modern physics or biology, but Socrates and his friends would have little trouble in following most current discussions of human affairs.

(Skinner, 1971, pp. 5–6)

However, arguably, the relevance of ancient Socratic philosophy to modern psychotherapy is not simply an embarrassing sign of slow progress in the field of scientific psychology but, rather, an indication that many concepts and strategies effective in helping people manage their emotions are fairly simple, and even perennial. (I would wager, incidentally, that a time-travelling Aristotle, or Socrates, would have been able to make his way through most of Skinner's own books fairly easily and to have more than held his own in a pretty interesting debate with him.) In any case, as Joseph Wolpe and Arnold Lazarus, two of the founders of behaviour therapy, wrote:

> While the modern behavior therapist deliberately applies principles of learning to his therapeutic operations, empirical behavior therapy is probably as old as civilization – if we consider civilization as having begun when man first did things to further the well-being of other men. From the time that this became a feature of human life there must have been occasions when a man complained of his ills to another who advised or persuaded him of a course of action. In a broad sense, this could be called behavior therapy whenever the behavior itself was conceived as the therapeutic agent. Ancient writings contain innumerable behavioral prescriptions that accord with this broad conception of behavior therapy.

(Wolpe & Lazarus, 1966, pp. 1–2)

Indeed, ancient literature can be seen as prescribing both *behavioural* and *cognitive* remedies, which bear a striking resemblance to some of those found in modern cognitive-behavioural therapy (CBT). By reconsidering the received wisdom concerning the history of these closely related subjects, we can learn a great deal about both philosophy and psychotherapy, under whose broad heading I also include potentially *solitary* pursuits such as "self-help" and "personal development".

- *Philosophers* can gain insight into how modern evidence-based psychotherapy might provide ideas for the practical application of familiar philosophical wisdom.
- Psychotherapists are likely to discover new practical techniques, strategies, and concepts, which may come as a surprise, as they are often consistent with modern therapy models but relatively neglected by them.
- Moreover, both therapists and philosophers may also discover the possibility of fitting the existing theory and practise of their profession into the

framework of a larger philosophical vision of the universe and man's place within it and even find a whole *way of life* consistent with their professional activities.

It almost goes without saying that ancient philosophical therapy techniques are *not* based upon randomized controlled trials (RCTs) and lack any direct empirical support of this kind. That may sit uncomfortably with modern proponents of evidence-based practise in psychotherapy. I should emphasize that I am not about to propose that empirically-supported treatments, or principles, should be abandoned in favour of a therapy that predates the Book of Revelations. However, as we shall see, modern psychotherapy is already indebted to certain aspects of classical philosophy, and this common ground may provide inspiration for deriving other concepts and techniques from ancient literature, which can themselves be put to the test empirically in due course.

The origins of philosophical therapy

Many modern psychotherapists appear to think that Sigmund Freud, the founder of psychoanalysis, was the *first* psychotherapist. Those who look a little further into the history of the subject will realize that Freud not only had contemporary rivals, such as Pierre Janet and Paul Dubois, but had himself trained, albeit briefly, in hypnotic psychotherapy. Freud visited the two leading centres of his day, attending the Salpêtrière lectures of Jean-Martin Charcot and the "Nancy school" of Hippolyte Bernheim.

Modern psychotherapy first began to coalesce toward the end of the nineteenth century, around the dominant schools of hypnotherapy. Hypnotic psychotherapy itself originated over half a century prior to psychoanalysis, in 1841, when the Scottish surgeon James Braid first attempted to take the therapeutic practises of Mesmerism and reinterpret them in the light of Scottish realist ("common sense") philosophy of mind, substituting the psychological laws of association, habit, sympathy, and suggestion, etc., for the supernatural theory of "animal magnetism". That is, broadly speaking, how I conceive of the origins of modern psychotherapy as a branch of scientific medicine (Robertson, 2009).

Of course, there may also be a recognition that psychotherapeutic practises resemble in some way the much older theological notions of pastoral religious counselling and confession. However, many *non*-Christians perceive the Christian approach as doctrinaire in a way that somewhat restricts the value of any analogy with modern psychotherapy. Some therapists are aware that ancient Oriental practises such as chanting or meditation may serve a kind of psychotherapeutic purpose, but these are often shrouded in exotic symbolism and religious ideas alien, and often inscrutable, to our culture.

There may even be a sense that throughout European history various authors have hinted at obscure self-help techniques or contemplative exercises, fragmentary and fleeting, which they appear to have stumbled across in seeking a balm for their own troubled minds. In the literature of theology, secular self-help, philosophy, biography, fiction, and poetry, nuggets of therapeutic advice, concepts, and even psychological exercises can be found. For instance, in the *Remedies for Love* of Ovid, the *Spiritual Exercises* of St Ignatius of Loyola, the *Consolations* of Boethius, in Montaigne and Bacon's *Essays*, Spinoza's *Ethica*, Bertrand Russell's *The Conquest of Happiness*, and Tom Wolfe's novel *A Man in Full*, to pick just a handful of the most pertinent examples.

However, there is an important sense in which psychotherapy, even as we know it today, can trace its roots much farther back, perhaps all the way back into prehistory, before such ideas were committed to writing. Modern psychotherapy, especially in the form of CBT, the most "modern" of our contemporary schools, can also be viewed as part of an ancient therapeutic tradition derived from the informal philosophical circle surrounding Socrates and, therefore, stretch back to Athens in the fifth century BC. Of the various schools of Socratic philosophy, the one that bears the strongest therapeutic orientation is undoubtedly Stoicism, especially that of the later Roman schools. According to Galen, physician to the Stoic Emperor Marcus Aurelius, Chrysippus, one of the founders of Stoicism, emphasized the role of philosopher as that of "physician of the soul", someone whom we would now refer to as a *psychotherapist* (see Sellars, 2003, p. 68).

Out of the various contemporary schools of psychotherapy, Socratic philosophy in general and the Stoic school in particular definitely bear the strongest similarity to CBT. Most forms of CBT are indebted to Aaron Beck's "cognitive therapy" approach, which styles its method on Socratic questioning, loosely construed. "Cognitive therapy uses primarily the Socratic method" (Beck, Emery, & Greenberg, 2005, p. 167). Narrowing our focus even further, the Stoicism of Epictetus and the rational emotive behaviour therapy (REBT) of Albert Ellis, a major precursor of CBT, are perhaps the two schools of thought through which the ancient and modern traditions of psychotherapy may come closest to meeting, and between them a bridge may perhaps be built which can allow a commerce of ideas to flow between ancient and modern traditions.

To return to the questions with which we began: *why*, then, should philosophers and psychotherapists be concerned with one another? First of all, the difference between what the ancients did and what modern therapy does lies largely, but not exclusively, in its *scope*. Philosophy answers a craving for something more expansive; it embraces the *totality* of things through their *essence*. It has the capacity to raise the head of modern psychotherapy and tilt its gaze upwards toward the vastness around us, perhaps even the whole of time and space, as Socrates and the Stoics actually recommended.

It is precisely this "bigger" philosophical picture that, I think, the psychotherapist-*qua*-psychotherapist must wrestle with at some point in his or her career. When therapists go home from work, leaving their clients behind, as they lie in bed at night, they must wonder about certain things. They must ask themselves what therapy *means* and what role it plays in *life*. Must its truths stay locked up in the consulting room when the lights are switched off and the doors locked shut overnight, or should they spread and grow, touching other areas of life, colouring things as a whole? How does a therapist relate to God? How does he or she relate to the *absence* of God? What do they *make* of life itself? What happens when, in quiet contemplation, they put *themselves* on the treatment couch, or when they attempt to think of their relationship with the universe itself, in its totality, using the intellectual tools of their trade? What is the *point* of doing psychotherapy? These are the philosophical questions that must surely stir in the minds of many professional psychotherapists, and which philosophy can at least strive to answer.

Recent decades have seen growing interest in movement called "philosophical practice" (Marinoff, 2002) and other attempts to promote philosophy outside of the academic institutions as something that "ordinary people" do in cafés, or apply to their own life problems in the form of individual counselling or group sessions with a quasi-therapeutic style. Even many academic philosophers appear to crave, quite understandably, a return to the days when philosophical discourse was meant to be rooted in corresponding behavioural and emotional transformation and not *merely* an "academic" pursuit abstracted from any practical application. The ancients conceived of the ideal philosopher as a veritable *warrior* of the mind, a spiritual hero akin to Hercules himself, but since the demise of the Hellenistic schools, the philosopher has become something more bookish, not a warrior, but a mere *librarian* of the mind.

James Bond Stockdale

James (or "Jim") Stockdale mentions the English philosopher Alfred North Whitehead once saying that if Plato were to return to life today he would first ask to be introduced not to an academic but to a *boxing* champion (Stockdale, 1995, p. 17). If the Stoic philosopher Epictetus had lived in modern times, the person he would have wanted to be introduced to would probably be *Stockdale* himself. Stockdale's story deserves to be mentioned here as a striking example of ancient Stoicism in the face of modern adversity.

> On September 9, 1965, I flew at 500 knots right into a flak trap, at tree-top level, in a little A-4 airplane – the cockpit walls not even three feet apart – which I couldn't steer after it was on fire, its control system shot out. After ejection I had about thirty seconds to make my last statement in freedom before I landed in the main street of a little [North Vietnamese] village right ahead. And so help me, I whispered to myself: "Five years down there [in captivity], at least. I'm leaving the world of technology and entering the world of Epictetus".
>
> (Stockdale, 1995, p. 189)

At the outbreak of US involvement in the Vietnam War, Stockdale (1923–2005) was captured by a mob of 15 villagers who beat him to within an inch of his life, snapping his leg and leaving him permanently crippled. The irony, not lost on him, was that he was left just like Epictetus, the crippled slave whose ancient *Handbook* (*Encheiridion*) of Stoic philosophy Stockdale had previously devoured after studying philosophy as a Master's student at Stanford University.

Stockdale was taken prisoner by the North Vietnamese and incarcerated in Hanoi where, as the highest-ranking US naval officer, the only wing commander to survive an ejection over enemy territory, he assumed charge of a community of captured soldiers, which, at its largest, numbered in excess of 400 men. Stockdale said he never actually saw a Vietnamese POW camp as portrayed in the movies. He was imprisoned in an old French colonial "dungeon", which formed part of a large communist prison called *Hao Lo* or the "Hanoi Hilton". He described it as part psychiatric clinic, part reform school. The Americans, kept alongside Vietnamese criminals, were subjected to constant attempted psychological reprogramming by professional torturers and prison officers. During that time, as a prisoner of war, for *seven and a half years*, Stockdale spent four years in isolation, two years in leg irons, and was tortured 15 times, in a manner known as "taking the ropes".

> And if I were asked, "What are the benefits of a Stoic life?" I would probably say, "It is an ancient and honorable package of advice on how to stay out of the clutches of those who are trying to get you on the hook, trying to give you a feeling of obligation, trying to get moral leverage on you, to force you to bend to their will". Because I first reaped its benefits in an extortionist prison of torture, I could go on and say, "It's a formula for maintaining self-respect and dignity in defiance of those who would break your spirit for their own end".
>
> (Stockdale, 1995, p. 177)

Stockdale's experience obviously bears comparison with the better-known story of Victor Frankl, a Jewish psychiatrist who was incarcerated in Auschwitz concentration camp during the Second World War and published his bestselling self-help book *Man's Search for Meaning* after his release (Frankl, 1959). However, although both men arrived at similar conclusions regarding their plight, Stockdale was already aware of Stoic philosophy before being captured and therefore made explicit use of it in coping with his extreme circumstances.

Indeed, throughout his time in captivity, Stockdale drew upon the Stoic philosophy he had studied, which suddenly appeared to him to be of more value than anything else he could imagine. He called the many portions of Epictetus' *Handbook* that he had learnt by heart and memorized his "consolation" and "secret weapon" during captivity.

> I'm not the only prisoner who discovered that so-called practical academic exercises on "how to do things" were useless in that fix. The classics have a way of saving you the trouble of prolonged experiences. You don't have to go out and buy pop psychology self-help books. When you read the classics in

the humanities, you become aware that the big ideas have been around a long time, despite the fact that they are often served up today in modern psychological "explanations" of human action as novel and "scientific".

(Stockdale, 1995, p. 24)

On his release, Stockdale was regarded as a military hero. He went on to campaign as a US vice-presidential candidate, supporting the independent Ross Perot. He was one of the most highly-decorated officers in the USA's naval history, and spent his later years lecturing on the relevance of Stoic philosophy to modern military life. A collection of his talks and essays was published in his book, *Thoughts of a Philosophical Fighter Pilot* (1995). It is surprising that more frequent reference is not made to Stockdale's story by cognitive-behavioural therapists, who claim to derive their inspiration from the same philosophical source, ancient Stoicism. I hope this short digression helps to illustrate how Stoic philosophy, like Frankl's existential psychotherapy, has been applied even to the most extraordinary psychological challenges imaginable in the modern world.

Summary

Critics might say it is actually a healthy sign that so little attention has been given to the historical and philosophical origins of CBT, because it is inherently a forward-looking, scientific approach to psychotherapy. Just because ideas are very old, it does not *necessarily* mean that they are particularly valid or useful today. However, there are a number of legitimate reasons for exploring this matter in more detail. As Stockdale wrote:

Most of what Epictetus has to say to me is "right on" for modern times. Will Durant [an American philosopher] says that human nature changes, if at all, with "geological leisureliness". According to me, not much has happened to it since the days of Homer. Epictetus lived a tough life: born a slave, crippled by a cruel master, went from boy to man in the murderous violence of the household of a totally indulgent Emperor Nero. And he read human nature across a spectrum like this, and by the standards of my spectrum it rings with authenticity.

(*ibid.*, p. 180)

Indeed, a handful of cognitive-behavioural therapists have already attempted to make some headway in the direction of increasing dialogue concerning the relationship between Hellenistic philosophy and REBT or CBT (Brookshire, 2007; Herbert, 2004; McGlinchey, 2004; Montgomery, 1993; Reiss, 2003; Robertson, 2005; Still & Dryden, 1999).

Moreover, there are still therapeutic concepts and techniques to be found in classical literature that have good "face validity", appear consistent with CBT, and may well deserve empirical investigation in their own right. Nevertheless, in his recent article, Herbert, while defending the notion that comparisons between ancient philosophy and modern psychotherapy are interesting and valuable in their own right, has called into question the extent to which correlation between their respective ideas can be taken as evidence of causation, that is, of a historical influence (Herbert, 2004). While I agree that the question of influence is a complex one, and perhaps something of a *diversion* from the bigger issues, in the following chapters I will discuss the extent to which the founders of both REBT and cognitive therapy have explicitly stated, in some of their principal texts, that Stoicism and other ancient philosophical traditions provided the "philosophical origins" of their approach. For example, "The philosophical origins of cognitive therapy can be traced back to the Stoic philosophers" (Beck, Rush, Shaw, & Emery, 1979, p. 8).

Hence, some of the key points of the following text might be summarized as follows, for the benefit of readers requiring an overview of what may seem a complex and somewhat interdisciplinary subject matter:

- The origins of modern CBT can be traced, through early twentieth century rational psychotherapists, back to the ancient therapeutic practices of Socratic philosophy, especially Greek and Roman Stoicism.
- The notion of Stoicism as a kind of "intellectualism", opposed to emotion, is a popular *misconception*. Stoicism has traditionally attempted to accommodate emotion, especially the primary philosophical emotion of rational love toward existence as a whole.
- Ancient philosophy offers a clear analogy with modern CBT and provides many concepts, strategies, and techniques of practical value in self-help and psychotherapy.
- The contemplation of universal determinism, of the transience or impermanence of things, including our own mortality, and the vision of the world seen from above, or the cosmos conceived of as a whole, constitute specific meditative practices within ancient Hellenistic psychotherapy.
- Contemplation of the good qualities ("virtues") found in those we admire and in our ideal conception of philosophical enlightenment and moral strength (the "sage") provides us with a means of modelling excellence and deriving precepts or maxims to help guide our own actions.
- The rehearsal, memorization, and recall of short verbal formulae, precepts, dogmas, sayings, or maxims resembles the modern practice of autosuggestion in hypnotherapy, affirmations in self-help literature, or the use of verbal coping statements in CBT.
- The objective analysis of our experience into its value-free components, by suspending emotive judgements and rhetoric, constitutes a means of cognitive restructuring involving the disputation of faulty thinking, or cognitive distortion. By sticking to the facts, we counter the emotional disturbance caused by our own internal rhetoric.

- Mindfulness of our own faculty of judgement, and internal dialogue, in the "here and now", can be seen as analogous to the use of mindfulness meditation imported into modern CBT from Buddhist meditation practices, but has the advantage of being native to Stoicism, the philosophical precursor of CBT, and to European culture and language.
- The enormous literary value, the sheer *beauty*, of many of the classics with which we are concerned marks them out as being of special interest to many therapists and clients, just as it has marked them out for many thousands of previous readers throughout the intervening centuries.
- Socratic philosophy has a broader scope than modern psychotherapy, it looks at the bigger picture, and allows us the opportunity to place such therapy within the context of an overall "art of living", or philosophy of life.

The modern *industrialization* of psychotherapy, the division of the therapist's labour, has compartmentalized it in a manner that is bound to cause certain contradictions. What was once a lifestyle and calling, a vocation in the true sense of the word, has now largely been degraded into a mere "job". By nature, however, we do *not* merely study the cure of human suffering in order to alleviate it but also to understand and transform *ourselves* and our relationship with life itself. Perhaps, as the ancients seemed to believe, the philosopher-therapist must first transform his *own* way of life, making it a living example of his views, in order to be able to help others. By contrast, if the goal of the "rational" or "philosophical" therapist is merely to do his job and leave it all behind him at the weekend, to treat what we call "psychotherapy" as just another profession, then perhaps that is not a very *rational* or *philosophical* goal.

Philosophers and psychotherapists have a great deal to talk about, and a better common ground is required on which the two traditions can meet each other and exchange ideas. I hope that this study of the philosophical precursors of modern CBT will help to clarify and strengthen the basis for further dialogue between philosophers and therapists in the future.

Revised second edition

Since the first edition of this book was published, in 2010, Stoicism has continued to grow in popularity. A nonprofit organization, now called Modern Stoicism Ltd., was founded by Christopher Gill, professor emeritus of Ancient Thought at Exeter University. Modern Stoicism's purpose is to conduct research on the application of Stoicism to modern life and to disseminate information on its uses. The author is one of the founding members of Modern Stoicism, along with a small multidisciplinary group of psychologists, philosophers, classicists, and therapists, led by Professor Gill.

Modern Stoicism created a website and a blog called Stoicism Today, which currently hosts over 500 articles about applying Stoicism in practice, written by people from all walks of life. The organization also developed an online course called Stoic Week, which runs each year. In 2018, over 8,000 participants from all over the world took part. Participants are taught how to apply different concepts and techniques from Stoicism to their lives each day. The Modern Stoicism team also developed the Stoic Attitudes and Behaviours Scale (SABS) to help collect data from participants. We then developed a longer, four-week, skills training course called Stoic Mindfulness and Resilience Training (SMRT), which was designed to focus on core psychological skills for the purposes of conducting more carefully controlled studies on the effects of Stoic psychological training. Modern Stoicism also organizes an annual international conference on applying Stoicism in daily life.

The research from Stoic Week and SMRT is still at an early stage and takes the form of pilot studies, although thousands of people have taken part. However, so far consistent improvements have been found in established measures of positive and negative mood and life satisfaction, following training in Stoicism, including at three-month follow-up. The team is planning to carry out more studies in the future to discover whether or not their initial findings will be confirmed using more rigorous experimental design. Our impression is that Stoicism may hold promise as a method of building emotional resilience and preventing future mental health problems, although additional research is required to test this hypothesis.

In addition to these developments, there have been a growing number of self-help books inspired by Stoicism. When the first edition of this book was being written, William Irvine had just published his popular self-help book *A Guide to the Good Life: The Ancient Art of Stoic Joy* (2009). Subsequently, though, Oliver Burkeman (2013), Nassim Taleb (2012), and Derren Brown (2016) have published popular books that introduced many more people to Stoicism as a philosophy of life. Ryan Holiday's *The Obstacle is the Way* (2014) and *The Daily Stoic* (2016), co-authored with Stephen Hanselman, have introduced Stoicism to a much larger audience, as has Tim Ferriss, who published his own edition of Seneca's letters (2017). Recently, excellent introductions to Stoicism have also been published by Massimo Pigliucci (2018), Brad Inwood (2018), Ward Farnsworth (2018), Chuck Chakrapani (2016), and others.

The first edition of this book focused on the rational emotive behaviour therapy of Albert Ellis and cognitive therapy of Aaron T. Beck. However, since its publication, the third-wave of CBT, also known as "Mindfulness and Acceptance-based CBT", has grown more influential. So the current revised edition incorporates more discussion of the relationship between third-wave CBT and Stoic philosophy.

As we'll see, although third-wave CBT practitioners have tended to draw more upon Buddhism than Stoicism, their approaches often bear a notable resemblance to key aspects of ancient Stoicism, which were not emphasized as much by Ellis, Beck, and other pioneers of CBT. In particular, the emphasis on mindfulness of our thinking, acceptance of unpleasant feelings, and living in accord with values are all themes that play a central role both in mindfulness and acceptance-based CBT and in ancient Stoic philosophy. The current edition of this book has therefore been updated with more references to third-wave CBT and an entirely new chapter dedicated to the comparison between these approaches and Stoicism.

Part I

Philosophy and cognitive-behavioural therapy

Chapter 1

The "philosophical origins" of CBT

Cognitive-behavioural therapy (CBT) is the predominant school of modern evidence-based psychological therapy. As the name implies, it employs both cognitive and behavioural interventions. Unfortunately, this name belies the fact that CBT is concerned with helping clients to deal with irrational or disturbing *emotions* and to cultivate rational, healthy, and proportionate ones in their stead. The terms "cognitive" and "rational" also suggest to some people's minds that CBT must be a form of *rationalization*, or that it neglects emotion, intuition, or practical experience. However, CBT is actually *anti*-rationalist, in this sense, given its emphasis upon the value of behavioural experiments and empirical observation. In other words, CBT emphasizes that, insofar as it is reasonable to do so, beliefs should be tested out in practice, in the laboratory of our personal experience.

Professor Keith Dobson, one of the leading authorities in the field of CBT, offers the following account of its "philosophical bases", that is, the common assumptions shared by variations of cognitive-behavioural therapy.

1 Cognitive activity affects behavior.
2 Cognitive activity may be monitored and altered.
3 Desired behavior change may be affected through cognitive change.

(Dobson & Dozois, 2001, p. 4)

Moreover:

> A number of current approaches to therapy fall within the scope of cognitive-behavioral therapy as it is defined above. These approaches all share a theoretical perspective assuming that internal covert processes called "thinking" or "cognition" occur, and that cognitive events may mediate behavior change.
>
> (*ibid.*, p. 6)

If we accept this definition, there are several different forms of therapy that potentially fall within the "broad church" of CBT. The two most influential and commonly cited ones are the rational emotive behaviour therapy (REBT) of Albert Ellis and the cognitive therapy (CT) of Aaron Beck. Dobson includes a number of other approaches that combine cognitive interventions, which modify the clients' thinking or internal dialogue with elements of earlier behaviour therapy. However, the philosophical bases of CBT described by Dobson are actually shared with several schools of ancient Greek philosophy. Stoicism, in particular, would certainly meet the criteria cited previously for classification as a species of CBT.

Moreover, as Beck's approach is probably the most influential one in the current field of CBT, it may be helpful to delineate the components of which his seminal cognitive therapy of depression is comprised (Beck, Rush, Shaw, & Emery, 1979, p. 4). The client is helped by the cognitive therapist to do the following:

1   To monitor his negative automatic thoughts, or cognitions.
2   To evaluate the relationship between his thoughts, feelings, and actions.
3   To carefully evaluate the evidence for and against his distorted or maladaptive cognitions.
4   To generate alternative cognitions and to substitute them for the negative ones.
5   To identify and modify underlying dysfunctional assumptions and beliefs which predispose him to negative automatic thoughts.

Once again, though, these and other strategies employed in cognitive therapy can be identified easily in the practices of various schools of classical philosophy, as we shall see, especially Stoicism.

Stoicism as the philosophy of REBT and CBT

Albert Ellis and Aaron T. Beck, the main pioneers of CBT, have both stressed the role of Stoicism as a philosophical precursor of their approaches. There is only a vague appreciation of this fact among many therapists today, however, so it is worth drawing attention to the key passages in their writings.

Ellis openly admitted that "much of the theory of REBT was derived from philosophy rather than psychology" (Ellis & MacLaren, 2005, p. 16). His first major publication on rational therapy, *Reason & Emotion in Psychotherapy* (1962), describes the philosophical basis of the approach as the principle that a person is rarely affected emotionally by outside things but, rather, "by his perceptions, attitudes, or internalized sentences *about* outside things and events" (Ellis, 1962, p. 54).

> This principle, which I have inducted from many psychotherapeutic sessions with scores of patients during the last several years, was originally discovered and stated by the ancient Stoic philosophers, especially Zeno of Citium (the founder of the school), Chrysippus (his most influential disciple), Panaetius of Rhodes (who introduced Stoicism into Rome), Cicero, Seneca, Epictetus, and Marcus Aurelius. The truths of Stoicism were perhaps best set forth by

Epictetus, who, in the first century AD wrote in the *Encheiridion*: "Men are disturbed not by things, but by the views which they take of them".

(ibid.)

Ellis adds that Shakespeare "rephrased" this idea centuries later when he portrays Hamlet saying "There's nothing good or bad but thinking makes it so". (This well-known quotation may stem from Shakespeare's own reading of the Stoics, incidentally, particularly Seneca.) Moreover, earlier in the same book, Ellis states:

> Many of the principles incorporated in the theory of rational emotive psy-chotherapy are not new; some of them, in fact, were originally stated several thousand years ago, especially by the Greek and Roman Stoic philosophers (such as Epictetus and Marcus Aurelius) and by some of the ancient Taoist and Buddhist thinkers. What probably is new is the application to psycho-therapy of viewpoints [such as these] that were first propounded in radically different contexts.

(ibid., p. 35)

However, as we'll see, Ellis was mistaken with regard to this latter point. Ancient Greek and Roman philosophers *did* consider themselves to be applying these principles as a form of psychological therapy. From Socrates onward, a "medi-cal model" was commonly used to interpret philosophy as analogous to a talking cure, a form of medicine for the soul. The term "therapy" (*therapeia*) was used by Greek philosophers to describe the use of philosophical doctrines and practices to alleviate psychological suffering. For instance, the third head of the Stoic school, Chrysippus, wrote a four volume work titled *On Passions*, about pathological desires and emotions, which concludes with a volume titled *Therapeutics*, on the Stoic therapy of the *psyche*. Psychotherapy, in other words, is *not* a modern con-cept. The ancient Greeks developed philosophical approaches to psychotherapy and even employed similar terminology to describe their approach.

In a later article specifically examining the relationship between REBT and Stoi-cism, Still and Dryden note that the saying of Epictetus quoted previously has become a "hallmark" of REBT and is "even given to clients during the early sessions, as a succinct way of capturing the starting point" (Still & Dryden, 1999, p. 146). They go on to say that although the specific therapeutic remedies found in REBT and Stoicism may differ in some respects, they both emphasize the role of responsibility, rational-ity, and self-disciplined observation of one's mind as a means of modifying irrational emotions and achieving psychological well-being (*ibid.,* p. 149).

Likewise, in his popular self-help book, *A Guide to Rational Living*, co-authored with Robert A. Harper, Ellis advised his lay readers of the relevance of Stoic philosophers for REBT,

> History gives us several outstanding instances of people who changed them-selves and helped change others by hardheaded thinking: Zeno of Citium, for

example, who flourished in the third century B.C., and founded the Greek Stoic school of philosophy; the Greek philosopher Epicurus; the Phrygian Epictetus; the Roman emperor Marcus Aurelius; and the Dutch Jew Baruch Spinoza. These and other outstanding rational thinkers, after reading about the teaching of still earlier thinkers (Heraclitus and Democritus among others), and after doing some deep thinking of their own, enthusiastically adopted philosophies radically different from their original beliefs. More to the point for the purposes of our present discussion, they actually began to *live* these philosophies and to *act* in accordance with them.

(Ellis & Harper, 1997, p. 5)

As we shall see, the Dutch philosopher Spinoza, though not a Stoic himself, was heavily influenced by the therapeutic concepts found in Hellenistic philosophy, particularly Stoicism.

Moreover, at the beginning of *Cognitive Therapy of Depression* (1979), taking their cue from Ellis, Beck and his colleagues explicitly claimed that the "philosophical origins" of their own approach also lay in the ancient Stoic tradition.

The philosophical origins of cognitive therapy can be traced back to the Stoic philosophers, particularly Zeno of Citium (fourth century BC), Chrysippus, Cicero, Seneca, Epictetus, and Marcus Aurelius. Epictetus wrote in *The Encheiridion*, "Men are disturbed not by things but by the views which they take of them". Like Stoicism, Eastern philosophies such as Taoism and Buddhism have emphasized that human emotions are based on ideas. Control of most intense feelings may be achieved by changing one's ideas.

(Beck, Rush, Shaw, & Emery, 1979, p. 8)

There are obvious similarities between these two passages from Beck and Ellis. Both happen to employ the same translation of a quote from Epictetus. They could have chosen from an enormous wealth of similar passages written by Epictetus or, indeed, the other Stoic authors, which communicate the same basic idea. Both Ellis and Beck, incidentally, make a small error in listing Cicero as a Stoic. Cicero was a follower of the Academic school of philosophy, founded by Plato. Nevertheless, he was highly educated in Greek philosophy and his surviving writings are among our most important sources for the teachings of Stoicism.

These quotations from Ellis and Beck are typical of the somewhat cursory manner in which Stoicism is acknowledged by proponents of CBT as the major philosophical precursor of their approach. Nevertheless, what seems clear is that Ellis, and subsequently Beck, attributed the philosophical bases of REBT and CBT primarily to the ancient Stoics and, to a lesser extent, to similar themes in Oriental literature. Little more can be drawn from these brief remarks except that Stoicism is very relevant to CBT and that this importance stems from the shared emphasis upon cognition (ideas, judgements, opinions, etc.) as both the cause and cure of emotional disturbance. There are, however, a handful of other references made by important figures in the field of CBT regarding ancient philosophies that may help to further illustrate the nature of the historical relationship between the two traditions.

Stoic philosophy in Beck's cognitive therapy

As Beck and his colleagues acknowledged, Ellis' REBT "provided a major impetus" to the historical development of cognitive-behavioural therapies in general (Beck, Rush, Shaw, & Emery, 1979, p. 10). Moreover, as we have seen, they clearly state that cognitive therapy shared exactly the same philosophical origins as REBT. In addition, Beck had opened his earlier book, *Cognitive Therapy and the Emotional Disorders* (1976), with the claim that:

> These assumptions converge on a relatively new approach to emotional disorders. Nevertheless, the philosophical underpinnings go back thousands of years, certainly to the time of the Stoics, who considered man's conceptions (or misconceptions) of events rather than the events themselves as the key to his emotional upsets.
>
> (Beck, 1976, p. 3)

Although Beck does not seem to have engaged any further with the Stoics' philosophical views, he scattered additional quotations from Stoic and Stoic-influenced authors throughout this book, his first on cognitive therapy. Beck used the famous quotation from Epictetus mentioned previously as the epigraph of his chapter on *Meaning and Emotions*. He likewise quoted Marcus Aurelius, saying the same thing: "If thou are pained by any external thing, it is not the thing that disturbs thee, but thine own judgement about it. And it is in thy power to wipe out this judgement now" (Marcus Aurelius, quoted in Beck, 1976, p. 263).

Beck introduced his chapter on phobias in this book with the following Stoic-sounding quotation from Spinoza: "I saw that all the things I feared, and which feared me had nothing good or bad in them save insofar as the mind was affected by them" (Spinoza, quoted in Beck, 1976, p. 156). However, apart from these few references, Beck does not appear to have had much more to say regarding the "philosophical origins", as he puts it, of cognitive therapy.

This is more surprising than it might seem at first. The Stoics do not merely present abstract philosophical theories loosely related to the clinical applications of cognitive therapy. They were the most practical and therapeutic in orientation of all the ancient philosophical schools. Their writings contain many specific psychological techniques or exercises, most of which are consistent with modern CBT, and some of which have been forgotten or neglected by modern psychotherapists, though still potentially relevant today. Indeed, A.A. Long, a leading scholar of Stoic philosophy, writes:

> Epictetus scarcely needs updating as an analyst of the psyche's strengths or weaknesses, and as a spokesman for human dignity, autonomy, and integrity. His

principal project is to assure his listeners that nothing lies completely in their power except their judgements and desires and goals. Even our bodily frame and its movements are not entirely ours or up to us. The corollary is that nothing outside the mind or volition can, of its own nature, constrain or frustrate us unless we choose to let it do so. Happiness and a praiseworthy life require us to monitor our mental selves at every waking moment, making them and nothing external or material responsible for all the goodness or badness we experience. In the final analysis, everything that affects us for good or ill depends on our own judgements and on how we respond to the circumstances that befall us.

(Long, 2002, p. 1)

Long is undoubtedly correct. What he and other classical scholars find in Epictetus is, self-evidently, a therapeutic system very similar in its assumptions to modern CBT, and certainly one that meets the criteria quoted at the start of this section. Both Stoicism and CBT place central emphasis upon the role of cognition in determining the cause and cure of emotional disturbance, as the previous quotations amply illustrate. However, although this is one of the most fundamental principles of Stoicism, there are others that logically precede it. Moreover, the philosophical core of Stoicism is also consistent with the theory and practice of CBT, as we shall now see.

The Serenity Prayer and Stoicism

The most fundamental principle of Stoic psychotherapy can be found in the very first sentence of the famous *Encheiridion* or Stoic "handbook" of Epictetus: "Some things are up to us and others are not" (*Handbook*, 1). The importance of this maxim and the wider implications of absorbing its meaning and implications are explored in detail throughout the ancient Stoic literature.

The *Encheiridion* is a condensed guidebook to Stoic life that draws upon the more lengthy *Discourses* of Epictetus, which claim to record discussions held between the Stoic teacher and groups of students. Just like the *Encheiridion*, however, the *Discourses* begin with a chapter dedicated to the theme "On what is in our power, and what is not". Epictetus begins by explaining the Stoic view that our judgements and opinions are pre-eminently within our power to control, whereas external events, especially sources of wealth and reputation, are ultimately in the hands of Fortune. Hence, the Stoic should always strive to cope with adversity by having ready "at hand" precepts that remind him "what is mine, and what is not mine, what is within my power, and what is not" (*Discourses*, 1.1.21). Indeed, Epictetus goes as far as to define Stoicism itself as the study of this distinction. "And to become educated [in Stoic philosophy] means just this, to learn what things are our own, and what are not" (*Discourses*, 4.5.7).

This distinction forms the premise for two closely related principles. First, that the Stoic should cultivate continual self-awareness, mindful of his thoughts and judgements, as these lie at the centre of his sphere of control. Second, that he should adopt a "philosophical attitude to life", as we now say, meaning that one should Stoically accept those things that are none of our concern or outside of our power to control. Epictetus attempts to sum up these notions in a laconic maxim of the kind that the Stoics meant to be easy to memorize and constantly ready to hand: "What, then, is to be done? To make the best of what is in our power, and take the rest as it naturally happens" (*Discourses*, 1.1.17).

Modern therapists will probably recognize this as the basis of the "Serenity Prayer", used by members of Alcoholics Anonymous and other therapeutic and self-help approaches, which usually takes the following form,

> God grant me serenity to accept the things I cannot change,
> Courage to change the things I can,
> And wisdom to know the difference.

It derives, allegedly, from a similar prayer written by the Protestant theologian Reinhold Niebuhr in the 1940s (Pietsch, 1990, p. 9). However, the resemblance to both Stoic doctrine and terminology is unmistakable to anyone familiar with the literature of the subject. As it happens, courage and wisdom are two of the four cardinal virtues of classical Greek philosophy, along with self-control and justice.

The basic Stoic precepts

Likewise, though it may have taken a lifetime to study the subtle implications of Stoic philosophy, its basic tenets were intended to be summed up in a few words, as Epictetus emphasizes (*Discourses*, 1.20.13–14): to follow nature and make good use of our impressions was the doctrine of Zeno, the founder of Stoicism (*Discourses*, 1.20.14–15). "Following nature", or "following the gods", in the Stoic sense, amounts to the same thing, and primarily requires serene acceptance of things that lie outside of our direct control. Correct use of impressions means exercising moral wisdom. This primarily requires questioning whether our impressions represent things genuinely within our control, such as value judgements, or whether they represent external things ultimately outside of our direct control, matters of "fortune" or the "facts of our situation", such as our material wealth and reputation.

To some people, the Serenity Prayer and these Stoic precepts appear counterintuitive at first, but this was not the philosophers' intention. Beck emphasized that cognitive therapy could be seen primarily as an extension of our common sense assumptions (Beck, 1976, pp. 6–23). Likewise, the Stoics considered their teaching to be grounded in "natural preconceptions". According to this view, we all possess certain deep-seated, intuitive, natural, and common sense assumptions but fail to apply them consistently or think their logical implications through.

> What, then, is it to be properly educated [as a philosopher]? To learn how to apply natural preconceptions [i.e., common sense] to particular cases, in

accordance with nature; and, for the future, to distinguish that some things are in our own power, others are not. In our own power are choice, and all actions dependent on choice; not in our power, children, country, and, in short, [the actions of] all with whom we associate. Where, then, shall we place the good? To what class of things shall we apply it? To that of things that are in our own power.

(*Discourses*, 1.22.9–11)

The wisdom of the enlightened Stoic sage consists primarily in his unwavering mindfulness and moment-to-moment attention to acts of his will and to his faculty of judgement. Emotional disturbance is the result of mindlessly becoming absorbed in external events, being overly attached to sensory pleasure, wealth, and the praise of others, and overly anxious about pain, poverty, and criticism.

> If we had acted thus, and trained ourselves in this manner from morning till night, then, by the gods, something would have been achieved. Whereas now, we are caught half asleep by every impression, and if we ever do wake up, it is only for a little in the lecture-hall. And then we go out, and if we see anyone in distress, we say, "He is done for"; if a consul, "Happy man!"; if an exile, "What misery!"; if a poor man, "How wretched for him; he has nothing to buy a meal with!"
>
> These harmful ideas must be eradicated; and to this our whole strength must be applied. For what is weeping and groaning? A judgement. What is misfortune? A judgement. What is sedition, discord, complaint, accusation, impiety, foolish talk? All these are judgements, and nothing more; and judgements concerning things outside the sphere of choice, taking them to be good or evil. Let anyone transfer these judgements to things within the sphere of choice, and I will guarantee that he will preserve his constancy, whatever be the state of things about him.
>
> (*Discourses*, 3.3.16–19, modified)

Of course, modern cognitive therapist would call these "cognitions", or irrational thoughts and beliefs, and Beck describes the process of distinguishing between internal *thoughts* and the external *facts* they claim to represent as cognitive "distancing" (Beck, 1976, pp. 242–243). This process of learning to monitor our spontaneous judgements and automatic thoughts (cognitions), such as "How wretched for him!", and reminding ourselves that they represent subjective attitudes rather than objective facts, is essential to both Stoicism and CBT.

Moreover, Epictetus' examples are essentially *value* judgements that express our own attitudes rather than objective features of the external world. Insofar as they arouse desire, anxiety, pity, or other emotions, these are self-inflicted disturbances, and not primarily the result of external events, which merely serve as the occasion, or vehicle, for them. Epictetus compares the mind to a bottle of water with a ray of light shining through it, representing our perception of external events. If the water is shaken, the light is refracted and disturbed. Likewise, when our mind, judgements, and perceptions are internally disturbed, external events look disturbing to us. We project our feelings on to external events. The sage sees everything in the same light because his mind is constant and he refuses to attach undue importance to anything outside his control. As Epictetus is previously quoted as saying, the values attributed to external events should, arguably, be transferred onto the judgements that make them appear that way. For example, a depressed patient may think "life is awful and depressing", blaming their feelings upon the world. However, it might be better and more accurate, for them to "blame" their depressed mood on their own way of looking at the world, on their own judgements and automatic thoughts. While there is little we can do to change the face of the world itself, we can take *responsibility* for our own thoughts and attitudes and, with some effort, learn to change them.

Hence, for the Stoics, the fundamental rule of their ethic can be viewed simply as the requirement for personal authenticity, or integrity. To Stoic students demanding therapeutic "rules" to live by, Epictetus replied:

> What am I to prescribe to you? Hasn't Zeus [i.e., nature] already done that? Has he not given you things that are *yours*, free from impediment and hindrance, and things that are *not yours*, which are subject to impediment and hindrance? What guidance did you have from him when you were born, what kind of rule?
>
> "Cherish completely what is your own, and don't seek after things that don't belong to you".
>
> Your integrity is your own; who can take it from you? Who but yourself will prevent you from using it? But how do you prevent it? When you are eager for what is not your own, you lose that very thing.
>
> (*Discourses*, 1.25.3–5, in Long, 2002, p. 187)

As he puts it elsewhere, "This law has god ordained, who says, 'If you want anything good, get it from yourself'" (*Discourses*, 1.29.4), by which he means that the highest value should be placed by man not upon wealth or reputation but upon the attainment of self-awareness and self-control, that is, the cardinal virtue of "wisdom".

By attending to our judgements, we can change the way we think about life, review the value we attribute to things, and gain control over our emotions. As Epictetus puts it, when we attach value to external things and treat them as if they had inherent worth, we run the risk of becoming forgetful of our freedom to choose, we enslave ourselves to external events (*Discourses*, 4.4.23).

Life is what we make of it: "The materials of action are indifferent; but the use that we make of them is not indifferent" (*Discourses*, 2.5.1). "Likewise, life is indifferent; but the use of it is not indifferent" (*Discourses*, 2.6.1). We shall return to this theme, which Epictetus expresses so well when he says that our judgements upset us rather than things themselves and which CBT practitioners sometimes refer to as the principle of "cognitive mediation", or the "cognitive theory of emotion". As we have seen, it is central to Hellenistic philosophy and therapeutics, to the Serenity Prayer, and to modern CBT.

Hans Eysenck and behaviour therapy

We have considered the influence of Hellenistic philosophy upon REBT and CBT and, as we have seen, the founders of "behaviour therapy" also saw major precursors of that approach in ancient literature (Wolpe & Lazarus, 1966, pp. 1–2). Along with Wolpe and Lazarus, Hans Eysenck was one of the pioneers of behaviour therapy in the 1960s. He has repeatedly drawn attention to the fact that some of the basic principles of behaviour therapy resemble "common sense" observations and were, therefore, anticipated in previous centuries, for example, in the writings of the German author Goethe (Eysenck, 1990, p. 137).

Eysenck also explicitly states that long before Freud developed psychoanalysis, often erroneously considered the beginning of psychotherapy, "there existed already the rudiments of the theory which was later to account for neurotic fears and anxieties in a much more economical and scientific fashion" (Eysenck, 1977, p. 42).

> These ancient theories were Greek in origin, but were voiced in their most convincing form by Marcus Tullius Cicero, in his *Tuscularum Disputationum*. In the first place, he points out that "*Ab earum rerum est absentium metus, quarum est aegretudo*": in neurotic disorders, anxiety is felt of things not present, the presence of which causes grief, or distress. This suggests immediately a learning process by means of which the distress properly associated with the "thing present" (the unconditioned stimulus, in modern parlance) is evoked when the "thing" is not present; that is, through a conditioned stimulus. Now, if we can remove the distress reaction, then the neurotic anxiety also will be taken away: "*Sublata igitur aegritudine, eadem impendentes et venientes timemus*". This, of course, suggests a method of extinction, whether through "desensitization", or "flooding", or "modelling".
>
> (Eysenck, 1977, pp. 42–43)

Although Cicero was not himself a Stoic, as noted earlier, *Tusculan Disputations* was nevertheless one of his most Stoic-influenced writings. Eysenck also finds in this text a precursor of his own theory of trait "neuroticism", an innate emotional instability and vulnerability to disturbance, which he considered to be largely genetically determined.

> Cicero finally caps his account by appealing to individual differences: "*At qui in quem cadit aegritudo, in eundem timor; quarum enim rerum praesentia sumus in aegritudine, eadem impendentes et venientes timemus*". Translated freely, this states that the man who is easily distressed is also an easy prey to anxiety and fear. For, when stimuli cause distress by their presence, we

are also afraid of the menace of their approach. In other words, people who have strong fear reactions to actual dangers and stressful situations also show strong learnt anxieties in the absence of these stimuli. We cannot follow Cicero into the details of his discussion, but the elements of our modern way of looking at neurosis are certainly contained in his account.

(*ibid.*, p. 43)

Eysenck, therefore, makes it clear that he considers Cicero to be describing a theory and practice similar to his own and to those of modern behaviour therapists in general. Although Eysenck, as a behavioural psychologist, places much greater emphasis than cognitive theorists such as Beck and Ellis upon genetic predisposition and simple processes of emotional conditioning and de-conditioning, these concepts still have some influence in the field of modern CBT, especially in the treatment of anxiety through "exposure" therapy. In any case, the remarks of Eysenck, Ellis, and Beck combine to illustrate how a range of key figures in the fields of *behaviour* therapy and *cognitive* therapy have found the "philosophical origins", or, at least, the "rudiments", or basic "elements", of their approach in Hellenistic philosophers such as Cicero and Epictetus.

Donald Meichenbaum and cognitive-behaviour modification

In concluding this chapter, it may be worthwhile mentioning some comments made by another influential cognitive-behavioural theorist, Donald Meichenbaum. His remarks are not notable because they tell us anything about the philosophical provenance of CBT but because they illustrate the peculiar way in which therapists seem to keep stumbling across relevant philosophical passages but fail to engage further with the ancient therapeutic tradition from which they stem. In discussing the use of his "self-instruction training", as a cognitive approach to managing pain, Meichenbaum observes:

> Individuals have used cognitive strategies for as long as man has experienced pain. For example, the Stoic philosophers believed that man could get the better of pain by force of reason, by the "rational repudiation" of pain. Descartes and Spinoza recommended that pain should be overcome through the "permeation" of reason.

(Meichenbaum, 1977, p. 17)

This is an over-simplification of the Stoic attitude toward controlling pain. However, it does lead to the discovery of an interesting and somewhat obscure philosophical text.

Meichenbaum (*ibid.*, p. 171) illustrates the use of cognitive distraction techniques by providing the following quotation from the great eighteenth century philosopher Immanuel Kant's impressively titled essay, "On the power of the human mind to master its morbid feelings merely by a firm resolution". Kant recommends the mental repetition of a word as a means of interrupting intrusive trains of thought that prevent sleep and also as a method of dissociating from pain and thereby overcoming insomnia.

> To be unable to sleep at one's fixed and habitual time, or also unable to stay awake, is a kind of morbid feeling. But of these two, insomnia is the worse: to go to bed intending to sleep, and yet lie awake. – Doctors usually advise a patient to drive all *thoughts* from his head; but they return, or others come in their place, and keep him awake. The only disciplinary advice is to turn away his attention as soon as he perceives or becomes conscious of any thought stirring (just as if, with his eyes closed, he turned them to a different place). This interruption of any thought that he is aware of gradually produces a confusion of ideas by which his awareness of his physical (external) situation is suspended; and then an altogether different order sets in, an involuntary play of imagination (which, in a state of health, is *dreaming*). . . . But it can happen to anyone, now and then, that when he lies down in bed ready to sleep he cannot fall asleep, even by diverting his thoughts in this way.
>
> (Kant, trans., 1996, p. 319)

Kant experienced a painful condition that he assumed to be gout. Finding that the discomfort often prevented him from getting to sleep, he employed a coping method that he derived from the ancient Stoic philosophers.

> But, impatient at feeling my sleep interfered with, I soon had recourse to my Stoic remedy of fixing my thought forcibly on some neutral object that I chose at random (for example, the name Cicero, which contains many associated ideas), and so diverting my attention from that sensation. The result was that the sensation was dulled, even quickly so, and outweighed by drowsiness; and I can repeat this procedure with equally good results every time that attacks of this kind recur in the brief interruptions of my night's sleep.
>
> (*ibid.*, p. 320)

It would be tempting to view this as an example of the contemplation of a role model (Cicero), a Stoic technique which we will examine in due course, but, in fact, Kant states that he chose the name at random, so we appear to be left merely with a kind of distraction technique. In fact, one of the first modern psychotherapeutic methods for overcoming insomnia, reported by the founder of hypnotherapy, James Braid, was the repetition of a banal phrase. Braid quotes from an earlier author to illustrate this method of inducing sleep,

> And again, M'Nish writes, "I have often coaxed myself to sleep by internally repeating half a dozen times any well known rhyme. Whilst doing so the ideas must be strictly directed to this particular theme, and prevented

from wandering". He then adds, that the great secret is to compel the mind to depart from its favourite train of thought, into which it has a tendency to run, "and address itself solely to the *verbal* repetition of what is substituted in its place"; and farther [sic] adds, "the more the mind is brought to turn upon a *single impression*, the more closely it is made to approach to the state of sleep, which is the total absence of all impressions".

(Braid, 2009, p. 363)

Although Meichenbaum and Kant refer this technique to the Stoics, and it may have been practised by them, monotonous distraction seems like rather a blunt instrument by comparison with the full armamentarium of techniques and strategies that they had at their disposal. Distraction techniques also tend not to be favoured by modern CBT researchers or clinicians because they can easily turn into a habit of avoidance.

In the second part of this book, I shall attempt to describe in detail many of the specific therapeutic methods employed in Stoicism and show how they may be integrated within modern CBT in a more sophisticated manner. All in all, Eysenck, Meichenbaum, and Beck say very little about the relationship between modern therapy and Stoicism, apart from a few tantalizing remarks. Albert Ellis says somewhat more in this respect, as we shall see. Before elaborating on the Stoic therapy techniques, however, I hope to shed some more light on how the theory and practise of modern cognitive therapy in general relates to Stoicism by examining a kind of "missing link" in the history of the subject, the early history of "rational psychotherapy" in the first half of the twentieth century, beginning roughly 50 years prior to the work of either Beck or Ellis.

Chapter 2

The beginning of modern cognitive therapy

The historical transition from philosophical therapy to modern CBT was not as abrupt as it might seem. Ellis' REBT was never fully embraced by researchers in the field of psychology. CBT in general did not really achieve mainstream popularity as a branch of psychotherapy until the late 1970s, when Beck's cognitive therapy began to develop more widespread popularity due to its growing evidence base. However, there were several early twentieth century schools of psychotherapy that were influenced by Stoicism and other forms of classical philosophy in a manner that prefigures the work of Ellis and Beck.

Paul Dubois and rational psychotherapy

Albert Ellis explicitly recognized that in addition to their ancient precedent in Stoicism, modern schools of cognitive therapy, including REBT, had many precursors within the field of psychotherapy. Ellis claimed not to have read the writings of Swiss psychiatrist Paul Dubois (1848–1918) until a few years *after* he developed REBT but acknowledged that, "rational emotive psychotherapy is by no means entirely new, since some of its main principles were propounded by Dubois (1904) and by many pre-Freudian therapists" (Ellis, 1962, p. 105). That's because some of the principles that REBT shared with Stoicism were already familiar to earlier generations of psychotherapists.

Indeed, at the First International Congress of Psychiatry and Neurology, in 1907, there was considerable opposition to Freudian psychoanalysis, the more conventional techniques of persuasion and suggestion being still considered central to psychotherapy.

> Dubois told of his method of treating phobias. Emotions, he said, always follow ideas, so the treatment should go to the root, namely, the erroneous idea the patient has allowed to creep into his mind.
>
> (Ellenberger, 1970, p. 797)

Moreover, the "rational persuasion" school of psychotherapy founded by Dubois had many advocates and, for a time, competed with Freudian psychoanalysis, especially in the USA.

> Thanks to the influence of Dubois, during the opening years of the twentieth century, there was a notable output of books expounding, with more or less modification, these ideas of treatment by rational persuasion and moralisation.
>
> (Baudouin & Lestchinsky, 1924, p. 139)

Dubois was professor of neuropathology at the University of Berne and became world renowned in his day as a highly successful psychotherapist. He treated several famous clients, reputedly including the novelist Marcel Proust. However, unlike Freud, he failed to organize his followers into a coherent professional body and so, despite being the first significant modern proponent of a "rational" or "cognitive" psychotherapy, which he described as the "education of the self", his work is scarcely known today. Like Ellis and Beck after him, Dubois also explicitly recognized Stoicism as the precursor to modern rational psychotherapy, although he had more to say on that subject.

Following the ancient philosophers before him, Dubois uses the terms "ethics" and "morality" in a different sense from their current usage, to denote the practical recommendations for individual *well-being* derived from philosophy and psychotherapy. Dubois believed that "ethical" ideas, or rather underlying human values, were largely forced upon us by our basic experience of living and therefore changed little over the centuries. The strategies used by Epictetus to cope with hardship were bound to be similar to those found helpful by James Stockdale in Vietnam, because they were ultimately based upon simple, common sense observations about human nature.

> If we eliminate from ancient writings a few allusions that gave them local colour, we shall find the ideas of Socrates, Epictetus, Seneca, and Marcus Aurelius absolutely modern and applicable to our times. In this field of ethical thought men remain the same.
>
> (Dubois, 1909, pp. 108–109)

Dubois' central contention was that most neurotic or emotional disorders may be seen as the consequence of an ongoing process of unintentional *autosuggestion*, of an irrational and unhealthy nature. So-called "hysterical" or psychosomatic illness can result from negative autosuggestion, but even genuine physical ailments could be made worse by the negative thoughts that supervene upon them.

> But we often suffer from functional [i.e., psychosomatic] troubles which are not caused by organic changes and in the development of which the mind plays an immense part. Even in the course of purely bodily illness there is

often the mediation of psychical symptoms which depend above all on the condition of our spirit. Man, in short, suffers quite differently from the animals and he suffers more than they. He does not content himself, so to speak, with brute suffering which is adequate for the physical disorders; he increases them by imagination, aggravates them by fear, keeps them up by his pessimistic reflections.

(Dubois & Gallatin, 1908, p. 20)

The work of the psychotherapist centres on motivating the client, educating him about the effect of mind upon body, and teaching him to adopt remedial "philosophical" attitudes. Dubois wrote, "by rational education of ourselves we modify our ideas and our sentiments and we make our temperament of a noble character" (*ibid.*, p. 57). Through self-monitoring of thoughts, the client learns to spot the beginning of harmful emotions, pause for reflection, and nip them in the bud.

We should react briskly, act enthusiastically for good, obey the impulse of our better feelings. But however spontaneous this reaction may be, we must nevertheless leave time for calm reason to exercise a rapid control. Our reason is that which as an arbiter judges finally the value of the emotions of sensibility which make us act. If it is a sentiment of goodness, of pity, which carries us away, reason very quickly gives its approval. But when we are about to give way to a feeling of anger, envy, vexation, reason should intervene to correct the first impression and modify the final decision.

(*ibid.*, p. 56)

Dubois, therefore, often speaks of his rational psychotherapy as involving stoicism. (Although he wrote it with a small "s", incidentally, it would be correct to capitalize the word to distinguish the Greek philosophy of Stoicism from the more simplistic modern concept of stoicism as a tough-minded coping style.) Of students who wrote reporting the benefits experienced by following his advice, Dubois comments,

I congratulate them and I beg them to remember well that in insisting upon the power of mental representations I have never wished to accuse their sufferings of being imaginary. I know all the effort which this stoical education demands.

(*ibid.*, pp. 62–63)

Likewise, of the benefits of adopting a rational philosophy of life, he remarks, "Those whose reflections lead them to be freethinkers find in themselves, in a stoicism free from egotism, strength to resist all which life brings them" (*ibid.*, p. 60).

Dubois on Seneca

However, referring more explicitly to classical Stoic philosophy, Dubois recognized the fact that Seneca, among others, had proposed a similar account of the role of erroneous ideas (cognitions) in emotional disturbance. It is worth emphasizing the fact that although the word "autosuggestion" was not available to the ancients, Dubois uses it throughout his writings to describe the manner in which judgement penetrates into the emotions and affects our physical health. In other words, Dubois interpreted the Stoics as emphasizing the role of autosuggestion in the cause and cure of emotional disturbance. Hence, he finds in Seneca's philosophy a clear precursor to his own rational psychotherapy.

> I do not hesitate to persuade my patients to neglect the painful phenomena. The idea is not new; the stoics have pushed to the last degree this resistance to pain and misfortune. The following lines, written by Seneca, seem to be drawn from a modern treatise on psychotherapy: "Beware of aggravating your troubles yourself and of making your position worse by your complaints. Grief is light when opinion does not exaggerate it; and if one encourages one's self by saying, 'This is nothing', or, at least, 'This is slight; let us try to endure it, for it will end', one makes one's grief slight by reason of believing it such". And, further: "One is only unfortunate in proportion as one believes one's self so".
>
> One could truly say concerning nervous pains that one only suffers when he thinks he does. I could quote numerous examples which show the possibility of suppressing more or less rapidly and often once for all such painful phenomena.
>
> (Dubois, 1904, pp. 394–395)

Dubois goes on to describe how he successfully treated a neurasthenic patient by a single motivating psychotherapy session, and having him study the literature of classical Stoicism. This patient wrote to Dubois, "When I feel my courage ebbing, I read the letters of Seneca to Lucilius!" (*ibid.*, p. 433).

Indeed, Dubois clearly admired the Stoic teachings of Seneca in particular. He also quotes Seneca's letters to illustrate the role of patience and acceptance, as opposed to worry, in helping us to cope with and avoid exacerbating physical illness. "We must turn here to the ancients in order to recover the idea of patience towards disease, that stoical philosophy which not only helps to support us in evils, but diminishes or cures them" (Dubois, 1909, pp. 224–225).

As an example of the ancient philosophical recognition of cognition's effect upon psychosomatic illness, he quotes Seneca's letter, beginning:

> I am going to tell you how consoled I am after having always insisted that the [philosophical] principles upon which I leaned would act upon me like

medicine. Honest consolation becomes in itself a remedy, and everything that lifts up the soul strengthens the body. My studies have saved me; I attribute my recovery, my return to health, to philosophy; I owe my life to it, but that is the least of my obligations.

(Seneca, quoted in Dubois, 1909, p. 225)

Dubois also refers to the Stoic principle that the fear of death is the underlying philosophical root of most other human fears. Bemoaning the confusing multitude of different remedies proposed by ancient physicians, Seneca writes:

But I not only give you a remedy for this illness, but a remedy for all your life: despise death. Nothing distresses us when we have ceased to fear it.

(Seneca, quoted in Dubois, 1909, p. 226)

"How far we are from this mentality!" exclaims Dubois, who was greatly concerned by the hypochondria among his patients, and their tendency to excessive neurotic worrying about death and illness. He saw this as a "second story" added to their suffering, adding another level to physical illness by escalating natural concern for one's health beyond its rational boundary, into anxious, pathological worrying.

Dubois proceeds to give a very homely but memorable illustration of this point:

A young man into whom I tried to instil a few principles of stoicism towards ailments stopped me at the first words, saying, "I understand, doctor; let me show you". And taking a pencil he drew a large black spot on a piece of paper. "This", said he, "is the disease, in its most general sense, the physical trouble – rheumatism, toothache, what you will – moral trouble, sadness, discouragement, melancholy. If I acknowledge it by fixing my attention upon it, I already trace a circle to the periphery of the black spot, and it has become larger. If I affirm it with acerbity the spot is increased by a new circle. There I am, busied with my pain, hunting for means to get rid of it, and the spot only becomes larger. If I preoccupy myself with it, if I fear the consequences, if I see the future gloomily, I have doubled or trebled the original spot". And, showing me the central point of the circle, the trouble reduced to its simplest expression, he said with a smile, "Should I not have done better to leave it as it was?"

"One exaggerates, imagines, anticipates affliction", wrote Seneca. For a long time, I have told my discouraged patients and have repeated to myself, "Do not let us build a second story to our sorrow by being sorry for our sorrow".

(Dubois, 1909, pp. 235–236)

He adds:

> We recognise here the example of concentric circles as showing increase in
> our physical and moral suffering. He who knows how to suffer suffers less.
> He accepts the trouble such as it is, without adding to it the terrors that preoc-
> cupation and apprehension produce. Like the animal, he reduces suffering to
> its simplest expression; he even goes further; he lessens the trouble by the
> thought, he succeeds in forgetting, in no longer feeling it.
>   What fine colour Seneca gave to this thought in his letter LXVIII to Lucil-
> ius: "Beware of aggravating your troubles yourself, and of making your posi-
> tion worse by your complaints. Grief is light when not exaggerated by the
> idea, and if we encourage ourselves, saying 'it is *nothing*', or at least, 'it is
> of small moment; let us endure it, it is about to stop', we render pain light
> by thinking it so". Yes; pain becomes light when we are able so to look at it,
> when we do not draw concentric circles around it, such as my patient ingen-
> iously described; when we do not multiply it by fear. That fine stoicism does
> not reign today.
>
> (*ibid.*, pp. 236–237)

In clinical practise, Dubois rejected the use of hypnosis, during the height of its
popularity, and resorted instead to vigorous psychological education and Socratic
dialogue, of this kind, designed to instil hope of cure in his clients, build confidence, and directly undermine their irrational beliefs and negative philosophies
of life.

Despite his emphasis upon cultivating a rational Stoic philosophy of life,
Dubois has little more to say about specific philosophical texts or theories. There
is one notable exception to this avoidance of academic debate, however, and that
is Dubois' criticism of the metaphysical theory of free will. Like the Stoics, who
were strictly speaking *compatibilists*, he argued in favour of universal causal
determinism. Dubois believed determinism to be a philosophical truth but he also
found its acceptance to be an important aid to psychotherapy because of its beneficial effect upon the emotions.

> from the beginning of human thought, philosophers like Socrates have under-
> stood the idea of moral determinism; [nevertheless] man has continued to
> think and to do good or evil. He has thought worse for being ignorant of
> the mechanism of thought; the neglect of these [deterministic] principles of
> psychology renders him less indulgent to the faults of others, without making
> him severe enough towards himself.
>
> (*ibid.*, pp. 47–48)

Although Dubois did not use hypnosis himself, he accepted the theory of suggestion, and several influential proponents of hypnotherapy (for example, Bernheim,

Baudouin, Morton Prince, and others), came to assimilate elements of Dubois' rational persuasion approach (*q.v.* Baudouin & Lestchinsky, 1924). In their hands, hypnosis or self-hypnosis could serve as an additional means to reinforce the internalization of healthy, rational beliefs. Dubois himself, though not a hypnotist, seems grudgingly to accept the relevance of his observations on autosuggestion to the practise of hypnotism.

> We are easily made victims by these auto-suggestions, as they are called today, when we have some plausible reason to believe them. I have often felt heat radiating from a stove which I was passing. I had understood that it was heated; when touched it was cold. There are people who have felt the oil and smelled the odour of petroleum when lifting a new lamp which has never contained any.
>
> One can recall thousands of examples of these errors of the senses which show the influence of imagination, the incredible power of mental representations. The success of hypnotism abundantly demonstrates this influence.
>
> (Dubois & Gallatin, 1908, pp. 27–28)

To some extent, the influence of Dubois' method of disputing pre-existing negative autosuggestions can be seen in modern cognitive-behavioural approaches to hypnotherapy, which are based upon the concept of "negative self-hypnosis" (NSH) introduced by Daniel Araoz (1981). Araoz and others effectively resurrected the old theory that holds that many forms of emotional disturbance, such as anxiety or depression, can be seen as partly due to the effects of negative autosuggestion or self-hypnosis. This notion was common in Victorian psychotherapy, and traces of it can even be found as far back as the 1840s in the writings of James Braid, the founder of hypnotherapy (Braid, 2009).

The notion of "negative self-hypnosis" was, of course, not available to the Stoics. If it *had* been, then they may have found it a useful analogy for their cognitive theory of emotional disturbance. Indeed, James Stockdale instinctively describes the Stoic concept of a "mental impression" (*phantasia*) as a form of autosuggestion.

> The Stoics gave that name to those bursts of suggestion that flash on the screen of your mind, usually when you're in tight straits, wooing you to believe that a crisis is imminent and that you should accede to the suggestion immediately and take counteraction. Stoics place great stock in man's obligation to exercise *stringent judgement* on whether to accept this suggestion at face value or use caution, play for time, and see if what you first believed you were being told was an exaggeration. Your response is both a judgemental and a moral act.
>
> (Stockdale, 1995, p. 235)

These "bursts of suggestion" (or, rather, "autosuggestion") are precisely what modern cognitive therapists mean by "automatic thoughts". As we have seen, Dubois himself did not combine the *techniques* of suggestion and autosuggestion with the *theory* of emotional disturbance as being due to autosuggestion. We can, however, find an example of an early twentieth century school of psychotherapy that not only saw autosuggestion as both the cause and cure of neuroses but also attempted to assimilate the philosophical precepts of Stoicism to this view.

Émile Coué and the new Nancy school

When the French pharmacist Émile Coué (1857–1926) was 28 years old, he met one of the pioneers of hypnotherapy, a country doctor named Ambroise-Auguste Liébault (1823–1904), and assisted him for about two years in his hypnotic clinic at Nancy. However, by 1910, Coué had abandoned classical hypnotism in favour of his technique of "conscious autosuggestion", in which subjects are taught how to use suggestion and imagination for themselves, without the use of a formal hypnotic induction. At this point, Coué founded a movement he termed the "new Nancy school", in reference to the Nancy school of Liébault, who had passed away a few years earlier. Coué became one of the most influential "self-help" gurus of the twentieth century, touring America with his public seminars and attracting an international following during the period when Paul Dubois' theories were still popular among psychotherapists.

Strikingly, Coué wrote, "Pythagoras and Aristotle taught auto-suggestion" (Coué, 1923, p. 3). Though his justification for this conclusion seems somewhat unclear, he could probably have found more material to explain and support it.

> We know, indeed, that the whole human organism is governed by the nervous system, the centre of which is the brain – the seat of thought. In other words, the brain, or mind, controls every cell, every organ, every function of the body. That being so, is it not clear that by means of thought we are the absolute masters of our physical organism and that, as the Ancients showed centuries ago, thought – or suggestion – can and does produce disease or cure it? Pythagoras taught the principle of auto-suggestion to his disciples. He wrote: "God the Father, deliver them from their sufferings, and show them what supernatural power is at their call".
>
> (*ibid.*, pp. 3–4)

The practise of repeating aphorisms, short verbal formulas, seems to have been associated with the ancient mystery religions and oracles, and the philosophical-therapeutic sect of Pythagoras which evolved from them.

> The Ancients well knew the power – often the terrible power – contained in the repetition of a phrase or formula. The secret of the undeniable influence

they exercised through the old Oracles resided probably, nay, certainly, in the force of suggestion.

(Coué, 1923, p. 27)

The most famous formulae associated with the Delphic Oracle of Apollo, a patron of philosophy, were "Know thyself" and "Nothing in excess". However, the dox-ographer Stobaeus recorded a list of 147 maxims attributed to the Delphic Oracle. They include a number of very Stoic-sounding sayings such as "Follow god", "Think as a mortal", "Master yourself", "Control anger", "Cling to discipline", "Long for wisdom", "Praise virtue", "Guard what is your own", "Shun what belongs to others", "Foresee the future", "Speak plainly", "Be happy with what you have", "Love your fortune", and "Be not discontented in life".

The Pythagoreans compiled their own lists of such aphorisms, which acquired cryptic symbolic meanings, and were referred to as *akousmata*, the "things lis-tened to", and *symbola*, the "symbols" or "watchwords". For example, according to Porphry, the precept "poke not the fire with a sword" was a reminder that one should not further provoke an angry person by attacking them with verbal criti-cisms; "eat not the heart", meant that one should not wallow in morbid emotions (Porphyry, trans., 1988, p. 131). These Pythagorean sayings, and those derived from the Greek Oracles, may well be the precursors of the Stoic precepts (*dog-mata*), which, as we shall see, appear to have performed a similar function.

Coué also makes insightful use of a passage from Aristotle that clearly out-lines the same mechanism of mind-body interaction that he took to underlie autosuggestion.

Even more definite is the doctrine of Aristotle, which taught that "a vivid imagination compels the body to obey it, for it is a natural principle of move-ment. Imagination, indeed, governs all of the forces of sensibility, while the latter, in its turn, controls the beating of the heart, and through it sets in motion all vital functions; thus the entire organism may be rapidly modified. Nevertheless, however vivid the imagination, it cannot change the form of a hand or foot or other member".

(Coué, 1923, p. 4)

Coué explains that this passage corresponds to two key principles of his own theory of autosuggestion,

1   The dominating role of the imagination.
2   The results to be expected from the practice of auto-suggestion must neces-sarily be limited to those coming within the bounds of physical possibility. (*ibid.*)

According to Coué's theory, which is not unlike the philosopher Spinoza's in this respect, the imagination is bound to evoke physical and emotional reactions more powerfully than the intellect alone can muster. We must fight fire with fire – use *empowering* images to counteract *enfeebling* ones. Even the Stoics did not depend *solely* upon the abstract power of reason. The prevalence of vivid imagery and potent rhetoric throughout all the major Stoic writings demonstrates their grasp of the extent to which the imagination, guided by reason, must be turned upon itself in order to effect real emotional change. As we shall see, a variety of mental exercises, including visualization techniques, were at the Stoic's disposal.

As an adolescent, Albert Ellis had studied Couéism, and he seems to have found it an attractive model of therapeutic self-help (Ellis, 2004, pp. 19–20). Ellis had initially claimed that the essence of rational emotive behaviour therapy (REBT) was that it emphasized what he called "autosuggestive insight", that is, helping the client to understand the role of ongoing negative autosuggestions in their problem (Ellis, 1962, p. 276). He acknowledges that Bernheim and Coué had emphasized the benefits of positive autosuggestion but argues that they had not fully addressed the role of *negative* autosuggestion in emotional disturbance. REBT, according to Ellis, was a novel approach because it encouraged clients to realize how negative autosuggestion is affecting them before they proceed to use positive counter-suggestions to change things. However, Coué and his school had already highlighted this notion of "autosuggestive insight" and, indeed, made it the essence of their own method.

> Autosuggestion is a double-edged weapon; well-used it works wonders, badly used it brings nothing but disaster. Up to the present you have wielded this weapon unconsciously, and made bad suggestions to yourselves, but that which I have taught you will prevent [you] from ever again making bad auto-suggestions, and if you should do so, you can only beat yourself upon the breast, and say: It is my own fault; entirely my own fault!
>
> (Coué, 1923, p. 102)

Coué's fundamental insight was that autosuggestion could be a force *either* for good *or* bad. We either use it for our benefit or allow it to work spontaneously and, perhaps, to our ruin. The most important part of Coué's method was that clients should come to share the same basic insight.

However, Ellis also criticizes Couéism for encouraging positive thinking without direct *disputation* of the original negative thoughts. He sees this as a kind of "magical thinking" that attributes too much power to positive affirmations.

> Many people think that rational therapy [REBT] is closely related to Emile Coué's autosuggestion . . . but it is actually just the reverse of these techniques in many ways. It is true that clients become emotionally disturbed largely because of their own negative thinking or autosuggestion, and that is why they sometimes snap out of their depressions and anxieties quite quickly – if temporarily – when they are induced to do some kind of positive thinking or autosuggestion. But accentuating the positive is itself a false system of belief,

since there is no scientific truth to the statements that "Day by day in every way I'm getting better and better". . . . In fact, this kind of Pollyannaism can be as pernicious as the negative claptrap which clients tell themselves to bring about neurotic conditions.

(Ellis, 2004, p. 37)

Ellis expresses this concern in his own notoriously forceful style, not unlike the blunt or even abrasive language sometimes adopted by Stoics like Epictetus, and the Cynic philosophers before him.

In REBT we do not merely stress positive thinking or autosuggestion, but a thoroughgoing revealing and uprooting of the negative nonsense which clients endlessly repeat. . . .
 Another way of putting this is to say that no matter how often a woman repeats, "Every day in every way I'm getting better and better", . . . if she keeps saying to herself much louder and more often, "I'm really a shit; I'm no fucking good; I'll never possibly get better", all the positive thinking in the world is not going to help her. Unless she is forcefully led to challenge and undermine her own negative thinking, as in effective cognitive psychotherapy, she is still a gone goose.

(*ibid.*, pp. 37–38)

To some extent, this criticism is justified, and the subsequent combination of Coué's methods with those of Dubois undertaken by Baudouin and others would help to redress this imbalance. However, in all fairness, Coué himself did insist that clients should become more aware of the negative autosuggestions they give themselves and thereby realize that they were both false and harmful.

Baudouin and Lestchinsky's *The Inner Discipline*

Coué wrote little and most of his books contain transcripts of seminars or exhortations aimed at the public. However, a follower of Coué, the French academic and psychotherapist Charles Baudouin, provided a more erudite account of the New Nancy School approach, into which he assimilated elements of early psychoanalysis and classical philosophy. Baudouin recognized the relevance of Stoicism to modern psychotherapy and self-help, and its particular similarity to the "rational persuasion" therapy of Dubois (Baudouin & Lestchinsky, 1924, p. 50). Hence, he and Lestchinsky dedicated a whole chapter of their short book *The Inner Discipline* (1924) to expounding the therapeutic principles of Stoicism and their relevance to psychotherapy.

Hellenistic philosophy in particular, and, indeed, much of classical philosophy in general, can be seen to prefigure modern cognitive-behavioural psychotherapy. However, like Ellis and Beck almost half a century later, Baudouin and

Lestchinsky saw *Stoicism* as the ancient precursor of rational psychotherapy *par excellence*.

> One of the most original characteristics of Stoicism was the stress it laid upon a vigorous discipline, upon the education of the character. That is why, in the present handbook, we select Stoicism for special consideration from among the classical philosophies.
>
> (*ibid.*, p. 89)

Baudouin and Lestchinsky recognize the emphasis found in Stoicism upon continual rehearsal of practical exercises as part of a therapeutic regime. "One of the most firmly established among such principles is the law of habit", they write, "and the need for *training*" (*ibid.*, p. 216). Exercises must be practised daily in Stoicism, something they compare to the Indian tradition of practising yoga exercises. They explain that their approach to rational psychotherapy also required regular practise. Likewise, modern CBT can be distinguished from other modalities of psychotherapy by virtue of the fundamental emphasis it tends to place upon daily practise of homework assignments. Clients are trained to develop cognitive and behavioural skills that are rehearsed in the consulting room under the supervision of the therapist before being practised at home, between sessions, until they become habitual.

Baudouin's enthusiasm for Stoicism is qualified by a preference for Christian self-help, and somewhat limited by the classical scholarship available to him. Nevertheless, he quotes both Epictetus and Marcus Aurelius over and over again, at much greater length than either Beck or Ellis, and clearly outlines the basic therapeutic philosophy of Stoicism. As such, Baudouin undoubtedly provides the best example to date of an attempt to assimilate Stoic literature within modern "rational" psychotherapy, the forerunner of CBT. He and Lestchinsky begin by recognizing the fundamental dogma of Stoicism: "One of the first of these philosophers' precepts is that we must thoroughly grasp the distinction between the things which are in our power and the things which are not in our power" (*ibid.*, p. 40). On this count, I believe Baudouin has surpassed Beck and Ellis in his grasp of Stoicism's relevance for psychotherapy. This principle, which reminds us to carefully distinguish what we do (thoughts and actions) from what merely happens to us (everything else), seems to be more fundamental to Stoicism than the maxim of Epictetus quoted most often in modern CBT literature, which attributes emotional disturbance to our judgements rather than to things themselves. As mentioned in the first chapter, this distinction quoted by Baudouin is the very first principle introduced in the *Encheiridion* of Epictetus, from which the other aspects of Stoicism follow.

Baudouin and Lestchinsky also recognize the relevance of other features of Stoicism for modern psychotherapy to a much greater extent than either Beck or Ellis did. They discuss the Stoic psychology of self-knowledge, determinism, and the Stoic attitude of acceptance toward that which is outside our control. Although the sages of classical antiquity seemed to them to overvalue reason, Baudouin and Lestchinsky think that they were basically right to see the proper use of man's rational faculty as a powerful means for the "inner discipline" of self-help and psychotherapy.

> In the first place it enables us to gain an accurate *knowledge* of ourselves and of things. Knowledge is power. "Know thyself", said the Greek philosophers, and Buddha voiced the same precept. The Stoics tell us that we must distinguish clearly between things in our power and things not in our power, in order to regulate our desire in the light of this distinction, and to avoid unreasonable wishes. Thus, for the philosophers of the Stoic school, an understanding of universal determinism, a recognition of the inexorable interlacement of causes and effects, was one of the first premises of wisdom. We cannot but be interested to note that, in our own day, Dubois founds his therapeutic method of moralisation upon the same principle of determinism.
>   But our reason has an additional task in this struggle with ourselves. We can use it in the form of the *rational persuasion* which Dubois has organised into a therapeutic system. We shall do well to remember that the Stoics had grasped the importance of this method, for their advice was that we should practise a pitiless analysis, that we might convince ourselves of the worthlessness of the objects towards which passion was leading us astray.
>   (Baudouin & Lestchinsky, 1924, pp. 217–218)

Baudouin and Lestchinsky's criticism of the overvaluation of reason in classical Socratic philosophy was once a common one. In previous decades, people often discounted Stoicism as being "overly rational" or "intellectual". However, to some extent, this may be based upon misconceptions caused by difficulties in translation. The Greeks and Romans used different words to describe different aspects of reasoning. Moreover, their emphasis upon the role of exercise and training, which these authors note, clearly implies that they appreciated various processes were involved in reasoning, some of which required repeated practise in order to instil change. Baudouin and Lestchinsky's addition, the concentrated repetition of autosuggestions, is not completely alien to ancient philosophy, though. It can be compared to various passages found in the Stoic literature and elsewhere, as we shall see. It will suffice at this stage to draw attention to the contradiction involved in dismissing Stoicism as "merely intellectual" when it is clearly characterized by a practical emphasis on the development of psychological self-discipline through specific daily exercises. As we shall see, Stoicism consists of both *cognitive* and *behavioural* exercises that constitute part of a therapeutic lifestyle and daily regime.

Moreover, despite his partial criticism of the philosophical approach to therapy in general, Baudouin did acknowledge the value of Stoic contemplative exercises. Central to Dubois' rational psychotherapy was the concept that simply encouraging clients to contemplate the meaning of universal causal determinism often had positive psychological benefits. Baudouin recognized that this particular method of philosophical contemplation, as a form of psychotherapy, was also fundamental to Stoicism. Both Dubois and Baudouin were psychotherapists who were forced to educate their clients in "plain English" rather than through abstract or technical philosophical jargon. Therapists today call this procedure of teaching their clients relevant psychological facts and theories "psycho-education". Baudouin, like Dubois, illustrated the contemplation of determinism to the layman simply by reference to the progress of modern science.

> Science, a philosophical knowledge of the world, discloses the existence of universal determinism, discloses the never-ending chain of causes and effects, and thus proves to us how numerous are the things which are not in our power.
>
> (*ibid.*, p. 40)

There are many ways in which one can contemplate determinism, and a variety of psychological benefits can be drawn from this kind of practise. As Baudouin points out, one benefit of this perspective is that it encourages a realistic and balanced attitude toward the question of which things are within our power to control and prevents us from expending energy wastefully by fighting against ourselves. Contemplation of determinism tends to promote a sense of emotional equanimity in many people, as the Stoics observed.

> For, as concerns things which are not in our power, there is but one manly attitude, that which is summed up in the Stoic maxim "*sustine et abstine*" – be steadfast, and forego. . . .
>
> Nothing should be done without a purpose. We must not wish for the impossible, or try to do what is impossible. We must not run our heads against a wall, for we shall only injure ourselves without breaking down the wall. If we follow these recommendations, we shall certainly economise our energies! This principle of economy of effort ("*abstine*") pervades the Stoical doctrine.
>
> (*ibid.*, pp. 42–43)

The slogan that Baudouin quotes in Latin was a well-known maxim of Epictetus and his Stoic school and is more commonly translated into English as "endure and renounce" or "bear and forbear".

Ancient Stoic novitiates probably began their training by learning both to *endure* the fear and pain caused by illusory harm, and to *renounce* the craving and sensory pleasure caused by illusory gain. By this was meant the loss or gain of external things – such as health, wealth and reputation – classed by the Stoics as fundamentally "indifferent", or rather as not worth worrying about. Instead, the student of Stoicism learns to place absolute value upon the cultivation of wisdom (*sophia*) and mental well-being (*eudaimonia*), the only things that truly matter in terms of the philosophical art of living. The Stoics believed that common sense tells us on reflection that people tend to disturb themselves by worrying too much about things that are outside of their control, banging their heads against a wall. However, it usually requires patient practise and self-discipline to train oneself to be on the outlook for this bad habit and to nip it in the bud. The price we pay for becoming overly preoccupied with external events, a natural human weakness, is that we tend to become forgetful of our own attitude toward life and neglect to look after our own mental health. The inner strength of the ideal Stoic sage begins with what Baudouin calls his "economy of effort"; he carefully avoids wasting his energy on futile preoccupations, allowing him to focus more of his attention on what he can actually change.

Moreover, Baudouin and Lestchinsky recognized that the Stoic concept of our sphere of control and responsibility offers a possible philosophical solution to the issue of morbid rumination over the past and the unhealthy and excessive sense of guilt, self-blame, etc., so common among clients in modern psychotherapy.

> As for regret and remorse, as for the tortures we inflict on ourselves on account of a past which we cannot change, these also fall within the category of the wishes that relate to things which are not in our power. They involve a futile expenditure of energy. Let us see to it that we do better in the future, but let us cease to deplore having done ill in the past. Phocylides, the poet and sage who lived in the sixth century B.C. wrote: "Do not let past evils disturb you, for what is done cannot be undone".
>
> (*ibid.*, p. 44)

Modern CBT practitioners often attempt to dispute irrational self-blame or unhealthy obsessions with past events in a similar manner, by drawing attention to our inability to change the past. If guilt serves a purpose, it is surely to motivate us to change *today*, in order to prepare for *tomorrow*, but not to condemn ourselves to endless complaining about *yesterday*. Likewise, as Baudouin notes, the Stoics advise us against attaching too much importance to the distant future, to the neglect of the present moment, because the future is both uncertain and beyond our immediate control. The true locus of our control, and therefore our primary concern, is the *here and now*, from moment to moment. It is in the present moment that lessons are learned *from* the past, and preparation is made *for* the future. Many modern therapists think of the "here and now" as an important concept derived from Buddhist thought, but it is an idea native to European philosophy, and a characteristic feature of Stoicism is its emphasis upon the here and now and learning to live more in the present moment. Indeed, the English phrase "here and now" is actually a direct translation of the Latin idiom *hic et nunc*, used by Aquinas and other medieval Christian philosophers.

Baudouin and Lestchinsky's writings have the virtue of expressing Stoic ideas in plain and simple language, although sometimes they may be guilty of over-simplification.

> Imagination and opinion are pre-eminently to be classed among the things which are within our power. There is a familiar adage: If we can't get what we like, we must like what we have. The Stoics held the same view, though on a somewhat higher plane. Instead of lamenting because we cannot change our lot, let us learn to love it. Happiness and unhappiness are, to a great extent, matters of imagination and opinion.
>
> (*ibid.*, p. 45)

Nevertheless, they provide a good introduction to Stoic thought and its role in psychotherapy and self-help. Moreover, as far as I am aware, this book is the only example of a detailed discussion of this topic in the literature of twentieth century psychotherapy. It certainly both predates the writings of Beck and Ellis and makes more explicit reference to Stoic therapy.

We have now looked at the way in which a range of "rational" or "cognitive" psychotherapists such as Dubois, Baudouin, Ellis, Beck, and others have drawn upon Stoicism and related philosophical literature. In doing so, we have already had the opportunity to mention some of the most important Stoic authors, to introduce some of the basic precepts of Stoicism, and to touch briefly on the kind of therapeutic exercises employed in ancient philosophy, such as the contemplation of universal causal determinism. We are now ready to focus our attention directly on the general concept of philosophical therapy in antiquity and the nature of Stoic theory and practise in particular.

Chapter 3

A brief history of philosophical therapy

To understand the relationship between Stoicism and psychotherapy, we need to consider the historical roots of the philosophy. As we shall see, it is likely that some therapeutic concepts and practises were already in use by the followers of one of the very earliest philosophers, the enigmatic Pythagoras of Samos (ca. 580–490 BC). Precursors of certain therapeutic concepts may perhaps even have been in use among the mystery cults, such as Orphism, from which Pythagorean philosophy probably evolved. However, to the endless frustration of modern scholars, these pre-Socratic traditions were notoriously secretive and clandestine, primarily oral traditions, and very little can be said about their practises or beliefs with confidence.

The Socratic schools of philosophical therapy

Socrates himself wrote nothing that survives, but his character and the events of his life made such a profound impression upon his contemporaries that, following his execution, he became a kind of philosophical martyr and propelled interest in philosophy to the forefront of Greek society. Ten schools or "sects" were founded by his immediate followers, most notably the famous Academy of Plato but also the sects of Antisthenes, a forerunner of the Cynics, and the briefly-lived school of the Greek general Xenophon, both of which particularly influenced the later Stoic school. "Of those who succeeded him", writes Diogenes Laertius, "and who are called the Socratic school, the chiefs were Plato, Xenophon, and Antisthenes" (*Lives*, 2.5). However, each of the ten "Socratic" schools developed his original ideas in different ways. Plato's Academy, probably the first institution of its kind, published numerous written *dialogues*, which portray the philosophical discussions of Socrates. However, Plato appears to have been increasingly drawn to more metaphysical speculations, influenced by contemporary Pythagoreans, such as his friend Archytas of Tarentum. The direction in which he took the Socratic teaching could be described, to some extent, as "academic", in the modern sense of being abstract and intellectual at the expense of practical application. According to Diogenes Laertius, in fact, after hearing Plato read his dialogue *Lysis*,

Socrates exclaimed, "By Heracles, what a number of lies this young man is telling about me!" because it attributed many things to Socrates that he had never said (*Digoenes Laertius*, 3.1).

It is important to appreciate that ancient philosophy in general had a *practical* emphasis that was lost over the centuries, and that most philosophers, even the Academics, were more concerned with moral and psychological self-improvement than modern-day academic philosophers tend to be. However, Plato and the Academy were traditionally contrasted with the Diogenes of Sinope and the Cynics, who represented a more extreme emphasis on the practical side of philosophy, as a means of developing strength of character. The Cynics generally sneered at the sort of abstract metaphysical discussions associated with Plato's Academy.

Diogenes the Cynic and Plato reputedly exchanged several barbed remarks. However, the Cynic tradition was sometimes said to have originated a generation earlier with a close friend of Socrates called Antisthenes. The name Cynic derives from the Greek word for *dog*, and refers to the frank and often abrasive manner, known as "plain speaking" (*parrhesia*), in which Cynics would address others, typically encouraging them to adopt a more virtuous lifestyle. Diogenes reputedly explained that while other dogs bite their enemies, the Cynics bite their friends, in order to help them. Antisthenes likewise mused that physicians must sometimes use bitter remedies to cure their patients.

The Cynics wrote and debated less than other schools, and focused instead upon adopting the practical lifestyle of the philosopher, renouncing all but the bare necessities and disregarding the esteem of others in an attempt to eschew social customs in favour of a life at one with nature. As we shall see, the Cynics were very closely aligned with the Stoics and may be seen as their more outlandish precursors. The ancient historian Diogenes Laertius actually refers to Antisthenes as "the founder of the more manly Stoic school" (*Lives*, 6.1). Indeed, throughout his *Discourses*, Epictetus refers to Diogenes of Sinope alongside Socrates as an example of the *ideal* philosophical role model for young Stoics.

The different Socratic schools, or sects, flourished to varying degrees. When Plato died, his most talented student, Aristotle, was snubbed, and Plato's nephew Speusippus took over running the Academy instead. This apparent act of nepotism triggered events of monumental significance for the history of philosophy, because Aristotle proceeded to set up his own rival school, the Lyceum, at the other side of Athens. Thus began a long-standing tradition of competition between increasingly sophisticated and well-organized philosophical schools. Despite the importance sometimes attributed to Freudian psychoanalysis, it only flourished for little over half a century, progressively superseded by humanistic and cognitive-behavioural approaches from the 1950s onward. By contrast, the "Cynic-Stoic" tradition originating with Socrates and his follower Antisthenes, leading through the Cynics, and concluding with the Stoics, down to the time of Marcus Aurelius, endured as an active therapeutic movement for *over six centuries*.

Zeno and the Stoic school

A few decades after Plato's death, following a shipwreck, Zeno of Citium found himself in Athens, where he obtained a copy of Xenophon's *Memorabilia* of Socrates. He was reputedly so impressed that he sought out the closest living person he could find to the sage-like figure of Socrates, and, thereby, became the student of the Cynic philosopher Crates. Around the end of the fourth century BC, having studied with the Cynics, Zeno started his own school of philosophy, which met in the famous Athenian *Stoa Poikile*, a large "painted colonnade" facing the Athenian agora, the wall of which was decorated with four paintings depicting historical and mythological battles. This setting was perhaps a foretaste of the militaristic theme that runs throughout much Stoic literature, where life is seen as a kind of psychological battle to be fought with philosophical weapons. Zeno's school consequently became known as "Stoicism", after the stoa or porch where they met.

   The Stoics appear to have seen themselves as more faithful to the lifestyle and ethics of Socrates than Plato's followers, but more moderate and willing to engage with society than the Cynics. It is, therefore, important to realize that at least some of the Stoics, most notably Epictetus, viewed themselves as the true followers of Socrates, and revered the story of his life and death, holding him up as a role model approximating to their ideal of the enlightened sage. Stoicism is self-consciously a *Socratic* sect, in other words. As we shall see, modern CBT tends to refer to itself as employing a "Socratic method", albeit without much recognition of what this phrase implies or the fact that ancient Stoicism constitutes the main sect of Socratic therapeutics.

The Hellenistic schools

To continue our historical sketch: a couple of generations after the death of Socrates, Alexander the Great, reputedly a student of Aristotle, rapidly spread his empire to the east following a series of stunning military victories. As a consequence, the influence of Athenian culture and philosophy expanded throughout the known world. During the "Hellenistic" period that followed, several dominant schools of Greek philosophy arose. After the final collapse of the Hellenistic regime in the first century BC, and the continuing rise to power of the Roman Republic, these schools began to play a role at the centre of Roman culture. Indeed, for centuries, many educated Romans employed Greek as the language of science and philosophy. For example, *The Meditations* of the Roman Emperor Marcus Aurelius, one of the most revered and influential Stoic texts, was written in Greek, although its author spoke Latin.

   Greek philosophers were highly respected and travelled to teach in Rome. Most notably, in 155 BC Diogenes of Babylon, the head of the Stoic school, travelled to Rome as part of an ambassadorial mission, along with an Aristotelian and Academic philosopher. These philosophers caused a sensation among the younger generation. However, the Stoic philosophy appears to have especially resonated with Roman values. Shortly after this event, Panaetius of Rhodes, the last head of the Athenian Stoic school, became the tutor of the famous general and politician Scipio Africanus the Younger, and his friends known as the Scipionic Circle.

Stoicism and other "Hellenistic schools" of philosophy continued to influence European culture until the rise of Christianity as the state religion of the Roman Empire many centuries later. The Hellenistic schools are usually identified as follows:

1   The Academy of Plato.
2   The Lyceum or Peripatetic school of Aristotle.
3   The Stoa or Stoic school of Zeno.
4   The Garden or school of Epicurus.
5   The movement known as Skepticism, which later took root within the Academy.
6   The movement known as Cynicism, which preceded and continued to be particularly associated with the Stoics.

We might also include reference to the survival of certain traces of the very ancient *Pythagorean* sect in the Hellenistic period, sometimes known as "Neopythagoreanism". As we shall see, in discussing Stoic philosophy, most of these other movements must be taken into account. It was not unusual for some philosophers to draw on ideas and techniques from rival schools. In particular, the Stoics refer favourably to aspects of Platonism, Cynicism, Epicureanism, and Pythagoreanism, though criticizing rival schools in other respects. Indeed, there are many positive references to ancient Pythagorean contemplative practises throughout the surviving Stoic literature, and this affinity may ultimately derive from a lost book, *On the Doctrines of the Pythagoreans*, reputedly written by Zeno, the founder of Stoicism (*Lives*, 7.1).

Psychotherapy in Hellenistic philosophy

All of these schools, to varying degrees, derive from Socrates, though they responded to his teachings in different ways, and in combination with other influences. All appear to have practised techniques and strategies designed to control unhealthy emotions and impulses and to achieve enlightenment and peace of mind. In them, "spiritual", "philosophical", and "therapeutic" practises merge together, or rather the modern *distinctions* between these categories were alien to ancient philosophy. Pierre Hadot, one of the leading scholars in this area, notes that all of the Hellenistic schools of philosophy defined the goal of life in terms that encompass some form of "peace of mind" (Hadot, 2002, p. 102). From this perspective, philosophy becomes a "remedy for human worries", a psychological therapy.

However, different sects explained the causes of suffering in different ways. For the Cynics, human misery was mainly due to the baneful influence of unnatural social conventions. For the Epicureans, it was the quest for false pleasures, and for the Skeptics false opinions in general. However, for the Stoics misery was ultimately due to the tendency to place too much value upon pleasure and the avoidance of pain, as well as the misleading influence of other people's false opinions. Hadot claims that whether or not they claimed descent from Socrates, all the Hellenistic schools agreed that human misery and vice are due largely to some form of ignorance. They tend to agree that evil and human suffering are maintained primarily by our faulty value judgements rather than external factors – good and evil exist within us, although we tend to look outside for their sources in life. Hadot concludes: "People can therefore be cured of their ills only if they are persuaded to change their value judgements, and in this sense all these philosophies wanted to be therapeutic" (Hadot, 2002, p. 102).

Perhaps because of the increasing commerce between different cultures during these centuries, a greater sense of anxiety and confusion prevailed. Struggling to cope with the rate of change, people sought a means of overcoming their emotional distress. In this respect, as many historians have commented, this period in history resembles our own, except that modern information technology has replaced ancient trade routes as a source of information that is sometimes confusing and overwhelming.

> As a matter of fact, people in antiquity were just as filled with anguish as we are today, and ancient poetry often preserves the echo of this anguish, which sometimes goes as far as despair. Like us, the ancients bore the burden of the past, the uncertainty of the future, and the fear of death. Indeed, it was for this human anguish that the ancient philosophies – particularly Epicureanism and Stoicism – sought to provide a remedy. These philosophies were therapies, intended to provide a cure for anguish, and to bring freedom and self-mastery, and their goal was to allow people to free themselves from the past and the future, so that they could live within the present.
>
> (Hadot, 1995, pp. 221–222)

From a modern point of view, the ancient philosophical practises that seem most relevant to psychotherapy and self-help can be divided into the following categories of cognitive and behavioural strategies.

1   Philosophical attitudes, or maxims, memorization, and acceptance of which helped to promote mental health.
2   Lifestyle changes, such as the adoption of moderate diet, regulation of sleep, physical exercise, plain clothing, etc.
3   Contemplative techniques involving mental imagery, such as visualization of the earth seen from above, or the mental rehearsal of anticipated events, etc.

4   Rhetorical exercises, involving reading of key texts, discussion of applied philosophical themes, and the keeping of a personal notebook or journal in which verbal exercises are performed on a regular basis.

Unfortunately, most of the techniques and concepts involved in classical philosophical therapy must be reconstructed by careful analysis of a wide range of texts that hint at them, take them for granted, or allude to them in passing. The lack of a clear outline of them handed down to us in the tiny proportion of classical texts that survive today is one reason why they have been largely overlooked in modern times.

Fortunately, the process of reconstructing philosophical therapeutic methods has already begun, thanks primarily to the seminal research of the distinguished French academic quoted previously, Pierre Hadot, who has published several books on the subject in recent decades. Although he describes a range of ancient therapeutic techniques and strategies with great precision, Hadot's research has been largely neglected by modern psychotherapists, who have yet to take the work of contemporary historical and philosophical scholarship and evaluate it from the applied perspective of clinical psychotherapeutic practise. A first step in this direction would be achieved by attempting to show the extent to which ancient philosophy and modern psychotherapy relate to each other. As previously discussed, of all the schools of Hellenistic philosophy, it is evidently the *Stoic* school, especially that founded by Epictetus and followed by Marcus Aurelius, which offers the most obvious parallel with modern psychotherapy.

CBT has been around for roughly 60 years now, since Ellis first began developing REBT in the mid-1950s. By comparison, the period from the founding of the Athenian Stoic school by Zeno around 301 BC to the death of the Emperor Marcus Aurelius, the last great Stoic philosopher, in 180 AD, spans nearly *five centuries*. The Stoics appear to have written many *thousands* of books and shorter works during this period. Chrysippus alone, their leading scholar, "industrious beyond all other men", was said to have written over 705 books (*Lives*, 7.7). However, like much of classical philosophy, virtually the entire output of the Stoic school was either destroyed or lost, and only a few fragments and sayings survive from the school's founders. Most of what now remains of the once voluminous Stoic literature consists in the letters and essays of Seneca, *The Discourses* and accompanying *Handbook* of Epictetus, *The Meditations* of Marcus Aurelius, and some fragments from earlier Stoics. We also have some commentary from writers of other schools, particularly Cicero and Plutarch, who subscribed to the Academic school. There are, arguably, also traces of Stoic influences in the writings of the Roman poets as well as in the *New Testament* and other early Christian literature. The *Acts of the Apostles* actually portrays Paul addressing a group of Stoic and Epicurean philosophers at the Areopagus in Athens, and quoting a couple of lines of poetry from Aratus, a student of Zeno (*Acts*, 17.16–31). Early Christians believed that Seneca knew the Apostle Paul, who grew up in a predominantly Stoic town called Tarsus, although there seems to be little evidence to support this claim.

Epictetus was originally a slave in the household of a freedman called Epaphroditus who served as a Greek secretary to Emperor Nero. Epaphroditus informed Nero that a conspiracy was being organized against him by a senator called Piso. Nero's response was a political purge, which included the execution of Seneca, whom he suspected of playing a role in the Pisonian conspiracy. At some point, Epictetus won his freedom and went on to become the most influential teacher of Stoic philosophy in the history of Rome. However, he never refers to Seneca, and neither does Marcus Aurelius (apart from some brief mentions in his private correspondence with Fronto).

On the other hand, Marcus Aurelius thanks his favourite Stoic tutor, Junius Rusticus, for giving him "The recognition that I needed training and therapy [*therapeia*] for my character", adding "And for introducing me to Epictetus' lectures – and loaning me his own copy" (*Meditations*, 1.7). Marcus refers to Epictetus more frequently in *The Meditations* than to any other philosopher. Although only four of the original eight volumes of Epictetus' *Discourses* survive today, Marcus quotes sayings from Epictetus not found in the surviving *Discourses* so it's likely he'd read the lost ones as well.

Epictetus was a crippled slave but he preached that only a Stoic like himself could truly claim to be a "king". He said that the aristocratic young men who attended his lectures were the real "slaves" because they were in thrall to their own strong desires and emotions, and to other people's opinions of them. Despite being one of the most powerful political and military figures in European history, Emperor Marcus Aurelius apparently dedicated his life to daily contemplation of Epictetus' teachings regarding the true meaning of inner slavery and freedom. "That an ex-slave actually shaped a Roman Emperor's deepest thoughts is one of the most remarkable testimonies to the power and applicability of Epictetus' words" (Long, 2002, p. 12).

Stockdale puts it rather more colloquially when he writes, "Epictetus, the great teacher, played his part in changing the leadership of Rome from the swill he had known in the Nero White House to the power and decency it knew under Marcus Aurelius" (1995, p. 187). The English historian, Edward Gibbon wrote of this period in his famous *Decline and Fall of the Roman Empire*:

> If a man were called upon to fix the period in the history of the human race was most happy and prosperous, he would without hesitation name that which elapsed from the accession of Nerva (A.D. 96) to the death of Marcus Aurelius (A.D. 180). The united reigns of the five emperors of the era are possibly the only period of history in which the happiness of a great people was the sole object of government.
>
> (Gibbon, 1909, p. 78)

This was the height of Stoicism's influence at Rome. After the death of Marcus Aurelius, however, Christianity gradually came to supplant pagan philosophy, including Stoicism.

A thousand years later, as the authority of Roman Catholicism gradually declined during the European Renaissance period, Stoicism experienced a revival in a form sometimes called "Neostoicism". Scattered traces of Stoic influence are found throughout the writings of many intellectuals from the early modern era. By this time, however, the practise of Stoicism as an art of living had long since disappeared and philosophy had become a largely bookish and academic subject. However, as we have so far discussed, the modern phenomenon of psychotherapy, originating within the nineteenth century medical field, has led to an indirect and gradual rediscovery of practical Stoic exercises in the guise of the various modalities of CBT.

Stoic philosophy as psychotherapy

What do the surviving texts tell us about Stoicism as a psychotherapy? Seneca said, "Without wisdom the mind is sick" (*Letters*, 15). Cicero described philosophy as "Socratic medicine" (*Socratica medicina*) and "medicine for the soul" (*animi medicina*), phrases which could equally well be translated simply as "Socratic therapy" or "psychotherapy". In the *Tusculan Disputations*, he argues that the philosopher will treat diseases of the mind (*animi morbum*) in the way that physicians treat diseases of the body, except that the philosopher will primarily be his *own* physician in this regard and take care of his own soul (Sellars, 2003, pp. 65–68). Likewise, Epictetus advised his students that philosophy was the study of their *own* "art of living", but that the art of living of another person was his own business (*Discourses*, 1.15.1–5).

However, it seems that although philosophers primarily focused upon applying therapy to their own psyche, they sometimes also attempted to assist others through their teachings. Indeed, the very fact that Epictetus and other philosophers took on students and lectured in public seems to illustrate that they assumed some benefit could be given to others in this regard. Moreover, it is a striking quirk of fate that the three main surviving primary sources for Stoic philosophy, which happen to be classics of great literary value, seem to represent three distinct *modalities* of philosophical psychotherapy: Seneca's letters illustrate the individual mentoring of a student, the transcripts of Epictetus record group discussions, and Marcus Aurelius' private journal records his personal Stoic regime of contemplation. These modalities can be seen, respectively, as analogous to modern individual *psychotherapy*, group therapy *workshops*, and self-help journals or *workbooks*.

The ancient Stoics would undoubtedly have perceived the similarity between modern CBT and their own therapy of the passions. By contrast, a modern academic professor of philosophy would, no doubt, be looked upon with incredulity by an ancient Stoic philosopher. The Stoics, like Socrates before them, would quite probably refuse to dignify the modern subject with the name "philosophy" at all – what we call academic "philosophy" today would arguably be closer in spirit to what they knew as "Sophistry". The Stoics generally disparaged mere rhetoric or wordplay, which they opposed to *practical* philosophy, or genuine love of wisdom.

As Hadot observes, most Hellenistic schools of philosophy shared the assumption that, with patient effort and training, man could rise above his circumstances and learn to conquer his desires and emotions. Underlying this conviction is the parallelism between physical and spiritual exercises: just as, by dint of repeated physical exercises, athletes give new form and strength to their bodies, so the philosopher develops his strength of soul, modifies his inner climate, transforms his vision of the world, and, finally, his entire being. The analogy seems all the more self-evident in that the *gymnasium*, the place where physical exercises were practised, was the same place where philosophy lessons were given; in other words, it was also the place for training in *spiritual* gymnastics (Hadot, 1995, p. 102).

Marcus Aurelius speaks of the Stoic philosopher training himself to become, "an athlete in the greatest of all contests – the struggle not to be overwhelmed by anything that happens" (*Meditations*, 3.4). However, over the course of European history, philosophers gradually left the open air of the ancient gymnasia and immured themselves in the basements of dusty libraries instead. The practical training, meditative regime, and disciplined lifestyle of the Socratic sects were abandoned. "Doing philosophy" slowly became synonymous with talking about philosophy. Philosophy, in short, became little more than a caricature of its former self. In the following chapters, by contrast, we will examine the specific means by which the Stoics and other sects trained themselves, through daily exercise regimes, to master the ancient Socratic art of living.

Chapter 4

Stoic philosophy and psychology

Stoic philosophy and psychology must be reconstructed by reference to what few texts remain. We must also contend with the fact that we are dealing with a tradition that spans two ancient languages, Greek and Latin, and the teachings of many individual philosophers living many centuries apart. However, there does seem to be a surprising consistency in the basic theory and practise that emerges upon a close analysis of the surviving writings.

The principle doctrines (dogmata) of Stoicism

Stoic philosophy was founded upon a system of basic doctrines, called *dogmata* ("opinions") or *kanones* ("rules of life"). As Hadot states, during the Hellenistic period, philosophical theories were reduced to "a theoretical, systematic, highly concentrated nucleus" of key doctrines, which could serve as a guide to life (Hadot, 1995, pp. 267–268). These had to be psychologically powerful enough to influence the emotions and behaviour of students and yet simple enough to be kept constantly ready to hand (*procheiron*). Hadot postulated that Stoicism and other branches of Hellenistic philosophy were expressed as tightly integrated systems not because the ancients wanted to provide a comprehensive theoretical account of the whole of reality but so that they could exert greater psychological force. A system based on a handful of core principles is more persuasive and easier to recall than a list of discrete stand-alone rules.

With respect to the role of these short maxims or sayings, it is important to remember that ancient philosophy evolved out of *oral* traditions of wisdom. Ancient poetry and oratory made use of rhetorical techniques, like metaphor and assonance, which are aesthetically pleasing but also aided memorization and recall. Likewise, early philosophers, most notably Socrates, did *not* write books but taught small circles of attentive students orally. The doctrines most likely to be passed down this way were the ones that happened to be most memorable, usually because they were expressed in a vivid and compelling manner.

Although writing down ideas in a book may have many benefits, it also discourages students from making the effort required to commit the essence of the teaching to memory. This has profound implications for a philosophy that aims to be *therapeutic*. The psychological effects of Stoicism and other therapeutic philosophies depend upon the complete internalization of certain key ideas, or rules of living, and their future recall in the face of stressful situations. The rhetorical power of oral tuition can assist this process of deep internalization but so can the deliberate use of a number of traditional *mnemonic* strategies. For example, the compiling of short lists, common in the Buddhist oral traditions but also found in notions such as the Epicurean "fourfold remedy", or Epictetus' Stoic three-fold rule of life, etc. Lists are equally popular in modern self-help literature, of course, such as Covey's well-known book, *The Seven Habits of Highly Effective People* (1989). Likewise, the use of diagrams and symbols, such as the Pythagorean *tetractys*, or acronyms and symbolic words and phrases, may also have been used to assist the process of memorization and recall of beneficial ideas.

The Stoic love of condensing philosophical doctrines into short summative phrases employs the rhetorical technique known as *aphorism*. The two most famous examples of such aphorisms used in Greek philosophy are probably the inscriptions from the Oracle of Apollo at Delphi: "Know thyself", and "Nothing in excess" (the principle of the Golden Mean, "all things in moderation"). These correspond with central principles of Socratic epistemology and ethics, respectively. At the top of the Stoic hierarchy of *dogmata* was a handful of core principles from which more elaborate formulations were derived. In this sense, paradoxically, the philosophical framework of Stoicism was both incredibly *simple* and incredibly *complex*. Its essence could be stated in a few words, but this simplicity was necessarily deceptive and required lifelong study to fully assimilate at a practical level into one's daily life.

However, the fact that Stoic philosophy was encapsulated in short, pithy aphorisms made it easier for students to thoroughly *memorize* the core doctrines, recall them, and focus all of their attention upon them once again when needed. In response to a student who complains that learning the Stoic art of living requires too much training and effort, Epictetus replied:

> What of it? Do you expect that the greatest of arts can be acquired with little study? And yet the principal doctrine of the philosophers is in itself very succinct. If you have a mind to know it read Zeno, and you will see. For it does not take long to say, "Our end is to follow the gods and the essence of good consists in the proper use of impressions". However, if you ask, "What, then, is god, and what is an impression? What is particular, what universal nature?", then the argument becomes lengthy.
>
> (*Discourses*, 1.20.14–16, modified)

The ancient concept of compressing a complex therapeutic idea into a much simpler and more memorable aphorism has several parallels in modern psychotherapy.

For instance, hypnotherapists, such as Baudouin, have long referred to the prac-tise of condensing a series of suggestions into a single phrase, or even one word, so that it can be easily repeated as a form of autosuggestion.

> We must be able to think of it mechanically; ere long in spite of ourselves, as if we were obsessed by it; in the same way as that in which we listen to the sound of running water.
>
> A very simple means of securing this is to condense the idea which is to be the object of the suggestion, to sum it up in a brief phrase which can readily be graven on the memory, and to repeat it over and over again like a lullaby. The state of hypnosis thereupon ensues, with the effortless [concentration] characteristic of this condition.
>
> (Baudouin, 1920, p. 151)

Modern self-help and "positive thinking" literature, since Coué's time, is replete with similar affirmations. Likewise, in modern CBT, clients take complex affirma-tions of healthy, rational belief and turn them into short "coping statements", brief phrases which can easily be committed to memory and made ready to hand during future adversities.

We have no definitive account of the core principles of Stoicism. However, the many references to them in ancient literature make it possible to make a number of inferences. Hadot summarized the common "Stoic attitude" as consisting of four main features (1998, p. 310ff.). I would paraphrase them as follows.

1   *The All is One.* Consciousness that no individual being exists in isolation, but that all things are parts of a larger whole, the universe considered in its spatio-temporal entirety.
2   *The only good is moral good.* The only things that matter for us are the things which we ourselves control, our acts of will, decisions, intentions, etc., as opposed to external events.
3   *The brotherhood of man.* Human beings are valuable in themselves because they possess volition and the capacity for wisdom and virtue; we should therefore think of all men and women as our kin, our bothers and sisters.
4   *The here and now.* The Stoic's sphere of control is centred upon the present moment, and hence it is in the here and now that his attention should be grounded.

However, although these are undoubtedly fundamental *concepts* in Stoicism, the surviving literature also contains certain core precepts or maxims. As we have seen, Epictetus said that the principal doctrine of Stoicism was to follow nature (or Zeus), and the essence of wisdom and goodness consists in the proper (rational) use of our impressions. It is to this doctrine that we shall now turn.

Follow nature/follow God

"Our motto, as everyone knows", said Seneca, "is to live in conformity with nature" (*Letters*, 5). Likewise, Diogenes Laertius reports that Zeno was the first, in his book *On the Nature of Man*, to designate the supreme goal as "living in agreement with nature", which we're told was synonymous with living virtuously, as following nature guides us toward virtue (*Lives*, 7.1). Zeno also wrote a lost book titled *On Life According to Nature*. Living in agreement, or accord with nature, meant fulfilling our own potential as rational beings by becoming wise and virtuous. However, it also came to mean living in agreement with the nature of the cosmos as a whole.

> For our individual natures are all parts of universal nature; on which account the chief good is to live in a manner corresponding to nature, and that means corresponding to one's own nature and to universal nature.
>
> (*Lives*, 7.1)

The ancient Pythagoreans reputedly taught that the goal of philosophy was to "follow God". As the Stoics were pantheists who identified nature with God, these two formulae, "follow nature"/"follow God", would be virtually synonymous to them.

The Stoics appear to have believed, as we shall see later, that it was important to meditate upon the totality of space and time and think of one's actions and events in life as part of the whole, part of a vast causal network of interconnected events in the universe. They also believed, as we shall continually encounter them saying, that it is important to recognize that which is beyond the sphere of choice or control of a human being, beyond our direct volition, and to accept it accordingly, to act as if we had willed our fortune to be as it is. I take this to be part of what they mean by following external nature, it resembles what theologians would call acceptance of the "Will of God". In a crude sense, when we speak of people from simpler times or older civilizations as being "Stoic" and "fatalistic" about life, assuming they ever were, what virtue exists in that simple outlook corresponds to the philosophical attitude of the Stoic sage. It contrasts with the "age of anxiety" in which we live, where man constantly finds himself at odds with his own circumstances, a notion Marcus Aurelius puts in more colourful terms,

> The human soul degrades itself above all, when it does its best to become an abscess, a kind of detached growth on the world. To be disgruntled at anything that happens is a kind of secession from Nature, which comprises the nature of all things.
>
> (*Meditations*, 2.16)

One aspect of Stoic writing that seems to deter many modern readers and perhaps clashes with the scientific world view of CBT is the emphasis on the role of a provident God named Zeus. However, some Stoics appear to have been willing to contemplate agnosticism or atheism as consistent with their philosophy. As Marcus Aurelius repeats to himself, whether the universe is "God or atoms", either way the basic precepts of Stoicism still stand firm. Most ancient Stoics did refer repeatedly, and often passionately, to their relationship with God. The Zeus of the Stoics is a *philosopher's* god, though, in relation to which the mythological Zeus is interpreted not literally but *metaphorically*. He is synonymous with fate itself, or the whole of nature, and, therefore, "belief in God" is arguably more a question of adopting a certain *perspective* on nature, for Stoics, than a metaphysical hypothesis.

The Neostoic Justus Lipsius represented Zeno as saying, "it matters not whether you call it Providence or nature" (2006, p. 65). Seeing the universe itself as divine is the *rational mysticism* of great scientists like Einstein, a question of one's attitude toward life, and not a question of believing that something exists. Note, for instance, that for a pantheist, the question "Does god exist?" would simply be another way of asking "Does the universe exist?", which is, arguably, a nonsensical question. The Stoic God is not really a "thing", a mythical superhuman being, to be believed in or not, like a glorified unicorn. Rather, it is a way of looking at the world, conceiving the universe itself, in its absolute entirety, as if it were *godlike*, as being divine, mystical, and sacred in its totality. The references to "God" in Stoicism, to put it bluntly, can therefore be replaced by the word "Nature" or "the Universe" without much loss of meaning, and doing so would probably render things easier to digest for modern CBT practitioners.

Stoicism as psychotherapy

In a recent analysis of Stoic psychotherapy, DeBrabander describes the doctrine of tranquillity as founded upon, "a diagnosis of the passions . . . in terms that immediately invoke their susceptibility to remedy", leading to the conception of "psychotherapy as the means to happiness, a means that is subject to individual agency and responsibility" (DeBrabander, 2004, pp. 198–199). However, it is Pierre Hadot who must be given credit for expounding in most detail upon the various exercises of a therapeutic nature to be found in classical philosophy. Having surveyed the available literature, he concluded that, although practical philosophical therapeutic exercises (*askeses*) are alluded to in many places and books on the subject are seemingly mentioned in other texts, no clear systematic account of them survives today. Nevertheless, one brief text entitled *On Exercise*, by the Stoic Musonius Rufus, does remain.

As Hadot notes, Musonius begins by asserting that students of philosophy must undertake certain exercises. He divides these into psychological exercises and ones that train *both* the mind and body. The former consist mainly in contemplating and "always having at one's disposition" the fundamental dogmas of Stoicism, as a guide to action, as well as the basic arguments supporting them. The psychological exercises of Stoic philosophy also include representing events to ourselves in certain ways, he says, and focusing our attention on the pursuit of wisdom and virtue. Hadot notes that Musonius' remarks show that the Stoic concept of *psychological* exercises was modelled on the Greek ideal of athleticism and the practise of exercises in the ancient gymnasia where philosophy was taught alongside sports such as wrestling. "Just as the athlete gave new strength and form to his body by means of repeated bodily exercises, so the philosopher developed his strength of soul by means of philosophical exercises, and transformed himself" (Hadot, 2002, p. 189).

Epictetus also compares philosophy to gymnastic training, the beneficial effects of which should be visible to all in the physique of the athlete, not just in their verbal claims (*Discourses*, 3.21.1–4). This metaphor is particularly fundamental to Stoicism, which consistently refers to the aim of developing good mental "tone" (*tonos*). The philosopher uses "spiritual exercises" to *tone* his mind, that is, in a manner analogous to an athlete toning the muscles of his body through physical exercises in the gymnasium.

The same athletic metaphor was adopted by Ellis, who recommended to his REBT clients that they vigorously seek out and dispute their own irrational beliefs, "Keep doing this, over and over, until you build intellectual and emotional muscle (just as you would build physical muscle by learning how to exercise and then by continuing to exercise)" (Ellis & MacLaren, 2005, p. 130).

In addition to this analogy with physical *exercise*, or athletics, Stoic philosophy was also compared to a sort of *medicine* or *therapy*. Epictetus said bluntly, "the philosopher's school is a doctor's clinic" (*Discourses*, 3.23.30). However, philosophy is a *psychological* therapy rather than a physical one. "It is more necessary for the soul to be cured than the body, for it is better to die than to live badly" (*Fragments*, 32). In other words, Stoic philosophy was originally defined as a form of psychotherapy concerned with both *cognition* and *behaviour*, or the "art of living" (*Discourses*, 1.15.2).

This was a common conception of ancient philosophy, especially among the schools that came after Socrates.

> Philosophy is what persons need in order to become properly themselves, to fulfil their natures, to achieve the happiness that is everyone's natural goal. It is the required route for anyone who wants "to live well". Epictetus can expect broad agreement to this general specification of philosophy across the competing schools of his day.
>
> (Long, 2002, pp. 98–99)

To illustrate what philosophy entails, Epictetus and the other Stoics consistently appeal to *physical* metaphors, especially athletic training, the military life, and medicine. However, philosophy relates primarily to "care of the self", to internal, *psychological* training, battle, and therapy.

As these metaphors serve to highlight, Stoic psychotherapy is bound to resemble those forms of modern psychotherapy that adopt an educational and skills training orientation, such as CBT, rather than, for example, psychoanalysis. It is very difficult to see how psychoanalytic therapy could be compared to military or athletic training, whereas cognitive and behavioural therapies have always defined themselves in this way. Epictetus describes his role as follows, in a dialogue with real Stoic students apparently transcribed directly from his seminars. If we were simply to modify the jargon, we could perhaps view this as an ancient predecessor of cognitive-behavioural group therapy sessions.

So I am your trainer and you are being trained in my school. And my project is this – to make you unimpeded, unrestricted, free, contented, happy and looking to God in everything great and small [i.e., always keeping your eye on the bigger picture]. And you are here to learn and to practise this. Why then don't you finish the job if you have the right intention and if I, besides the intention, have the right qualifications?

What is missing?

When I see a craftsman who has available material, I expect the artefact. The craftsman is here, and so is the material.

What are we lacking? Is the thing not teachable?

It is teachable.

Is it, then, not up to us?

It is the only thing in the world that is so. Wealth isn't up to us, nor is health or reputation or anything at all except the correct use of impressions. This alone is naturally unhindered and unimpeded.

So why don't you finish the work? Tell me the reason. For either it is due to me or to you or to the nature of the thing. The thing itself is possible and the only thing up to us. Therefore the failing is mine or yours or, more truly, it pertains to us both.

Do you want us to begin, here and now, to execute this project? Let's say goodbye to the past. Let's simply begin, and trust me, you will see.

(*Discourses*, 2.19.29–34)

This resembles a fragment of dialogue in *The Meditations* of Marcus Aurelius, which may be a quotation from one of the lost *Discourses* of Epictetus:

"So the dispute", he [Epictetus] said, "is over no slight matter, but whether we are to be mad or sane". Socrates used to say, "What do you want? To have the souls of rational or irrational beings?" "Of rational beings". "And of what kind of rational beings, those that are sound or depraved?" "Those that are sound". "Then why are you not seeking for them?" "Because we have them". "Then why all this fighting and quarrelling?"

(*Meditations*, 11.38–39)

The philosopher's school, therefore, is a doctor's clinic although the goal of Stoicism is not physical but mental health. However, it's a specific form of mental health, or sanity, that's meant, grounded in the Stoic conception of wisdom and moral virtue and achieved by rigorous training in Stoic philosophy and its psychological exercises.

The most important precepts for Stoic students to rehearse, derived from the lectures of Epictetus, appear to have been carefully collected together by his follower Arrian. "After hearing his first few lectures, he is reported to have exclaimed something like, 'Son of a gun! We've got to get this guy down on papyrus!'" (Stockdale, 1995, p. 186). Stockdale was told by his philosophy lecturer, who handed him a copy of Epictetus' *Handbook*, that Frederick the Great never went on campaign without a copy of it in his kit. So what techniques does Epictetus' handbook of Stoic therapy actually contain?

The philosophers' handbook (Epictetus)

The famous *Encheiridion* or "Handbook" of Stoic philosophy was intended to provide guidance on the philosophical art of living, employing an armamentarium of therapeutic concepts and techniques. Its name can also mean "sword", and it contains the precepts with which a Stoic would arm himself, having them memorized and constantly "ready to hand" (*procheiron*). Rather than the book itself being handy, as the English expressions "manual" or "handbook" happen to imply, the Stoics meant that the contents of the *Encheiridion*, the *ideas* and *maxims* it contains, are to be made constantly "ready to hand" by those studying the art of living.

The *Encheiridion* contains the famous piece of guidance offered by Epictetus to his students which, as we have seen, is quoted, in different translations, throughout the CBT literature as the basis for the "cognitive mediation" model: "It is not the things themselves that disturb people but their judgements about those things" (*Encheiridion*, 5).

However, as the psychotherapist Baudouin appears to have recognized half a century earlier, this Stoic precept is derived from a more fundamental premise, which I originally called the "Stoic Fork" but modern followers of Stoicism now frequently refer to as "the Dichotomy of Control". The importance of this fundamental principle is highlighted by the fact that it has pride of place as the opening sentence of the *Encheiridion*: "Some things are up to us and others are not" (*Encheiridion*, 1).

As we have learnt already, this simply means that some things in life are more directly under our voluntary control than others, or, rather, strictly speaking, that only a *handful* of things are genuinely within our sphere of control. As we have also discussed, the Stoics summarized their philosophy in short precepts, meant for memorization, which were then elaborated at length in discussion or writing.

The *Encheiridion*, therefore, immediately goes on to explain what this precept means, defining it in more detail.

> Things in our control are opinion, intention, desire, objection, and, in a word, whatever are our own actions. Things not in our control are body, property, reputation, status, and, in one word, whatever are not our own actions.
>
> The things in our control are by nature free, unbounded and unhindered; but those not in our control are weak, slavish, constrained, not our own. Remember, then, that if you suppose things which are naturally slavish to be free, and what belongs to other people to be your own, then you will be enslaved. You will complain, you will be distraught, and you will condemn both gods and men.
>
> But if you suppose only that which is your own to be your own, and what belongs to others to belong to others (as it really is) then no one will ever bully or enslave you. Further, you will find fault with no one and blame no one. You will do nothing against your will. No one will hurt you, you will have no enemies, and nothing will harm you because you cannot be harmed.
>
> (*Encheiridion*, 1, modified)

These are, presumably, the first precepts that a Stoic would be expected to study, understand, and internalize. They make it very clear that the first step in Stoicism consists in learning to carefully distinguish between our own voluntary judgements and intentions, for which we have responsibility, and external events and the actions of others, which lie outside of our direct sphere of control.

The cognitive triad and Stoic threefold rule

One of the basic concepts in Beck's cognitive model of depression, developed in the 1960s, is that of the primary "triad" of negative cognitions (Beck & Alford, 2009, pp. 225–226; Beck, Rush, Shaw, & Emery, 1979, pp. 10–11). Beck found that depressives tended to show a fundamental pattern of negative cognition in relation to three dimensions: their *self*, *world*, and *future*. Ellis claimed to have already made a similar distinction, in the late 1950s, which acquired increasing prominence in REBT (Ellis & MacLaren, 2005, p. 32). REBT distinguished between three major categories of irrational belief, responsible for emotional disturbance, which relate to *self*, *life* (or world), and not the future but one's view of *others*. Ellis argued that the client should counteract unreasonable demands placed upon self, life, and others by adopting a philosophical attitude of fundamental, unconditional acceptance. He compared the notion of unconditional acceptance in REBT to the Stoic-sounding advice contained in the Serenity Prayer (*ibid.*, p. 87).

The Stoics likewise describe a basic threefold distinction, similar to Ellis' dimensions of self, life, and others. However, as pantheists, the ancient philosophers

equated the environment, one's "life" or the "world", with the divine, also referred to as fate. Marcus Aurelius outlines the following triadic model:
    Three relationships:

1   With the body you inhabit. [Self]
2   With the divine, the cause of everything in all things. [World/ Life]
3   With the people around you. [Others]. (*Meditations*, 8.27, modified)

This triad appears to correlate with a more explicit and well-known threefold division of the Stoic training curriculum into the fields of "physics", "ethics", and "logic" (Diogenes Laertius, *Lives*, 7.1). These terms carried a very different connotation in ancient philosophy than they do today, especially within the context of Stoic therapeutics. The three theoretical subjects also appear to correlate with three practical topics in Stoic therapy described, as follows, by Epictetus.

> There are three areas of study, in which a person who is going to be good and noble must be trained. That concerning desires and aversions, so that he may neither fail to get what he desires nor fall into what he would avoid. That concerning the impulse to act and not to act, and, in general, appropriate behaviour; so that he may act in an orderly manner and after due consideration, and not carelessly. The third is concerned with freedom from deception and hasty judgement, and, in general, whatever is concerned with assent.
>
> (*Discourses*, 3.2.1–2)

The Stoic disciplines, as we shall see, which deal with passion, action, and judgement, also appear to correspond with the common distinction between feelings, actions, and thoughts, or affect, behaviour, and cognition, often used in CBT. We may explain the three areas of Stoic study as follows.

1   The Stoic topic of Ethics appears to correspond with our relationship to other people (individually and collectively), the virtue of justice, and Epictetus' Discipline of Action, which we can relate to the domain of action or behaviour in CBT.
2   The Stoic topic of Physics appears to correspond with our relationship to the whole world (cosmos), the virtues of courage and temperance, and Epictetus' Discipline of Fear and Desire, which we can relate to the domain of feelings in CBT.
3   The Stoic topic of Logic appears to correspond with our relationship to our own inner nature (reason), the virtue of wisdom, and Epictetus' Discipline of Assent (or judgement), which we can relate to the domain of thought or cognition in CBT.

Physics: the discipline of desire and aversion

This is the discipline of the passions. The Stoic must be trained to master his desires by transferring them to those aspects of his experience under his direct control, i.e., his own judgement and intentions. By doing so, he also masters anxiety by avoiding falling into that which he seeks to avoid, as he is primarily concerned to avoid misuse of judgement, which is also under his control. Epictetus considered training in this discipline most urgent and important for beginners and felt that they should not trifle in logic until they have mastered their own desires in practise, through patient training in Stoic exercises (*Discourses*, 3.2.3). Perhaps this is a bit like saying the clients in modern CBT are often best advised to begin by making gradual changes to their behaviour and learning to manage their habits, emotions, and other symptoms before focusing directly on challenging their core beliefs. It seems the Stoics often thought that until the "passions", or, rather, emotional disturbances, are brought under our control, we are not fully capable of listening to reason.

The discipline of the passions entails Stoic *acceptance* because it requires cultivating an attitude of relative indifference (*apatheia*) toward the normal objects of our fear and desire. What has this got to do with "physics"? Stoic physics was probably closer to what we would now term cosmology, metaphysics, or even theology. As we shall see, it is the Stoic's insight into the nature of the world and his own place in the cosmos that helps him to see external events, and the opinions of others, as *transient* and, therefore, to avoid excessive emotional attachment to things outside his immediate control. The cardinal meditative technique of Stoic metaphysics is the "View from Above", which we will discuss in due course. The philosopher becomes dispassionate by contemplating the "bigger picture", expanding his perspective to encompass the whole world or the totality of space and time. It is this contemplation of cosmology and metaphysics that the Stoics used to induce feelings of serenity and which helps to illustrate the initially surprising link between Stoic physics and the practical conquest of irrational fears and desires. This is the Stoic therapy of contemplating their pantheistic God, "Nature", or what we would call "the nature of the universe", and it appears to have been a basic strategy for self-regulation of emotions and for cultivating a sense of Stoic acceptance toward life. Seeing things as relatively transient and indifferent, and having regained his equanimity, the Stoic novitiate was prepared to begin his training in social action and cognitive analysis.

Ethics: the discipline of action

The Stoic trains himself to act with due consideration and purpose, and not carelessly. He acts in a manner appropriate to his natural circumstances and relationships as a human being. 'I should not be unfeeling like a statue, but should preserve my natural and acquired relations as a man who honours the gods, as a son, as a brother, as a father, as a citizen' (*Discourses*, 2.2.4). The Stoic study of "ethics" deals largely with one's relationships with others both individually and collectively, and ultimately one's relationship with humankind in general. However, the study of ethics in Greek and Roman philosophy often meant the study, not of anything resembling Biblical moral rules, but rather the practical question of what actions contribute to genuine happiness and fulfilment, which is essentially a psychotherapeutic question. This discipline concerns the self-management of our intentions and actions in light of a rational consideration of what is "appropriate" in relation to society and to others (Long, 2002, pp. 113–116).

Nevertheless, the discipline of action entails cultivating our natural prosocial instincts or, as the Stoics put it, extending "natural affection" (*philostorgia*) to others. We are to treat others as our brothers and sisters, with wisdom, and in accord with the social virtues of justice, fairness, and kindness, i.e., wishing to help them insofar as that is possible. The Stoic study of rational and "appropriate" social action, as a practical skill, might perhaps be compared to the role of topics such as social skills training, communication skills, and assertiveness training in CBT.

Logic: the discipline of assent

The Stoic trains himself to avoid hasty judgements, and to test every impression by the laws of logic. Epictetus thinks this field should be left until last, and only to those who have already made progress in self-mastery and ethics, as a means to secure their achievements by developing the faculty of reason, "so that even in dreams, or drunkenness or melancholy, no untested impression may catch us off guard" (*Discourses*, 2.2.5). This emphasis upon *cognitive* change at a philosophical level as a means of stabilizing emotional and behavioural change over the longer term resembles the role of cognitive modification of underlying beliefs in relapse prevention during modern CBT. Epictetus seems to imply that Stoics typically progress through the three disciplines in this sequence, learning to moderate their fears and desires first, before training themselves in appropriate social action and, finally, securing these emotional and behavioural changes by working on their judgements or cognitions.

Stoic Logic isn't what we mean by formal logic today, though. It's a much broader concept, encompassing our relationship with reason, or thought, in more general terms. For Stoics, the most important aspect of it appears to have been the ability to separate our opinions, particularly our value judgements, from the external events to which they refer. We call this "cognitive distancing" in modern cognitive therapy, or "verbal defusion" in the third-wave behaviour therapies. For the Stoics it's closely associated with our ability to represent things *objectively*, without imposing strong emotions or value judgements.

These three disciplines and topics form part of the infrastructure of the Stoic system of philosophical psychology, and, therefore, of Stoic therapy. Many incidental references to this threefold rule of life can be found in the surviving literature. One of the passages in Marcus Aurelius' *The Meditations* has been translated simply as asserting "Apply them constantly, to everything that happens: Physics, Ethics, Logic" (*Meditations*, 8.13). Elsewhere he elaborates:

> Objective judgement, now, at this very moment. [Logic] Unselfish action, now,
>   at this very moment. [Ethics]
> Willing acceptance – now, at this very moment – of all external events.
>   [Physics]
> That's all you need. (*Meditations*, 9.6, modified)

Within the framework or "curriculum" for the Stoic art of living, a number of specific therapeutic strategies and self-help interventions seem to have been employed, including various semantic and visualization techniques. We will explore these in more detail in subsequent chapters.

Philosophy as habit conditioning and the effort of training

One aspect of the Stoic approach to therapy which many people struggle to understand at first is the need for repetitive practise. Albert Ellis emphasized a similar point in his "REBT Insight Number 3", the notion that people are only likely to become less emotionally disturbed by powerfully and consistently practising thoughts, feelings, and actions that counteract their irrational beliefs. The ancient philosophers, likewise, did not merely think about the challenges of living and arrive at a conclusion once. They found it necessary to repeatedly go over and over the same line of reasoning in their minds on a daily basis, sometimes reviewing a single idea in relation to many different concrete situations, or elaborating it by means of different analogies and modes of expression. In other words, it takes effort and perseverance, in many cases, to change our habits of thinking and overcome destructive emotional responses.

In order to understand any form of cognitive or philosophical therapy, and avoid the accusation of "mere intellectualism", it helps to distinguish between the superficial kind of insight that makes little or no difference to behaviour and deeper or more profound insight, which is capable of transforming action, emotion, habit, and even character.

> In order to obtain this result, they had, on the one hand, to develop and teach their philosophical doctrines, but, on the other hand, they were perfectly conscious of the fact that the simple knowledge of a doctrine, beneficial as it was, did not guarantee its being put into practice. To have learned theoretically that death is not an evil does not suffice to no longer fear it. In order for this truth to be able to penetrate to the depths of one's being, so that it is not believed only for a brief moment, but becomes an unshakable conviction, so that it is always "ready", "at hand", "present to mind", so that it is a "*habitus* of the

soul" as the Ancients said, one must exercise oneself constantly and without respite – "night and day", as Cicero said.

(Ilsetraut Hadot, quoted in Hadot, 1995, pp. 22–23)

Although these "are certainly exercises of meditation", she adds, they are not mere intellectual exercises but must evoke the imagination and emotions in order to be effective, something requiring "all the psychoagogical means of rhetoric". Achieving an insight is of little benefit if it is quickly forgotten, and it seems that many of the realizations pertaining to practical wisdom are especially vulnerable. In particular, under unusual stress, people tend to revert back to irrational ways of thinking and speaking, easily making basic errors of reasoning, such as overgeneralization.

Epictetus describes the process of training in Stoic precepts in a manner that sounds highly reminiscent of modern psychological accounts of habit conditioning.

Every habit and capacity is preserved and strengthened by the corresponding actions, that of walking, by walking, that of running, by running. If you want to be a reader, read; if a writer, write. But if you fail to read [aloud] for thirty days in succession, and turn to something else, you will see the consequence. So also if you lie down for ten days, get up and attempt to take a fairly long walk, you will see how enfeebled your legs are. In general, then, if you want to do something, make it a habit; and if you want not to do something, abstain from doing it, and acquire the habit of doing something else in its place. This is also the case when it comes to things of the mind. Whenever you get angry, be assured that this is not only a present evil, but that you have strengthened the habit, and add fuel to the fire. . . . For habits and faculties must necessarily be affected by the corresponding actions, and become implanted if they were not present previously, or be intensified and strengthened if they were.

This is, of course, how philosophers say that sicknesses grow in the mind. When you once desire money [for its own sake], for example, if reason is applied to bring you to an awareness of the evil, the desire is curbed, and the governing faculty of the mind regains its authority: whereas, if you apply no remedy, it no longer returns to its former state, but when it is excited again by a corresponding impression, It is inflamed by desire more quickly than before, and, by frequent repetitions, at last becomes callous: and by this infirmity the love of money becomes fixed.

For he who has had a fever, and then recovers, is not in the same state of health as before, unless he was perfectly cured; and something similar happens in sicknesses of the mind too. Certain traces and weals are left behind in it, which, unless the person concerned expunges them utterly, the next time he is flogged in the same place, not weals but wounds are created.

(*Discourses*, 2.18.1–11)

Socrates emphasized that caring for one's soul requires philosophical training. For instance, in the *Gorgias*, Plato has him forcefully argue the point that "a person who wants to be happy must evidently pursue and practice self-control" (*Gorgias*, 507d). This theme continues throughout the teachings of subsequent philosophical schools. Hence, throughout Xenophon's *Memorabilia* of Socrates, it is emphasized that just as people's bodies do not function at their best unless trained by repeated exercise, so also the mind of the philosopher cannot be improved without a similar kind of repeated training.

Epictetus, therefore, explained to his students that they must be prepared for many setbacks, and must be ready to pick themselves up time and time again, and continue when they feel that their best intentions have failed them in the face of adversity. They must be relentless, never giving up their commitment to the philosophical ideal of the sage. He specifically advises a lapsed Stoic as follows:

> So, in the first place, pass judgement on your [faulty] actions; but when you have condemned them, do not give up on yourself, nor be like those mean-spirited people who, when they have once given way, abandon themselves entirely, and are, so to speak, swept off by the flood. Rather, learn from the wrestling trainers. Has the boy fallen down? "Get up", they say, "and wrestle again, until you have gained strength". You too should think in some such way as that; for you should know this, there is nothing more tractable than the human mind. You have only to will a thing [in the mind], and it comes to pass, and all is put right; and yet, on the other hand, you have only to doze off, and all is ruined. For both ruin and recovery come from within.
>
> (*Discourses*, 4.9.14–16, modified)

Skinner's strategy of "shaping", or successive approximation to some target, is central to behaviour therapy and CBT. However, the basic concept is a natural feature of any therapy that adopts a skills training approach. Hadot writes that in the philosophical exercises of Stoicism the basic principle is always found that one should begin by practising on easier things in order to gradually develop a stable change in habit over time (Hadot, 1995, p. 86).

Coué made the same point beautifully when he exclaimed to his students that even Christ stumbled and fell, more than once, as he carried his cross to Calvary (Coué, 1923, p. 42). The best of us encounter setbacks and temporary relapses, but the crucial difference between failure and success is the attitude of relentless perseverance, the indomitable spirit of the ideal Stoic student who keeps picking himself up and starting again with renewed vigour, each time refusing to give in.

The Cynics seem to have been one of the earliest schools to place particular emphasis upon rigorous training of this kind. Diogenes the Cynic taught that exercises involving enduring hardship and ridicule could improve our character:

> And he used to allege as proofs of this, and of the ease which practice imparts to acts of virtue [moral excellence], that people could see that in the case

of mere common working trades, and other employments of that kind, the artisans arrived at no inconsiderable accuracy by constant practice; and that any one may see how much one flute player, or one wrestler, is superior to another, by his own continued practice. And that if these men transferred the same training to their minds they would not labour in a profitless or imperfect manner. He used to say also, that there was nothing whatever in life which could be brought to perfection without practice, and that that alone was able to overcome every obstacle; that, therefore, as we ought to repudiate all use-less toils, and to apply ourselves to useful labours, and to live happily, we are only unhappy in consequence of most exceeding folly.

(*Lives*, 6.2)

Likewise, writing in the seventeenth century, Descartes, the father of modern philosophy, describes how his famous epistemological meditations led him to develop a moral code, based upon three central maxims. The first two of these refer to respect for custom and consistency in life. However, Descartes account of his third maxim provides a striking expression of certain Stoic doctrines, which he'd assimilated.

My third maxim was always to try to conquer myself rather than fortune, and to change my desires rather than the order of the world, and generally to accustom myself to believing that there is nothing that is completely within our power except our thoughts, so that, after we have done our best regarding things external to us, everything that is lacking for us to succeed is, from our point of view, absolutely impossible. And this alone seemed to me sufficient to prevent me in the future from desiring anything but what I was to acquire, and thus to make me contented. For, our will tending by nature to desire only what our understanding represents to it as somehow possible, it is certain that, if we consider all the goods that are outside us as equally beyond our power, we will have no more regrets about lacking those that seem owed to us as our birthright when we are deprived of them through no fault of our own, than we have in not possessing the kingdoms of China or Mexico, and that, making a virtue of necessity, as they say, we shall no more desire to be healthy if we are sick, or to be free if we are in prison, than we do to have a body made of a material as incorruptible as diamonds, or wings to fly like birds.

(*Discourse on Method*, 3.25–26)

This is one form of the Stoic contemplation upon necessity and determinism. It is clear, as the ancient philosophers observed, that nobody really feels pity for an infant because it cannot walk or speak, although we may feel differently about an adult who is dumb or lame. People do not become frustrated because they cannot grow wings and fly, but they do often envy the wealth and possessions of others. Accepting that something is outside of our control often means that we give up our desire for it, but people seem to torture themselves with goals that, although possible for others or for them at another stage in life, are not currently within their power to achieve (*Discourses*, 1.21). For example, many people wish they could change the past, or wish that they were rich and famous, demands which are either illogical, physically impossible, or unrealistic given the limitations of their current circumstances.

> But I admit that long exercise is needed as well as frequently repeated meditation, in order to become accustomed to looking at everything from this point of view; and I believe that it is principally in this that the secret of those philosophers [such as Socrates and the Stoics] consists, who in earlier times were able to free themselves from fortune's domination and who, despite sorrows and poverty, could rival their gods in happiness. For occupying themselves ceaselessly with considering the limits prescribed to them by nature, they so perfectly persuaded themselves that nothing was in their power but their affection for other things, and they controlled their thoughts so absolutely that in this they had some reason for reckoning themselves richer, more powerful, freer, and happier than any other men who, not having this philosophy, never thus controlled everything they wished to control, however favored by nature and fortune they might be.
>
> (*Discourse on Method*, 3.26)

Hence, writing many centuries later, Descartes nevertheless appears to share the Stoic view that philosophy can serve a therapeutic purpose, but that doing so is a practical application of psychology which typically entails "long exercise" and "frequently repeated meditation". Indeed, despite the relative brevity of these comments, Descartes has been credited with being an especially astute scholar of Stoicism, in particular the philosophy of Epictetus (Long, 2002, p. 266). Epictetus himself continually emphasizes the effort required for training in Stoicism. "Make a desperate push, man, as the saying goes, to achieve happiness and freedom, and nobility of mind" (*Discourses*, 2.16.41).

> You see, then, that it is necessary for you to become a student, that creature which every one laughs at, if you really desire to make an examination of your judgements. But this, as you are quite aware, is not the work of a single hour or day.
>
> (*Discourses*, 1.11.39)

In the *Handbook*, he stresses that the Stoic must define for himself the person he wishes to become, modelling the wisdom of sages, and train himself to maintain that habit of character, whether alone or in the company of others (*Encheiridion*, 33).

> For this reason philosophers exhort us not to be contented with mere [theoretical] learning, but to add practice also, and then training. For we have been

long accustomed to do the opposite of what we should, and the opinions that we hold and apply are the opposite of the correct ones. If, therefore, we do not also adopt and apply the correct opinions [in our daily lives], we shall be nothing more than interpreters of the judgements of others.

(*Discourses*, 2.9.13–14)

Philosophers ought to study precepts of action, write about them every day, and regularly exercise themselves in their application. The Stoic should be able to show the improvements that philosophy has wrought in his character through training, in the same way that an athlete's fitness can be seen in his physique. The philosopher who shows off his knowledge of books to impress others is like an athlete who shows off his training weights, rather than using them properly (*Discourses*, 1.4.13).

As we have seen, the medical model (philosophy as therapy) and the skills training model (philosophy as athletics) are two recurring analogies for philosophy found in Stoic literature. Both are also central to the modern understanding of cognitive-behavioural psychotherapy. This overtly practical conception of philosophy, therefore, highlights the essential role of mental and physical exercise (*askesis*) in overcoming emotional disturbance. In subsequent chapters, we shall examine a number of specific techniques, interventions that might be seen as connecting points between ancient philosophy and modern psychotherapy. However, first we must consider the role of the "passions" in Stoicism and the nature of the changes Stoic therapy sought to make.

Chapter 5

Rational emotion in Stoicism and CBT

As we have seen, Beck and Ellis say relatively little about the philosophical roots of their respective therapies. What we can conclude from the comments made by them is that they both consider Stoicism and CBT (or REBT) to share the same fundamental premise: the cognitive theory of emotion. Stoicism was the first major psychological therapy to emphasize the role of cognitions in determining our emotions. Both Stoicism and CBT therefore conclude that by changing our cognitions we are often able to change our emotions. Each embodies both a cognitive *theory* and *therapy* of emotional disturbance: cognitions are central to both the *cause* and *cure* of emotional disturbance. It should be noted that this does not necessarily exclude the possibility that other, *non*-cognitive, factors are implicated in the causation of emotional disorders, or even in their treatment. It simply places central emphasis upon the role of cognition.

That "passions" are irrational judgements

In Stoicism, the passions, or irrational emotions, are conceived of as emotionally charged cognitions; they definitely embody beliefs and are, therefore, susceptible to disputation.

> Stoic psychotherapy is directed at extirpating the [irrational] passions. The fact that passions are irrational judgements means not only that they are susceptible of treatment but also that they admit of complete and utter remedy. To treat a passion is just to clarify the poor cognition inherent in it and thereby to render its inherent judgement rational. Thus, Stoic therapy effectively involves transforming the passions, making them give way to *eupatheiai*, or rational emotions. Accordingly, rational emotions are defined by reasonable or prudent judgements of the true value of things. The Stoic teaching that there are four root passions underlying all passions is a further indication that the passions lend themselves to extirpation: eradicate the basic constituent passions and you eradicate their derivatives as well. Stoic psychotherapy is a process of replacing basic passions with basic rational emotions, which give rise to derivatives in their own right.
>
> (DeBrabander, 2004, pp. 202–203)

This is obviously an important area of common ground between Stoic psycho-therapy and modern CBT. In their article on the relationship between REBT and Stoicism, Still and Dryden observe that whereas we generally think of ethical obligations as extending mainly to our *behaviour*, the Stoics thought that we had a duty to take responsibility for our emotions as well (1999, p. 148).

Reviewing the relationship between the Stoic philosophical psychology of emotion and modern research in this area, the philosopher Lawrence C. Becker recently concluded that:

> There is a fairly impressive convergence between Stoic positions and con-temporary psychology – even psychotherapy – on the general nature of moods, feelings, emotions, and passions. . . . Contemporary Stoics will have to make some adjustments to the ancient doctrines, but nothing, I think, that will undermine their claim to being Stoics.
>
> (Becker, 2004, pp. 254–255)

Indeed, Becker also observes that the "most obvious" example of a modern cor-relate of Stoicism would be Ellis' REBT. He also mentions the related work of Arnold Lazarus, one of the pioneers of behaviour therapy and the founder of mul-timodal therapy (MMT). Similar analogies can just as easily be made between Stoicism and Beck's "cognitive therapy", but also with the writings of many other authors in the broad cognitive-behavioural tradition.

Emotional reductionism

One of the first philosophical obstacles to surmount in addressing the cognitive theory of emotion is caused by the common tendency to think of terms such as cognition and emotion as referring to mutually exclusive categories. Apples and oranges are two completely distinct types of physical object, two types of fruit. However, thinking and feeling are not two completely distinct psychological pro-cesses. We should remember that they both occur in the *same person* and refer to aspects of experience that are potentially overlapping. In comparing REBT to Stoicism, Still and Dryden (1999, p. 150) note that other schools of psychotherapy tend to reify cognition, treating it as a fundamentally separate entity (or process) from emotion, this is probably a false dichotomy whereas the Stoics avoided this mistake insofar as they realized that emotion is essentially a form of thinking.

There is an important semantic and conceptual confusion at stake here, with which cognitive therapists frequently struggle, or else by which they become ensnared. As Beck and his colleagues note, the terms "rational therapy" and "cognitive therapy" have been frequently *misinterpreted* by critics as implying a kind of intellectualism that ignores the role of feelings (Beck, Rush, Shaw, & Emery, 1979, pp. 34–35). Indeed, Ellis apparently changed the name he used for his approach, "rational therapy", to "rational emotive therapy", in part, to help overcome the misconception that "rational" implies an approach neglectful of the emotions. He also attempted to tackle the misunderstanding head-on and discussed the conceptual problems at some length in his early writings (Ellis, 1962). Ellis, therefore, seems to have been repeatedly forced to defend himself against the accusation of "over-*rationalization*" of clients' problems, which is indeed far from being a viable criticism and really little more than wordplay on the part of his detractors. His response was crystal clear: "The critic who accuses the rational emotive therapist of ignoring or intellectualizing feeling and emotion is making a false dichotomy between so-called emotion and so-called thought" (*ibid.*, pp. 332–333).

Indeed, it is the "critic" who is guilty of a kind of *reductionism* which attempts to oversimplify the relationship between different psychological processes by treating them all as if they were fundamentally distinct entities, resembling physical objects such as apples and oranges, rather than complex interweaving and overlapping concepts at different levels of abstraction.

> The theoretical foundations of RT [rational therapy, later REBT] are based on the assumption that human thinking and emotion are *not* two disparate or different processes, but that they significantly overlap and are in some respects, for all practical purposes, essentially the same thing. Like the other two basic life processes, sensing and moving, they are internally interrelated and never can be seen wholly apart from each other.
>
> (*ibid.*, pp. 38–39)

Unfortunately, the conceptual overlap that he alludes to raises some extremely complex problems; in fact it is a philosophical minefield. Ellis is perhaps right that, for practical purposes, the safest option is simply to remind ourselves that many of these processes (cognition, emotion, volition, perception, etc.) can *potentially* refer, under different aspects, to the same underlying process in a human organism.

> Rational Emotive Behaviour Therapy is based on the assumption that cognition, emotion, and behavior are not disparate human functions but are, instead, intrinsically integrated and holistic. When we feel, we think and act; when we act, we feel and think; and when we think, we feel and act? Why? Because humans rarely, except for a few moments at a time, just feel, or just think, or just behave.
>
> (Ellis & MacLaren, 2005, p. 3)

Nevertheless, even Ellis, who attempts to clarify these matters philosophically, seems to struggle and become ensnared by them sometimes, by frequently talking as though certain cognitions or beliefs must *cause* specific emotions. Still and Dryden, as advocates of REBT, admit in their discussion of Stoicism that, although Ellis shared the Stoic view that cognitions constitute part of the fabric of emotion, the founder of REBT was "less consistent than the early Stoics in maintaining that reason and emotion are essentially linked and not separate faculties" (1999, p. 154).

I will not dwell on this issue at length but simply mention one practical consequence of the residual philosophical morass. If therapists take frequently-uttered statements such as "cognition *causes* emotion" literally, then it becomes natural for them to ask clients questions such as "What were you thinking just *before* you became angry?" This assumes that cognition and emotion are completely distinct events in a (chronological) causal sequence, which they are not. However, if we think of cognition as frequently constituting an *aspect* of emotion, combined with other elements such as physical sensations, facial expressions, desires to perform certain actions, etc., then such a chronological cause-effect sequence becomes unnecessary, though still possible. In that case, we might do better to ask clients to try to translate their emotions in words in an attempt to find out the cognition that *constitutes* the emotion rather than looking for one which supposedly *precedes* it. To put it crudely, one might just as well ask, "Could you describe your feeling *as if* it were a thought?", rather than, "What thought came just before your feeling?"

This may seem to introduce an element of interpretation on the client's part, which is arguably always present in any case. However, closing the gap between cognition and emotion has the advantage of conceptualizing emotion in terms which emphasize self-control. Stoic passions are voluntary – or at least *potentially* under our control. Emotions, in this sense, are activities we engage in, things we *do*. James Stockdale said, "The Stoic thinks of emotions as acts of will", by which he meant that judgements are, in principle, under our voluntary control, and to that extent the emotions which incorporate them are as well.

> Fear is not something that darts out from behind a bush and settles itself on you in the dark. You fear because you decided to fear, you fear because you want to fear. The same with grief, pity, affection, and so on.
>
> (Stockdale, 1995, pp. 181–182)

In other words, the Stoic philosophy goes somewhat further than some accounts of CBT, in very explicitly conceptualizing the emotions themselves as *being*, at least in part, cognitions, judgements which may be either true or false. To the extent that we choose what to think, we also choose what to feel. However, when we assume that feelings *are not* thoughts, self-control slips further from our grasp, and we perceive ourselves as mere victims of our passions, forgetful that we may perhaps *decide* what we feel.

The Stoic terminology of "passion"

Just as Ellis appears to have been misunderstood because of his use of the word "rational", one of the greatest obstacles to a modern understanding of Stoicism is perhaps caused by the conventional use of the English word "passion" to translate the Greek word *pathos*. Stoicism is widely misinterpreted as a kind of cold intellectualism because translations of Stoic literature and academic discussion of it tend to talk about Stoic therapy as if it were about removing all *passion or emotion.*

> A successful rehabilitation of Stoic ethics will have to defeat the idea that there is something deeply wrong, and perhaps even psychologically impossible, about the kind of emotional life that Stoics recommend. The image of the austere, dispassionate, detached, tranquil, and virtually affectless sage – an image destined to be self-refuting – has become a staple of anti-Stoic philosophy, literature, and popular culture. It has been constructed from incautious use of the ancient texts and is remarkably resistant to correction.
>
> (Becker, 2004, p. 250)

The notion of completely eradicating all emotion is so counter-intuitive that we should at least pause for a moment to ask whether a practical philosophical therapy based upon common sense principles, shared by so many people, could feasibly have survived, for so many centuries, by promoting such a palpably absurd and *unworkable* goal. Of course, this is categorically *not* what Stoicism recommends but a frustratingly common *misconception*, which, although it goes back to antiquity, is reinforced in our own time by the difficulty of translating the Stoic word for "passion".

In Greek philosophy generally, but especially in Stoicism, the word *pathos* specifically denotes emotions which are irrational, unhealthy, and excessive. Long emphasizes that the Stoic feels rational positive and negative emotions and defines the "passions" from which he seeks to free himself as "faulty judgements manifested in 'excessive' or 'irrational' impulses" (Long, 2002, pp. 244–245). Still and Dryden, therefore, recognize that the Stoic concept of "passion" is akin to the "irrational" beliefs and emotions central to REBT (1999, p. 151), and, perhaps, we might even view them as equivalent. These are, essentially, the kind of pathological emotions that common sense would suggest are in need of therapy and are contrasted with rational, healthy, and proportionate feelings. The English word "passion" has come to denote strong emotion in general, including healthy emotions like courage, friendship, and love. A quick glance at most Stoic writings should make it apparent that these are definitely not feelings which the ancient Stoics would seek to remove but, rather, things they wish to promote and reinforce.

This problem of translation was noted even by Roman philosophers who sought to translate Greek philosophical terms into their native Latin. In the third volume of his *Tusculan Disputations*, dealing with the emotions, Cicero proposed to translate *pathos* into Latin as *morbus*, meaning not "passion" or "emotion" but rather "disease" – in other words these are *morbid* feelings we're talking about. In fact, the English word "passion" derives from the Latin *pati*, "to suffer", the same root shared by the word "patient", that is, a *therapist's* patient, who can be diagnosed in terms of *psychopathology*, a cognate term, alluding to mental disease, suffering, or morbidity. The English word "patience", likewise, derives from the same Latin root and refers to the virtue required to philosophically *accept* and *endure* certain forms of emotional suffering.

Seneca also wrestled with the problem of translating the Greek word *apatheia* into Latin as *impatientia*, its nearest equivalent, which carried slightly different connotations. He concluded that it would be preferable to explicitly state that the term refers to a mind that is "invulnerable", or "above all suffering", rather than one that is completely unemotional (*Letters*, 9). The word "passive" derives from the same root and from the fact that *pathos*, or passion, originally denoted the kind of emotion from which we suffer or of which we are victims, feeling *passive* in relation to it because it seems out of control. By contrast, for the Stoics, we become (cognitively) *active* in relation to our rational emotions in the sense that we have chosen to experience them. We therefore perceive ourselves as having more control of them insofar as we can choose whether or not to change our thinking.

Stoic ethics, self-interest, and psychotherapy

One of the reasons why modern psychotherapists have neglected classical philosophy is simply that the word "psychotherapy" is, of course, something of a modern invention and does not occur in translations of ancient texts. Yet, there are numerous well-known references to the philosopher acting as a "physician" of the psyche, or to philosophy as a psychological "medicine", which arguably amounts to exactly the same thing. Moreover, the Stoics did refer to their philosophy as a "therapy" (*therapeia*) of the psyche. As we've seen, Chrysippus, the third head of the school, wrote a book titled *On Therapeutics*. Marcus Aurelius also refers to his Stoic mentor Junius Rusticus, who gave him a copy of the *Discourses* of Epictetus, as having pointed out Marcus' need for correction and "therapy" of this kind (*Meditations*, 1.7).

Apart from this, classical literature had several other names for something akin to psychotherapy and, perhaps surprisingly, the most important term in this regard was probably "*ethics*". It is essential to realize that the popular notion of ethics as little more than a system of moral dogmas is a *degraded* version of the original concept found in ancient philosophy. Outside of academic circles, in the minds of the general public, and among most psychotherapists, there appears to be some confusion between ethics and what we might call *moralizing*. To some extent this may be due to the intervening influence of Christianity and the simplistic notion of Christian ethics as a set of rules, frequently seeming quite arbitrary in nature, laid down by God in book form and interpreted by his clergy. As Nietzsche would say, Christians or not, we still live in the shadow of a metaphysical system of morality which literally harks back to the Dark Ages.

Prior to the rise of Christianity, most ancient systems of philosophy were based upon the central assumption that what was right or ethical for a person was precisely what contributed to their happiness and well-being. That is, the question as to what is *therapeutic* was the basis of ancient ethics. Socratic ethics itself, to a large extent, is the study of what we would now consider self-help or psychotherapy. The word "ethics", we should remind ourselves, originally meant the study and development of excellence in one's character or personality (*ethos*). The Stoics, in particular, used the word "ethics" to mean something closer to the improvement of the human character (*ethos*) rather than what we now mean by "morality". We can try to reconstruct the core principles of Stoic ethics from the writings of the various sources available. One of our most important sources in this regard is Cicero's *De Finibus*, in which he portrays the Stoic Cato of Utica giving a fairly systematic account of Stoic ethics.

The basic presupposition was that all animals are constituted by nature to act with self-interest, so that they tend to seek their own well-being and self-preservation. Human infants are similar to non-human animals in this regard. However, as children develop the capacity for language and self-awareness they become increasingly capable of reasoning, which the Stoics believed sets humans fundamentally apart from other animals. For a human being, as a rational animal, self-preservation is not merely a matter of preserving the body but, more importantly, it becomes a matter of preserving the mind. Our *identity* is increasingly associated with our sense of self-consciousness and our capacity to think. The Stoics were therefore aware that the question of ethics, if referred to self-interest, must ultimately wrestle with the question of personal identity.

> So make your choice straightforwardly, once and for all, and stick to it. Choose what's best. – Best is what benefits *me*. As a rational being? Then follow through. Or just as an animal? Then say so and stand your ground without making a show of it. (Just make sure you've done your homework first.)
>
> (*Meditations*, 3.7)

Reason gives us the capacity to question our initial impressions about things and modify our reactions in a way that animals cannot. For example, to realize that although eating "junk food" may be pleasurable at the time, it may damage our health in the long-term, or that exercise might be temporarily painful but benefit us over time. More fundamentally, however, in order to preserve our ability to make these individual rational decisions, we need to act self-reflexively. That is, we need to preserve our general ability to think clearly and rationally first and foremost, as our ability to cope rationally with pain and pleasure will depend upon this. Marcus Aurelius opposes both egotism and hedonism to preservation of one's "sanity" by attaching value primarily to the integrity of one's own actions.

> Ambition means tying your well-being to what other people say or do. Self-indulgence means tying it to the things that happen to you. Sanity means tying it to your own actions.
>
> (*Meditations*, 6.51)

We might refer to this as the distinction between *ordinary* self-interest, based on hedonistic or egotistic gratification, and *enlightened* self-interest, based on a more philosophical attitude toward life. I know that pork pies are bad for my long-term health, but I am attracted by the short-term pleasure of their taste. The question "What should I *do*?" might depend upon the question "Who *am* I?" Do I *identify* more with reason or the passions, man or animal, mind or body? What is the relationship between these two apparently conflicting perspectives? To follow my own interest, to be true to myself and "authentic": does it mean being true to my animal nature or to my intellect? As we have seen, perhaps this is a false dichotomy, in which case to be "true to our passions" is, perhaps, merely to be forgetful of the extent to which our feelings are suffused by thoughts, and careless of whether they are true or false, rational or irrational. We cannot ultimately escape our reasoning nature, only temporarily neglect or suppress it through a form of self-deception akin to what the existential philosophers following Sartre called "bad faith".

In a particularly Stoic moment, Dubois writes, candidly, "The sole motive for every action of man is *the desire for happiness*". He explains:

> In man the desire for happiness is so much to the fore that he often prefers death to the loss of what he considers his happiness. To be fit physically, intellectually, or morally is the sole aim of every human creature, and whatever may be the mind, conduct, opinions, or aspirations of the individual, at the bottom of his soul will always be found this primitive desire for happiness. The question is where to look for this joy for which humanity is athirst.
>
> (Dubois, 1909, pp. 19–20)

Even the religious fanatic who flays himself does so because, in a definitional sense, that is what he believes will make him happy, perhaps by extirpating his sins. The modern depressive who self-harms frequently reports some emotional relief, albeit transient, or at least a subjective experience of satisfaction from doing so. People do what they believe will make them happy. They often sacrifice their long-term happiness and well-being for the kind of pleasant sensation which does little but temporarily mask unhappiness, however. As the Stoics put it, the basic, common sense, preconception that we should seek happiness and well-being (*eudaimonia*) is correct, but we frequently fall into error when applying this to specific cases in our daily lives. As the human mind is the key to fulfilling our natural function, its well-being is the essence of our natural obligation to pursue our own self-interest, in an enlightened manner. Self-preservation of the body evolves, with humanity, into self-preservation of the intellect.

The ideal state of the human mind is not irrational indulgence in mere sensory pleasure (*hedonism*), therefore, but something known as *eudaimonia*, a Greek term that encompasses *rational* fulfilment, happiness, and well-being. If "daemon" were taken simply to mean mind, then the word *eudaimonia* could be literally translated as meaning "mental health", although this does fail to do justice to the metaphysical connotations of the Greek word, which can also be taken to mean being on good terms with one's inner daemon or guide, a precursor in some ways of the Christian idea of conscience. In any case, the cardinal virtue or quality (*arete*) that contributes to *eudaimonia* is simply wisdom (*sophia*). Knowing this leads us to value and pursue the cultivation of human wisdom above all else, which is illustrated in the very word "philosophy", the *love of wisdom*. Philosophy in this concrete sense, the *everyday* pursuit of wisdom, is, therefore, defined as the *art of living*, the highest human purpose, though different schools of ancient philosophy differed on their interpretation of specifically how this was to be put into practise. It should be evident that for Socrates and the Stoics, the notion that the goal of human life is the pursuit of wisdom does not equate to saying that the "meaning of life" is that one should spend it reading books on philosophy but, rather, that one should strive for practical wisdom in facing everyday challenges.

This line of reasoning leads to the famous Stoic conclusion that virtue is the only true good. Everything else, including sensory pain and pleasure, and social approval or disapproval, is "indifferent". "Thus, the aspiring Stoic philosopher is not concerned with wealth or social standing; like Socrates, his only concern is to take care of his soul. It is to this end that the art of living is directed" (Sellars, 2003, p. 58). To many modern readers this seems like an extreme view, but that is, at least in part, due to confusion over some of the subtleties at stake and the difficulty of translation. First, bear in mind that, for the Stoic, *arete* means *psychological* virtue and not just *moral* virtue, for want of a better way of putting it. The cardinal "virtues" of Greek philosophy were wisdom, justice, courage, and moderation. The possession of these excellent character traits is the key to happiness and well-being (*eudaimonia*) in the Stoic view.

Moreover, according to the Stoics it is rational to *prefer* having external "goods", such as food, wealth, sex, social praise, etc., over pain and poverty, so long as these things are sought within reasonable bounds and not at the expense of our mental health or well-being. The Stoic by no means claims that "all pleasure is bad", which would be the opposite of "indifference" in any case. He simply does not see it as inherently important. The Stoic technical term sometimes translated as "serenity" or "indifference" (*apatheia*) actually means an absence of irrational or excessive passion (*pathos*). As we've seen, Seneca suggested that it would be preferable to explicitly emphasize that the Stoic term *apatheia* refers to a mind which is "above all suffering", i.e., free from irrational or excessive passions.

The Stoic can, therefore, take worldly things or leave them, but either way he does not get overly worked up about them. Wealth and fame, sensory pleasure or social praise, can only be either good or bad in a trivial sense, but genuine happiness is ultimately down to our attitude toward life, and the use we make of our intellect. Just because we find pleasure in something it does not necessarily make us truly happy and fulfilled. Many of the things people derive pleasure from can be harmful if abused or if we become too dependent upon them. As Musonius Rufus, one of the great Stoic teachers, put it:

> Training which is peculiar to the soul [i.e., psychological training] consists first of all in seeing that the proofs pertaining to apparent goods as not being real goods are always ready to hand, and likewise those pertaining to

apparent evils as not being real evils, and in learning to recognise the things which are truly good and in becoming accustomed to distinguish them from what are not truly good. Second, it consists of practice in not avoiding any of the things which only seem bad, and in not pursuing any of the things which only seem good; in shunning by every means those which are truly bad and in pursuing by every means those which are truly good.

(Musonius Rufus, Fragment 6, modified)

To paraphrase in terms more familiar to modern psychotherapy: Stoic mental training consists primarily in memorizing certain rational arguments until they influence habitual patterns of thinking: for example, statements which help one to distinguish more objectively between the genuine advantages and dis-advantages of different courses of action. Furthermore, this is supplemented by systematic attempts to face the objects of one's irrational fears and prevent responses, or courses of action, which, on reflection, are found to maintain emo-tional disturbance. If this seems, on reflection, to be little more than common sense, then I think the Stoics would be very happy to have got their point across. The Stoic is not necessarily a "cold fish", but, rather, someone whose art of living involves seeing things for what they are, that is, preferring things which are genuinely in his best interests over those which are appealing but ultimately harmful.

Hedonism and eudaimonism

Albert Ellis made a similar distinction in his philosophy between *short*-range and *long*-range hedonism, which he derives explicitly from Stoicism. He observed that people often suffer because they irrationally sacrifice their long-term happi-ness for the lure of short-term pleasure. A person may be quite miserable about being overweight, but continue to indulge in fattening "comfort foods" because the distant goal of being slim and healthy seems less motivating than the immedi-ate gratification that comes from indulgent eating.

It is sometimes alleged that RT [rational therapy] is too crassly hedonistic and that it teaches people to enjoy themselves at the expense of their deeper or more rewarding commitment. This is a false charge, since one of the main tenets of rational emotive psychotherapy is the Stoic principle of long-range rather than of short-range hedonism. . . .

Instead of being encouraged to do things the "easy way", the patient is helped to do them the more *rewarding* way – which in the short run, is often more difficult. RT, while embracing neither the extreme views of the Epicu-reans nor those of the Stoics, strives for a more moderate synthesis of both these ways of life.

(Ellis, 1962, pp. 363–364)

In classical philosophy, a distinction is often made between more passive sensory "pleasure" (*hedone*) and the kind of "happiness" (*eudaimonia*) that comes from rational activity in accord with the psychological virtues. According to this view, true happiness is constant and self-generated; it comes from *within*, as the cliché goes. For example, an *authentic* sense of happiness may come from the knowledge that one has acted freely and with genuine integrity, courage, and wisdom, in accord with one's highest psychological strengths and values. The pleasure that comes from indulging in sex, food, drink, drugs, or glorying in praise from others is passive in the sense that it depends upon external stimulation. It is, therefore, transient and not entirely under our control but depends upon fortunate circumstances. The happiness that comes from loving truth, reason, integrity, and wisdom, by contrast, is *autonomous*; it depends only upon itself.

Ellis actually appears to employ the term "hedonism" to mean not just the pursuit of rational long-term pleasure but also the pursuit of genuine happiness, obscuring the underlying similarity of his position to that of the Stoics (Dryden & Ellis, 2001, p. 298). The Stoics make a distinction between rational pleasure (*chara*, "joy") and irrational pleasure (*hedone*), which is similar Ellis' distinction between long-term and short-term pleasure. Unlike Ellis, however, they reserve the term *hedone* for irrational, unhealthy, or excessive pleasures (i.e., "hedonism"). *Chara* is the enjoyment of things that are actually healthy for us, which for the Stoics means primarily the virtues themselves. This would be better described as *eudaimonism* rather than hedonism. In any case, the indebtedness of REBT to Stoicism is here, as elsewhere, quite apparent.

Rational emotions in Stoicism

The Stoics did not promote the absence of emotion or desire, therefore, but, rather, the cultivation of *rational* and adaptive emotions (*eupatheiai*). Stoic philosophical psychology made the following distinction between the primary emotions according to Diogenes Laertius:

> There are also three good dispositions of the mind: joy, caution, and wishing. And joy they say is the opposite of [irrational] pleasure, since it is a rational elation of the mind; so caution is the opposite of fear, being a rational avoidance of things, for the sage will never be afraid, but he will act with caution; and wishing, they define as the opposite of [irrational] desire, since it is a rational choice. Just as certain unhealthy passions fall under the primary ones, so too with the primary good feelings. And accordingly, under the head of wishing, are classed kindness, generosity, warmth, affection; and under the head of caution are classed respect and modesty; under the head of joy, we speak of delight, sociability, and good spirits.
>
> (*Lives*, 7.1)

The translation of these terms becomes a little strained, as distinctions have to be maintained with other concepts in ways that do not necessarily correspond to English language distinctions. The Stoics classed both desires and emotions under the same broad heading. We could perhaps translate these three rational feelings into more modern language as "enjoyment" (rational pleasure), "mindfulness" (rational aversion), and "preference" (rational desire). Their recognition of these rational feelings directly undermines the misconception that Stoicism recommends the extirpation of *all* desire and emotion. On the contrary, the Stoic aimed to remove *unhealthy* desires and emotions only, counteracting them by cultivating the corresponding *rational* desires and emotions instead, as shown in what follows:

- Elation (*eparsis*, i.e., pleasure or joy)

  - *Hedone*, usually translated "pleasure". Irrational, excessive, unhealthy indulgence in sensory pleasure, i.e., hedonism.
  - *Chara*, usually translated "joy". Rational, moderate, healthy enjoyment, i.e., authentic happiness.

- Aversion (*ekklisis*, i.e., avoidance or concern)

  - *Phobos*, usually translated "fear". Irrational, excessive, unhealthy fear, i.e., phobia.
  - *Eulabeia*, usually translated "caution" or "watchfulness". Rational, moderate, healthy concern, i.e., mindfulness or circumspection.

- Desire (*orexis*)

  - *Epithumia*, usually translated "appetite" or "lust". Irrational, excessive, unhealthy desire, i.e., a craving or compulsion.
  - *Boulesis*, usually translated "willing" or "wishing". Rational, moderate, healthy desire, i.e., a light preference for something.

As "elation" (*eparsis*) refers to the satisfaction of the corresponding state of desire (*orexis*) in Stoic psychology, we are left with only *two* primary states: *orexis* and *ekklisis*, desire and aversion. These refer quite simply to the anticipation of future *harm* or *gain*, respectively, and have both rational and irrational variations. The healthy alternative to craving is rational preference; the healthy alternative to fear is rational caution. This simple and relatively common sense distinction has many parallels in modern psychology, for example the distinction between approach and avoidance behaviour in Skinner's operant conditioning.

In Epictetus' interpretation, desire and aversion should be transferred from external objects and other people's opinions, which the Stoic sees as ultimately indifferent, onto one's own judgements and intentions. These are the only things of primary value because they confer value on everything else and are therefore more deserving of our concern. For Stoics, in other words, the fear of death should be more of a concern than death itself. We fear social censure and physical pain, but mindlessly run into the more serious affliction that results from placing too much value on these things by mistake. Like a frightened deer, we run blindly from the noise of the beaters straight into the hunters' waiting nets, from the false impression of external danger to the hidden reality of it lurking within our own character (*Discourses*, 2.1.8).

The Stoic should learn that true benefit and harm lie not in his external fortune but within his own mind. We should rationally desire, or wish, to follow reason and nature in all things, and feel rational aversion, or caution, lest our faulty judgements lead us once more into the grip of irrational or neurotic passions. The transposition of fear and desire into the realm of judgement, as we shall see, forms the basis of Stoic mindfulness, the famous *self-possession* of the ideal sage. Because the only thing truly under our control is our own will, our ability to make decisions, the sage makes himself psychologically "invincible", as the Stoics put it, by attaining "desire that never fails in its achievement; aversion that never meets with what it would avoid" (*Discourses*, 2.8.24).

The Stoic reserve clause

The "reserve clause" (Latin, *exceptio*; Greek, *hupexhairesis*) is perhaps one of the most basic underlying concepts of Stoicism. In a sense, it merely formulates from a different perspective what I have termed the "Stoic Fork", the distinction between that which is under one's control and that which is not. It is a verbal clause added to the end of each sentence concerning one's own actions or intentions. Or, rather, it is the *concept* that would be implied by adding such a clause, the idea that it expresses, because I would assume that Stoics went from learning to merely *say* the reserve clause to actually *experiencing* it. The clause itself can take several forms, for example, "God willing", "fate willing", "nature permitting", "if nothing prevents me", etc. In each case, however, the underlying idea is essentially the same. The same idea is expressed in an old saying: "Do what you must; let happen what may". Nowadays, we say, "All that anyone can ask is that you try your best".

Seneca writes that the Stoic sage undertakes every action with the reserve clause: "If nothing shall occur to the contrary" (*Letters*, 34).

> The wise man considers both sides: he knows how great is the power of errors, how uncertain human affairs are, how many obstacles there are to the success of plans. Without committing himself, he awaits the doubtful and capricious issue of events, and weighs certainty of purpose against uncertainty of result. Here also, however, he is protected by that reserve clause, without which he decides upon nothing, and begins nothing.
>
> (*On Benefits*, 4.34)

He defines the reserve clause by the following formula, "I want to do such and such, as long as nothing happens which may present an obstacle to my decision"

(Seneca, *On Peace of Mind*, 13). He gives the example, "I will sail across the ocean, if nothing prevents me", and elaborates,

> Nothing happens to the Sage contrary to his expectations, for he foresees that something may intervene which prevents that which he has planned from being carried out. . . .
> What he thinks above all is that something can always oppose his plans. But the pain caused by failure must be lighter for one who has not promised success to himself beforehand.
>
> (*On Benefits*, 4.34)

The Stoic, therefore, makes a point of qualifying the expression of every intention by introducing a distinction between his will and external factors beyond his control. He thereby holds two complementary propositions in mind simultaneously, *viz.*,

1 I will do my very best to succeed . . .
2 . . . while simultaneously accepting that the ultimate outcome is beyond my direct control.

It implies, "I will try to succeed, but am prepared to accept both success and failure with equanimity", and, thereby, recognizes human fallibility. Centuries later, Christian theologians would signify the same notion by appending the letters "DV", or *Deo Volente* ("God Willing"), to their correspondence. Muslims express a similar idea by saying "inshallah".

The concept of goal-directed behaviour was traditionally illustrated in classical philosophy by the metaphor of an archer. (Apollo, one of the patron gods of philosophy, was also the god of archery.) The archer can notch his arrow and draw his bow to the best of his ability, but once the arrow has flown he can only wait to see if it hits the target. An unexpected gust of wind could blow it off course or the target could move. The intention is under his control, as is the act of setting the arrow in motion, but the result is outside his sphere of direct influence and, at least in part, down to "fate", by which is meant merely external variables. In the third book of *De Finibus*, Cicero portrays the Cato of Utica using this analogy of the archer shooting an arrow at a target to explain Stoic ethics. His ultimate wish is to hit the target, but he can only do everything within his power to shoot his arrow straight. Shooting straight as opposed to actually hitting the target must be his primary concern, and so it is with life in general. Marcus Aurelius likewise writes, "Thanks to action 'with a reserve clause' . . . there can be no obstacle to my intention" (*Meditations*, 5.20).

> Remember that your intention was always to act "with a reserve clause", for you did not desire the impossible. What, then, *did* you desire? Nothing other than to have such an intention; and *that* you have achieved.
>
> (*Meditations*, 6.50)

Epictetus puts it as follows:

> For can you find me a single man who cares how he does what he does, and is
> interested, not in what he can get, but in the manner of his own actions? Who,
> when he is walking around, is interested in his own actions? Who, when he
> is deliberating, is interested in the deliberation itself, and not in getting what
> he is planning to get?
>
> *(Discourses*, 2.16.15)

This is a little like saying, "It's not what you do; it's the way that you do
it". The Stoic *Handbook* of Epictetus likewise recommends that, in addition
to reminding oneself to avoid attaching emotive language to external things,
we should undertake any action with this reservation: that we may always be
thwarted by others, or by fortune. We should remind ourselves to view the
future realistically, and to prepare to accept any obstacles calmly rather than
feel frustration (*Encheiridion*, 4). The reserve clause can probably be corre-
lated with the Serenity Prayer, insofar as it makes a basic distinction between
courageously doing what is under our control while Stoically and serenely
accepting what is outside of our control, the outcome or consequences of our
actions.

The reserve clause and REBT

We have seen that the Stoics acknowledge both irrational and rational forms of
desire, which could be translated in terms of the distinction between "craving"
and "preference". The reserve clause, which appears to typify the concept of
"wishing" or rational preference (*boulesis*) in Stoicism, bears an obvious resemblance to the concept of "rational preference" in REBT. Ellis considered irrational
demands, the major underlying source of most emotional disturbance, to be exemplified by "must" and "should" statements:

> So REBT encourages your clients to feel strongly about succeeding at impor-
> tant tasks and relationships, but not to fall into the human propensity to raise
> their strong desires to absolutistic demands – "I *must* succeed or else I am
> worthless!" These produce dysfunctional negative feelings, especially panic
> and depression, that block their desires.
>
> (Ellis & MacLaren, 2005, p. 21)

The healthy alternative prescribed by Ellis is to adopt a philosophy of flexible
preference, which expresses a desire but also accepts the possibility of it being
frustrated. For example, "I must succeed, failure would be awful!", *becomes*,
"I strongly *prefer* to succeed, but even if I fail I will accept myself fully".

This is, of course, essentially the same "philosophical" attitude toward success
or failure that the reserve clause embodied for the Stoics. To put it another way,

"I intend to act with wisdom and integrity, fate willing, but will accept the result of my actions with a philosophical attitude".

We might call this philosophical stance the "take it or leave it" attitude of the Stoic sage, who is willing to meet success or failure with equal composure. These are the Stoic qualities Marcus Aurelius sought to model from his adoptive father, Emperor Antoninus Pius. They were exemplified by the way he handled the material comforts that fortune had supplied him in such abundance without arrogance and without apology. If they were there, he took advantage of them. If not, he did not miss them.

This "take it or leave it" aspect of Stoicism was, of course, one of the themes in Kipling's famous poem, *If*.

> If you can meet with Triumph and Disaster
> And treat those two impostors just the same . . .
> Yours is the Earth and everything that's in it, And – which is more – you'll
> be a Man, my son!
>
> (Kipling, 1994, p. 605)

This is sound wisdom and illustrates, once again, the extent to which Stoicism embodies a "perennial philosophy" which permeates the history of European civilization, from philosophy and theology to poetry and the arts.

Stoicism and rationalism (Ellis)

Toward the end of his life, Ellis explicitly distanced REBT from the suppression of emotion popularly (and falsely) associated with Stoicism and claimed that REBT was more Epicurean than Stoic, because of the connotation that "Stoic" meant lacking in emotion. However, this is definitely a misconception and an unfortunate one on the part of Ellis. Ancient Stoicism no more favoured a life lacking in or suppressing emotion than REBT does. On the contrary, the Stoics repeatedly encourage the development of positive and healthy emotions just as Ellis suggested REBT should.

It is essential to challenge this image of Stoicism because it is so deeply entrenched as an objection to the philosophy. It acts as a kind of *barrier* that prevents people who know virtually nothing of Stoicism from learning even the basics. It has prevented cognitive-behavioural theorists like Ellis from fully recognizing the extent of their indebtedness to Stoicism and the potential for benefiting from further engagement with ancient philosophy.

> Throughout its history Stoicism has been popularly characterised as a philosophy that is tantamount to emotional repression, a mentality not only egoistically unimpassioned but also insensitive towards the fortunes, whether good or bad, of other people. . . . Yet, the unimpassioned mentality (*apatheia*) of the ideal Stoic is not equivalent to a complete absence of emotion . . . it

signifies a mind that is free from "irrational" passions such as lust, craving, anger, dread, jealousy, envy, irritability, and worry. The Stoics set against these "morbid" emotions a category of attitudes that they called "good feelings" (*eupatheiai*), classifying these under three broad headings – joy, caution, and well-wishing. Under these headings they included such attitudes as cheerfulness, sociability, respectfulness, kindness, and affection.

(Long, 2002, p. 244)

Epictetus clearly and emphatically states, that the Stoic is someone

dealing with positive and negative impulses, and, in a word, with what is appropriate [*kathêkon*], in order to act methodically, with good reason, and not carelessly . . . for I ought not to be unmoved [*apathês*] like a statue, but I should maintain my natural and acquired relationships, as a dutiful man and as a son, brother, father, and citizen.

(*Discourses*, 3.2.2–4)

The "Stoic indifference" of the sage is, therefore, not an absence of all desire and emotion but merely an absence of irrational "passions", or their transmutation into rational ones.

The Sage's indifference is not a lack of interest with regard to everything, but a conversion of interest and attention toward something other than that which monopolises the care and attention of other people. As for the Stoic sage, as soon as he discovers that indifferent things depend not on his will but on the will of universal Nature, they take on infinite interest for him. He accepts them with love, but he accepts them all with *equal* love; he finds them beautiful, but all of them inspire him with the same admiration. He says "Yes!" to the entire universe and to each of its parts and events, even if specific parts and events seem painful or repugnant.

(Hadot, 2002, p. 222)

The Stoics, therefore, believed that, fundamentally, humans experience basic positive or negative emotions toward things that depend upon their value judgements. Desire is the emotional response we feel when we judge something to be good, aversion when we judge it to be bad. Ellis proposed a similar account of emotion, quoted here from an earlier work published in 1956.

An individual *emotes* when he evaluates something strongly – when he clearly perceives it as being "good" or "bad", "beneficial" or "harmful", and strongly responds to it in a negative or positive manner. Emoting usually, probably always, involves some kind of bodily sensations which, when perceived by the emoting individual, may then reinforce the original emotion. Emotions may therefore simply be evaluations which have a strong bodily component, while so-called nonemotional attitudes may be evaluations with a relatively weak bodily component.

(Ellis, 1962, p. 44)

The aim of the Stoic is simply to value things according to their true worth, rather than according to false impressions. That is what is meant by rational *vs.* irrational desire and aversion. From rational evaluations, emotional responses and inclinations to action should follow, so that the Stoic overcomes his excessive fear of sensory pain or social condemnation and becomes more able to endure them if needs be. He overcomes his excessive craving for sensory pleasure or social approbation and feels able to forego these things if necessary. Instead, he feels a love of wisdom (*philosophia*) coupled with a strong inclination to pursue happiness (*eudaimonia*) and becomes mindful and alert so as to avoid lapsing back into error.

Philosophical strengths and virtues

A further source of confusion, when reading about ancient philosophical therapy, stems from the use of the English word "virtue" to translate the Greek *arete*. There is a notorious problem with the translation of this term, because the English "virtue" still carries moralistic connotations derived from medieval Christianity, which are largely alien to pagan philosophies like Stoicism. As is often the case, the English language does contain traces of the original meaning, which have become somewhat muddied over the centuries. The basic meaning of *arete* is not some kind of moral righteousness, but a strength or positive quality "*by virtue of which*", as we might say, something excels at its natural or allotted function. Famously, in the philosophical sense, a house has *virtue* if it is well built, a tree if it grows strong and bears fruit, or a horse if it is strong or runs fast.

Consequently, when Stoics discuss "virtue" they could often be best understood as referring to the moral or psychological *strengths* of the ideal human being, the strengths of character, by virtue of which he achieves optimum happiness and well-being. By comparison with modern psychotherapy, the "virtues" of the Stoic are simply the positive character traits that contribute to mental health and emotional well-being. In classical philosophy, the cardinal virtues are traditionally fourfold: wisdom, justice, courage, and moderation in the following.

- Wisdom (*sophia* or *phronesis*), specifically moral or practical wisdom that consists in grasping the nature of the good; it often seems to be associated also with truthfulness toward oneself and others.
- Justice (*dikaiosune*), sometimes translated as "righteousness" in the past because it really refers more generally to social virtue, including fairness and kindness toward others.

- Courage (*andreia*), previously translated "fortitude", it is the virtue required to live with wisdom and justice instead of being pulled off course by pain or fear, also encompasses endurance and determination.
- Moderation (*sophrosune*), often translated as "temperance", it is the virtue required to live with wisdom and justice instead of being sidetracked by pleasure or desire, it also implies a kind of self-awareness, perhaps even *mindfulness*.

However, for the Stoics, as followers of Socrates, these are all conceived of as unified in wisdom; the other virtues are ultimately *aspects* of philosophical enlightenment: *All virtues are one.* It is by virtue of practical philosophical wisdom – the kind of wisdom that finds expression in justice, courage, and moderation – that the Stoic finds genuine tranquillity, happiness, and well-being.

Marcus Aurelius cajoles himself, writing, "You've wandered all over and finally realised that you never found what you were after: how to live". He reminds himself the answer is not to be found in abstract logic, nor in wealth, fame, or sensory indulgence.

- Then where is it to be found?
  - In doing what human nature requires.
- How?
  - Through first principles. Which should govern your intentions and your actions.
- What principles?
  - Those to do with good and evil. That nothing is good except what leads to [the virtues of] justice, and self-control, and courage, and free will. And nothing bad except what does the opposite? (*Meditations*, 8.1)

He likewise writes:

> If, at some point in your life, you should come across anything better than [the cardinal virtues] justice, truth, self-control, courage – than a mind satisfied that it has succeeded in enabling you to act rationally, and satisfied to accept what's beyond its control – if you find anything better than that, embrace it without reservations – it must be an extraordinary thing indeed – and enjoy it to the full.
>
> (*Meditations*, 3.6)

By virtue of these strengths of character the Stoic hopes to manage his feelings rationally and transform them into the rational love of universal Nature, corresponding with the philosophical ideal of enlightened and healthy passions.

Proto-passions and "raw affect"

One of the key areas where modern psychology might be seen to have settled a dispute within the field of Stoicism is with regard to the extent to which unhealthy emotions can be permanently extinguished by cognitive training. It seems that the Stoic Chrysippus believed that the perfect Stoic sage would be completely free of any risk of excessive unhealthy emotion. The later Stoic Posidonius argued that even the sage would have to endure some primitive emotional reactions, but could recover from them more easily due to his cognitive self-mastery. This seems to be a well-known caveat in Stoicism. Seneca discusses it in relation to a young philosopher whom he admired, despite his habit of nervously blushing.

> This I rather suspect will remain with him even when he has built up his character and stripped it of all weakness – even when he has become a wise man [i.e., a Stoic sage]. For no amount of wisdom enables one to do away with physical or mental weaknesses that arise from natural causes; anything inborn or ingrained in one can by dint of practice be allayed, but not overcome.
>
> (*Letters*, 11)

He proceeds to discuss phenomena such as trembling, stammering, sweating, etc., as examples of nervous reactions which Stoic training may help one to cope with better without necessarily curing completely. Philosophy does not have absolute dominion over our physical nature, he concludes, and even a perfect sage may initially blush or stammer under certain circumstances, although he may regain his composure later.

As Becker observes, modern psychology supports the later Stoic view that even the sage must continue to cope with certain emotional reactions.

> This does not mean that subsequent cognitive responses are ineffective in controlling such affect. It only means that this sort of affective *arousal* and its immediate emotional and passional consequences cannot be eliminated by cognitive (Stoic) training, any more than Stoic training can eliminate perspiration. Stoics with bad gallbladders will just have to cope with anxiety, whether they are sages or not; similarly for people who have brain injuries, or brain tumours, that excite affective structures. Modern medicine is clear that cognitive training is not always the treatment of first choice for such affective disturbances.
>
> (Becker, 2004, pp. 255–256)

Indeed, the formal codification of psychiatric disorders found in *DSM IV-TR*, the main classification system in psychopathology, distinguishes between anxiety disorders proper and anxiety that is due to a general medical condition or is substance induced.

Common sense suggests that the Stoic who is generally anxious because he drinks too much coffee or depressed because he drinks too much alcohol might be better advised to change his habits of consumption than simply trying to change his mood directly by thinking about things differently, and the same holds true for the use of modern cognitive therapy. However, as Becker observes, this should be as obvious as the observation that the Stoic who suffers from thirst would be better to drink water than to try to overcome his desire for rehydration. It is unlikely that these qualifications should raise any serious objections to the overall philosophy.

> Moreover, the affects generated solely by subcortical structures in our brains correspond to the sort of primal impulses or excitation so often discussed by Stoics as leading more or less involuntarily to proto-emotions (*propatheiai*), and thence transformed by further cognitive processes into full-fledged emotions. They thus fit comfortably into a contemporary Stoic account.
>
> (*ibid.*, p. 256)

The sage will never completely rid himself by *preventative* means of the "raw affect", which the body may generate as the precursor to certain unhealthy emotions. Nevertheless, modern psychologists generally agree that these primitive impulses may often be modified and possibly tamed to some extent by subsequent cognition, so the "cure" remains the same. This is probably true for the majority of ordinary emotional reactions with which the Stoic has to contend in daily life, and exceptions mainly pertain to those cases where affect is substance induced or due to a general medical condition.

> All affective states – or at least all of those above the level of pure primal impulse – have at least implicit, controlling beliefs, and are ultimately subject to the agent's ability to control those beliefs. Thus Stoic psychotherapy is a form of cognitive therapy – an effort to focus on, and then to correct, the cognitive errors that underwrite pathology.
>
> (*ibid.*, p. 257)

As Becker observes, even sages are eventually overcome by illness and disease. The common sense conclusion here seems to be that the Stoic should be able to identify whether the nervous states preceding his fully-fledged emotions are determined primarily by his own cognitions or by physical factors outside of his direct control.

As we've noted earlier, both Stoics and cognitive-behavioural theorists seem to have struggled to clarify the precise nature of the relationship between cognition and emotion. Sometimes, cognition is assumed to be the *cause* of emotion, sometimes a *constituent* of emotion. On careful reflection, it should become clear that these are two crucially different things. Without entering into this, nevertheless, very important area in more detail at this stage, it should be observed that the notion of cognition as a *constituent* of emotion is probably more consistent with the findings of empirical psychology. Nevertheless, the key issue is that changes in cognition appear to reliably result in emotions changing. This is not so very difficult to understand, as Becker very clearly illustrates with the following example:

> Suppose you enter a room in which your lover – whose back is turned to you – is cursing you angrily, shockingly, without warning, blaming you by name for some unnamed injury and breaking off your relationship with finality. You have a rush of sudden feeling and emotion – a rush, bewilderment, anger, hurt. And in the next moment, you see that your lover is reading a script – rehearsing a part in a play that has nothing to do with you. What happens to your emotions? The bewilderment, anger, and hurt drain away immediately, replaced by relief, hilarity, perhaps self-mockery. What happened? What changed? Cognition changed. Beliefs changed, and evidently drove the change in affect, including not only the conative impulse (whatever it was) but even the underlying state of physiological arousal. And we can multiply such examples without end. Psychotherapists quite generally go even farther than this, by acknowledging that many pathological emotional states are also transformable by changes in the subject's beliefs. Consequently, treatment regimes for many sorts of psychological illnesses – including depression, anxiety, phobias of various sorts – rely heavily on what can only be called Stoic principles. (At least one current variety of psychotherapy acknowledges this explicitly: rational emotive behaviour therapy.) This sort of change is commonplace, and naturally enough suggests the Stoic hypothesis – namely, that for rational agents (e.g., humans at or above the age of reason) beliefs underwrite the *original* emotions in such examples as well.
>
> (*ibid.*, p. 274 n.)

One of the clearest discussions of the role of proto-passions, or "raw affect" preceding fully-fledged emotion, is provided in Seneca's *On Anger*:

> In order that you may know how emotions begin, or grow, or are carried away, the first movement is involuntary, like a preparation for emotion and a kind of threat. The second movement is accompanied by will [or choice], not an obstinate one, to the effect that it is appropriate for me to be avenged since I am injured, or it is appropriate for him to be punished since he has committed a crime. The third movement is by now uncontrolled, and wills to be avenged, not if it is appropriate, but come what may, and it has overthrown reason.
>
> We cannot escape that first shock of the mind by reason, just as we cannot escape those things we mentioned which befall the body either, so as to avoid another's yawn infecting us, or avoid our eyes blinking when fingers are suddenly poked toward us. Reason cannot control those things, though perhaps familiarity and constant attention may weaken them. The second movement, which is born of judgement, is removed by judgement.
>
> (*On Anger*, 2.4)

Seneca appears to have clearly described a Stoic theory of emotion that, though different, can perhaps be compared in some ways to Ellis' ABC model, which is central to REBT. We could describe this is Seneca or Stoicism's own ABC model:

1   **A**: Initial Raw **A**ffect. An initial precursor of full-blown emotion (a "proto-passion") arises in a manner resembling a physical reflex such as blinking, e.g., increased heart rate and physical tension in response to a sudden shock. This is accompanied by the initial impression that something external is very good or bad. We can describe these as the initial phase of "automatic" thoughts and feelings triggered by external events.
2   **B**: Irrational **B**eliefs. A judgement is made that confirms the initial impression, giving assent to it. The wise man can avert this, of course, by transferring his judgement that something is bad or harmful from the external object onto the passion itself and the belief underlying it – telling himself that it's not events that harm us but our judgements about them.
3   **C**: Passionate **C**onsequences. The initial proto-passion escalates into a full-blown passion, which can feel difficult to control, although it's mediated by voluntary cognitions. Chrysippus compares this to a man running so fast that he finds it hard to stop or change direction to avoid obstacles.

Of course, in Seneca's model, the initial "activating event" is the incipient sensation of anger rising, the proto-passion. Although Ellis also allows internal sensations to perform this function in his ABC model, he tends to focus on the external event that is perceived as triggering the emotion. However, the Stoic model of emotion has also been expressed in terms of the cognitive reaction to the initial "appearance" or "impression" of an external event,

> The mere appearance is not yet a judgement and not yet an emotion because a judgement – and, hence, an emotion – is the assent of reason to the appearance. Ordinary people not trained in Stoicism may give the assent of reason so automatically that they do not realise that assent is a separate operation of the mind from receiving appearances. But Stoicism trains you to stand back from appearances and interrogate them without automatically giving them the assent of your reason.
>
> (Sorabji, 2004, p. 97)

Indeed, this is exactly how Ellis and MacLaren describe the role of emotive beliefs in REBT.

> People's evaluative Beliefs about Adversities are often automatic and unconscious; but they are also frequently conscious. What is largely unconscious is their knowledge that their Beliefs lead to (or at least significantly contribute to) their feelings. They usually have the illusion that they just feel bad about Adversity – that A "causes" C. Actually A B = C. But since

C frequently may occur almost instantly after A, they fail to see that B also importantly "causes" C.

(Ellis & MacLaren, 2005, p. 28)

These initial "appearances" evoke initial reflex responses, proto-emotions, which cognition turns into fully-fledged emotions. Hence, Marcus Aurelius reminds himself to pause over his initial impressions before adding any further value judgements or unfounded assumptions.

Noting but what you get from first impressions. That someone has insulted you, for instance. That – but not that it's done you any harm. The fact that my son is sick – that I can see. But "that he might die of it", no. Stick with first impressions. Don't extrapolate. And nothing can happen to you.

(*Meditations*, 8.49)

Elsewhere he writes,

The mind is the ruler of the soul. It should remain unstirred by agitations of the flesh – gentle and violent ones alike. Not mingling with them, but fencing itself off and keeping those feelings in their place. When they make their way, into your thoughts, through the sympathetic link between mind and body, don't try to resist the sensation. The sensation is natural. But don't let the mind start in with judgements, calling it "good" or "bad".

(*Meditations*, 5.26)

Sorabji recounts an anecdote reported by the grammarian Aulus Gellius in his *Attic Nights*, written in the second century AD (Sorabji, 2004). During a stormy trip at sea, a Stoic philosopher on a boat was seen to become pale and nervous. Once ashore, a curious passenger asked, "Tell me, how is it that you, a Stoic, who are supposed to have no emotions, grew pale in the storm?" The Stoic made light of the question, but then Gellius himself came forward and asked more earnestly, "No, please tell me really why you grew so pale in the storm?" The Stoic defended himself by taking out a copy of Epictetus' *Discourses*, and showing his audience a passage, which happens to be from the lost fifth book.

In this fragment, Epictetus explains that even the perfect Stoic sage is vulnerable to these sudden and frightening impressions, and the "first movements" of nascent emotion, which we would call symptoms of nervous arousal. The difference being that the sage has trained himself to refrain from making them worse by giving his assent to what they seem to say. He might say firmly to himself, "Even though I feel myself growing pale, I know it is just my body reacting to the choppy waves, which will soon pass, and there is no real danger for me to fear". By contrast, a non-Stoic might allow himself to dwell on the feelings, worrying about them, reinforcing them, and creating a vicious circle of nervous arousal and worried thoughts until they spiral into panic. Aulus Gellius paraphrases from Epictetus' lost discourse as follows:

> The way things look to the mind (what philosophers call "impressions") have an immediate psychological impact and are not subject to one's wishes, but force human beings to recognise them by a certain inherent power. But the acts of approval (what philosophers call "assents" [i.e., cognitions]) are voluntary and involve human judgement. So, when some terrifying sound comes from the sky or from a falling building, or when sudden news comes of some danger, or something of this sort happens, even the wise person's mind is necessarily affected, shrinks back, and grows pale for a moment, not because he forms a judgement that something bad is about to happen, but because of certain rapid and unconsidered movements which prevent the mind and reason from functioning properly. But soon the wise person in that situation does not give approval to (that is, "he does not assent to, or confirm by his judgement") "this type of impression" (that is, the fact that things look terrifying to the mind), but rejects them and dismisses them completely, and sees in them no reason why he should be afraid. They say that this is the difference between the mind of the foolish and wise person. The foolish person thinks that those things that initially strike the mind as dreadful and horrifying really are what they first appear, and, as if they were properly to be feared, he approves them by his assent "and confirms them by his judgement" (the word that the Stoics use when they discuss this topic). But the wise person, although affected superficially and briefly in colour and expression "does not assent", but keeps this consistency and firmness of judgement which he has always had about things that look like this to the mind, namely that they are not proper objects of fear at all, but that they frighten with a false face and empty terror.
>
> (Epictetus, *Fragment* 9)

Once again, we may compare Ellis' REBT conceptualization. He says that human adults typically experience thought and emotion acting in a "circular cause-and-effect relationship" and that they are in certain (but not all) respects "essentially the *same* thing" (Ellis, 1962, p. 49). Thoughts often develop into emotions and vice versa. Ellis says, though, that emotions can exist without thoughts, e.g., if a car suddenly comes toward you and you immediately become afraid without having time to consciously think "It's about to hit me!" On the other hand, it may be that the sentence flashes very rapidly through your mind and "perhaps this thought or internalised speech *is* your emotion of fright".

> In any event, assuming that you don't, at the very beginning, have any conscious or unconscious thought accompanying your emotion, it appears to be almost impossible to *sustain* an emotional outburst without bolstering it by repeated ideas. For unless you keep telling yourself something on the order

of "Oh, my heavens! How terrible it would have been if that car had hit me!"
your fright over almost being hit by the car will soon die.

(Ellis, 1962, p. 49)

Ellis argues that certain forms of neurological or chemical stimulation might
maintain emotional arousal but thinks that these are the exceptions that prove
the rule and are of little relevance to the process of ordinary self-help or psychotherapy. In any case, his example is similar enough to the tale of the seasick Stoic
to illustrate, yet again, the extent to which REBT in particular appears to parallel
ancient Stoic thought.

Reason vs. passion in the Medea

To attack a common misconception about reason and emotions, the Stoics
employed the famous example of the character Medea from Euripides' ancient
play of the same name. Medea is spurned in favour of another woman by her
husband, the legendary Greek hero Jason. Renowned both for her intellect and
temper, in a seemingly insane act of revenge, Medea murders her own children in
order to punish her husband. She wrestles with her thoughts and feelings in solilo-
quy, but finally settles on the decision to go ahead. This well-known story was
probably quoted to the Stoics as an example, a "case study", of passion seemingly
overpowering reason in a very dramatic manner. However, pre-empting criticism,
they attempted to use it to clarify and defend their own position rather than accept
it at face value.

> A person, then, cannot think a thing advantageous to him, and not choose it.
>   He cannot.
>   But what of Medea, who says, "Yes, I understand what evils I propose,
> but passion overwhelms my resolutions?" For it is just this, the gratification
> of her anger and the taking of vengeance on her husband, that she regards as
> more advantageous than the saving of her children.
>   Yes; but she is deceived. Show to her clearly that she is deceived, and she
> will not do it; but as long as you have not shown it, what else has she to fol-
> low but what seems true to her?
>   Nothing.
>   Why, then, are you angry with her, because, poor woman, she has fallen
> into error on the most important points, and instead of being a human being,
> has become a viper? Why do you not, if anything, pity her instead, and, as we
> pity the blind and lame, so likewise pity those who are blinded and lamed in
> their ruling [rational] faculties?

(*Discourses*, 1.28.6–9)

Medea claims that she knows that she is doing wrong, and acting against her own
self-interest, but feels emotionally compelled to seek revenge anyway. However,

Epictetus disagrees with Medea's own interpretation of her actions. Rather than thinking of passion and belief as opposing forces he thinks passions themselves are partially *constituted* from certain emotive beliefs. Medea drives herself mad by placing too much value upon the love of Jason, her unfaithful husband. She absolutely *demands* that he should be faithful to her, but she cannot control his actions. So she feels infuriated and driven to violence by his infidelity with another woman. Epictetus elsewhere advises Medea:

> Do not desire the man for your husband, and nothing which you do desire will fail to happen. Do not desire to keep him to yourself. Do not desire to stay at Corinth . . . and who shall hinder you, who shall compel you?
>
> (*Discourses*, 2.17.22)

Moreover, at a "metacognitive" level, in terms of her higher-order beliefs, Medea can be viewed as someone who *believes* that it is better to give in to her passion, and *let* it rule her actions, than to try to counteract it, for example, by killing *herself*, or sending her children to safety. She is *not* simply a clever woman overcome by her emotions, but someone who holds *contradictory* beliefs, the stronger of which prevails. Intelligent people, like Medea herself, sometimes do stupid things, especially when strong feelings are involved. Ellis could have been describing Medea when he wrote, "Neurosis, then, is illogical behaviour by a potentially logical individual" (Ellis, 1962, p. 55). On the one hand, she knows that it is insane to kill her children out of spite, but, on the other, she believes she should give in to her passions rather than fighting them; perhaps she believes that she has no other option – but she certainly cannot escape the accusation that her beliefs guide her actions just as much as her passions do. She seeks to avoid responsibility for her horrific actions by blaming them on her feelings but according to the Stoics this is self-deception: she will always be responsible for the set of beliefs that made her experience those feelings in the first place.

Cognitive therapists refer to something similar by the term "emotional reasoning", the tendency to justify an irrational decision because it *feels* like the right or only thing to do. It is, for example, possible to imagine another Medea saying *not* "passion rules my decisions" but, rather, "the stronger the passion for revenge becomes, the more likely it is to pervert my judgement, and so I should not let my feelings rule me any more". Although this might be difficult to conceive, it is, nevertheless, possible, and the Stoics can acknowledge the difficulty of Medea's inner struggle without conceding that, even in her extreme case, reason is merely the slave of the passions.

The rational love of the sage

We have seen that Stoicism is not just arid intellectualism. In order to counter the misconception of the Stoic as a "cold fish", I was tempted to begin my exposition under the heading of "Stoicism as a philosophy of love". Indeed, the founder of the school, Zeno, reputedly wrote a book titled *The Art of Love* (*Lives*, 7.1). This may refer to love between individual people. For example, according to Seneca, the Stoic philosopher Hecato prescribed the following salutary advice, "I shall show you a love philtre compounded without drug or herb or witch's spell. It is this: if you wish to be loved, love" (*Letters*, 9).

However, we may also speak of the "love" of the philosopher toward wisdom, or the universe itself. The cultivation of an intellectual, or philosophical, love of universal Nature (*Amor Dei Intellectualis*) was the explicit goal of Spinoza's system of philosophical therapy, and his ideas do seem particularly influenced by his Stoic precursors.

Indeed, the whole system of Stoic philosophy could be interpreted from as an attempt to define the meaning of love as the basis of a grand ethical and episte-mological system. Epictetus clearly states that it is part of human nature, common sense, to love what we perceive to be good and conducive to happiness, but men differ over the details, seeing different things as deserving of love.

> Whoever, therefore, has knowledge of good things would also know how to love them; and he who cannot distinguish good things from evil, and things that are neither good nor evil from both of these, how could he still have the power to love? *It follows that the wise man alone has the power to love.*
>
> (*Discourses*, 2.22.1–3, my italics)

The Stoic philosopher aims to reconcile love and reason, to love what is truly good. Stressing this simple point is perhaps the best rhetorical strategy to adopt in countering the fundamentally mistaken portrayal of Stoicism as espousing a kind of repression of all human emotion. To the question, "How, then, shall I be affectionate?" from one of his students, Epictetus replies:

> As becomes a noble-spirited and happy person. For reason will never tell you to be abject and broken-hearted, or to depend on another, or to reproach either god or man. Be affectionate in such a manner as to observe all this. But if from affection, as you call it, you are to be a slave and a wretch, it is not worth your while to be affectionate.
>
> (*Discourses*, 3.24.58–59)

The sage loves without demanding that he be loved in return, and without the kind of emotional attachment that presupposes that things are set in stone and cannot change. He, therefore, reminds himself of the transience of all things, including the lives of his loved ones, whom he views, rationally, as mortals, subject to change and death. With this qualification in mind, we can affirm that the sage feels love, and does so as a philosopher should, unconditionally, and toward all mankind. Likewise, in the preface to his *The Meditations*, Marcus Aurelius describes the Stoic ideal exemplified by his tutor Sextus of Chaeronea as follows: "Not to display anger or other emotions. To be free of passion and yet full of love" (*Meditations*, 1.9).

Given that many modern readers would, by contrast, consider "love" the archetypal passion, this passage shows just how distorted our view of Stoicism has become. Not many people would assume that the aim of Stoicism would be to be "full of love", as Marcus Aurelius writes, or that the sage alone is capable of love, as Epictetus puts it, with typically provocative rhetoric. I feel justified, therefore, in claiming that, contrary to popular misconception: Stoicism is essentially a philosophy of love.

Chapter 6

Stoicism and Ellis' rational therapy (REBT)

As we have seen already, the most obvious analogies between classical philosophy and modern CBT are probably to be found in the influence of Stoic, and, to some extent, Epicurean, philosophy upon the rational emotive behaviour therapy (REBT) of Albert Ellis. Indeed, Still and Dryden go further in their discussion of REBT and Stoicism by emphasizing that "this general similarity is homologous rather than analogous since Ellis drew some of his account of the control of emotions by reason directly from Stoic writings, and from the Stoicism present in popular morality" (1999, p. 154). According to Ellis, therefore, the central aim of REBT is that of "inducing the patient to internalise a rational philosophy of life" and to directly uproot and counteract the core irrational beliefs which he has inherited or developed since childhood (Ellis, 1962, p. 65).

> By direct statement and implication, then, modern thinkers are tending to recognize the fact that logic and reason can, and, in a sense, must, play a most important role in overcoming human neurosis. Eventually, they may be able to catch up with Epictetus in this respect, who wrote – some nineteen centuries ago – that "the chief concern of a wise and good man is his own reason".
>
> (Ellis, 1962, p. 109)

The origin of REBT

Ellis was originally a *psychoanalytic* therapist. In 1953, after ten years of psychoanalytic practise, he finally broke away decisively from that tradition and began practising what is widely considered to be the first *modern* cognitive therapy, or at least the first major cognitive approach of the post-war period. Ellis originally referred to his method as "rational therapy" (RT), subsequently changing the name to "rational emotive therapy" (RET) to counter the misconception that his approach was "rationalistic" and neglected emotional factors. He finally settled on the name "rational emotive behaviour therapy" (REBT) in order to acknowledge of the role of direct behaviour change in his therapeutic approach. The name came to encompass the three main response systems – reason, emotion, and behaviour – addressed by any psychotherapy. It is worth noting that Ellis had originally considered other names such as "logical", "persuasive", "objective", and "realistic" therapy (Ellis, 1962, p. 120).

Ellis claimed that from adolescence onwards he was interested in philosophy and was keenly aware of the fact that classical philosophers had developed systems of thought for dealing with emotional problems (Ellis, 2004, p. 12). In an interview about REBT, Ellis explained that in the early 1950s, when he broke from psychoanalytic tradition, he returned to his long-standing interest in classical systems of philosophy, rereading the Stoics in order to integrate their ideas into his new "rational" and "philosophical" system of psychotherapy.

> My main influences [in the 1950s] were philosophical. I happened to have a hobby of philosophy since the age of fifteen. There were some cognitive influences, but I really got my main theory that people largely upset themselves from ancient philosophers, some of the Asians, but also from the Greeks and Romans.
>
> (Ellis, 2004, p. 83)

Ellis makes similar comments concerning his debt to ancient philosophy throughout his writings. For instance, an article co-authored with Windy Dryden explains:

> Ellis had a long-standing interest in philosophy and was particularly influenced by the writings of Stoic philosophers such as Epictetus and Marcus Aurelius. In particular, the oft-quoted phrase of Epictetus, "People are disturbed not by things but by their view of things", crystallized Ellis' view that philosophical factors are more important than psychoanalytic and psychodynamic factors in accounting for psychological disturbance.
>
> (Dryden & Ellis, 2001, p. 295)

Ellis even goes so far as to claim: "I am happy to say that in the 1950s I managed to bring Epictetus out of near-obscurity and make him famous all over again" (Ellis & MacLaren, 2005, p. 10). This is probably an exaggeration, though it is true that Epictetus experienced a temporary period in obscurity until around the 1970s (Long, 2002, p. 2).

Ellis also mentions that he was influenced by the writings of modern philosophers such as Bertrand Russell and John Dewey, as well as Asian philosophers of the Buddhist traditions (Ellis, 2004, p. 12). As a teenager, he was interested in Couéism, which seemed to him the pre-eminent school of self-help available at the time. As we have seen, Couéism also has a strong cognitive orientation and Coué's follower Baudouin was one of the first modern "rational" psychotherapists to draw explicitly upon Stoic philosophy, though there does not seem to be any evidence that Ellis had read Baudouin's work.

Hypnotism and autosuggestion

The essence of REBT is encapsulated in the ABC model of Ellis, which we will consider shortly. However, he also described the three "insights" that follow as central to REBT theory (Ellis & MacLaren, 2005, p. 38).

1   Emotional disturbance is caused by a combination of adversity and irrational beliefs.
2   Despite the potential historical or developmental origins of emotional disturbance, it is largely maintained by ongoing irrational beliefs in the here and now.
3   Changing engrained irrational beliefs takes considerable effort and practise.

In his earliest writings, Ellis makes it very clear that he understood the role of irrational beliefs to resemble that of negative *autosuggestions*, which the client had internalized and was in the habit of repeating. Though his use of hypnosis seemed to diminish over time, Ellis initially employed it with many clients and wrote several articles on the subject. However, he felt that direct suggestion had certain limitations in psychotherapy and needed to be supplemented by rational *persuasion* techniques.

> Man is a uniquely suggestible as well as a uniquely rational animal. Other animals are to some degree suggestible and reasoning, but man's better equipped cerebral cortex, which makes possible his ability to talk to himself and others, gives him unusual opportunities to talk himself into *and* out of many difficulties.
>
> (Ellis, 1962, p. 104)

Insofar as it regarded a client's problems as primarily due to irrational autosuggestion and the solution as primarily a matter of rational disputation and persuasion, early REBT bore considerable resemblance to Paul Dubois' rational psychotherapy, as Ellis later acknowledged (*ibid.*, p. 105). However, Dubois never developed anything like the system or armamentarium of specific strategies and therapy interventions that Ellis came to employ.

Ellis seemed convinced that traditional hypnotists, from Braid's discovery of hypnotism in 1841 to Bernheim, who founded the Nancy school of psychotherapy, had completely overlooked the role of negative autosuggestion in psychopathology. He wrote:

> Bernheim [in Suggestion and its Therapeutic Applications, 1887] was one of the first to realise that suggestion, with or without hypnosis, is often a most effective therapeutic tool. But neither he nor any of his followers seem to have grasped very clearly *why* this is so – probably, ironically enough, because the answer to the problem is so simple.

The answer to this riddle, in the light of the theory of rational-emotive psychotherapy, is simply that suggestion and autosuggestion are effective in removing neurotic and psychotic symptoms because *they are the very instruments which caused or helped produce these symptoms in the first place.* Virtually all complex and sustained adult human emotions are caused by ideas or attitudes; and these ideas or attitudes are, first, *suggested* by persons and things outside the individual (especially by his parents, teachers, books, etc.); and they are, second, continually *autosuggested* by himself.

(*ibid.*, p. 277)

However, *pace* Ellis, Braid, Bernheim, and other Victorian hypnotists certainly *did* mention this phenomenon, albeit under different names. Braid, the founder of hypnotherapy, referred to the role of pre-existing "dominant" or "fixed" ideas in the pathogenesis of hysteria and carried out many experiments to prove that hysterical symptoms such as fainting or paralysis could be induced by suggestion. Of one client, suffering from "hysterical" or psychosomatic illness, Braid writes:

It was not, therefore, the induction of the *nervous sleep* [hypnotism] alone which effected the cure, but my knowledge of how to *direct the influence* DURING the sleep, so as to break down the pre-existing, involuntary fixed, dominant idea in the patient's mind, and its consequences.

(Braid, 2009, p. 97)

Couéism developed this idea further, emphasizing to clients the central role of morbid autosuggestion in psychogenic illness and other nervous disorders.

From our birth to our death we are all the slaves of suggestion. Our destinies are decided by suggestion. It is an all-powerful tyrant of which, unless we take heed, we are the blind instruments. Now, it is in our power to turn the tables and to discipline suggestion, and direct it in the way we ourselves wish; then it becomes auto-suggestion: we have taken the reigns into our own hands, and we have become masters of the most marvellous instrument conceivable.

(Coué, 1923, p. 6)

Moreover, like Coué, Ellis concludes that the main underlying issue is that the client should come to perceive their internal dialogue as a form of autosuggestion and to realize that they are continually re-indoctrinating themselves into irrational or neurotic belief systems.

The best kind of solution to this problem, therefore, is not his or the therapist's vigorous counter-suggestion, but the patient's attaining clear insight into his autosuggestive process and is using this insight so that he can effectively keep contradicting and challenging his negative, self-destroying autosuggestions.

(Ellis, 1962, p. 357)

Just over one hundred years after Braid's time, as we have seen, Ellis arrived at a similar conception of the role of "fixed ideas" or *autosuggestions* in emotional disturbance. In addition to its roots in ancient Socratic philosophy, therefore, the cognitive model of psychological disturbance was clearly prefigured by the writings of James Braid, the father of hypnotherapy. The cognitive model continued to develop throughout Victorian and early twentieth century psychotherapy and self-help, long before it reached its current form in the rational and cognitive psychotherapies of Ellis and Beck.

The ABC model

Perhaps the most famous component of REBT is Ellis' "ABC model", sometimes called the "activation-belief-consequence" model:

1   Activating event, which could be internal or external.
2   Irrational beliefs, mediate the response.
3   Consequences, particularly unhealthy emotions but also other symptoms of psychological disturbance.

According to this simple schema, although people often think of their emotional disturbance as being the direct consequence (C) of some activating event or "adversity" (A), the first step in therapy is to help them become more aware of the role irrational beliefs (B) play in determining the nature of their response.

In other words, most people tend to describe their emotional reactions in broadly *stimulus-response* ("A causes C") language. For example, someone might think to themself "he shouted at me" (environmental stimulus or "A") "and that made me cry" (emotional response or "C"). However, Ellis and other cognitive therapists are keen to emphasize the intermediate role of clients' cognitions. For example, "he shouted at me" (A), "I told myself 'That's awful, I can't stand it, he's an idiot!'" (B), "and that made me cry" (C). As Ellis put it:

> Sparked by philosophy, I worked on my psychotherapeutic theory from 1953 to 1955, and finally came up with what I called Rational Therapy (RT) in January 1955. In it, I presented the rather unique ABC theory of emotional disturbance. This held that when people were confronted with Adversity (A) and reacted with disturbed Consequences (C), such as severe anxiety and depression, it was largely their Belief System (B), together with A, that led to their dysfunctions. Thus, A + B = C. This theory significantly differed from psychoanalytic, conditioning, and other theories of emotional disturbance that were popular in 1955.
>
> (Ellis & MacLaren, 2005, p. 10)

This simple ABC framework serves very well as a working model of therapy, used to explain things to the client. However, on closer inspection, its application can become a little more complex. First, the activating event is not necessarily an *external* stimulus but may be a memory or some other internal event such as a physical sensation of tightness in the chest. The consequences evoked are seldom *only* emotional but also consist of cognitive, behavioural, and physiological responses. Moreover, as we have seen, the distinctions made between these concepts are not hard and fast, they are not mutually exclusive things, an issue that ultimately requires subtle conceptual analysis of the terms employed in such theories. To his credit, Ellis acknowledged these philosophical problems,

> While REBT theory does stress the role played by cognitive factors in human functioning, cognition, emotion, and behavior are not viewed as separate psychological processes, but rather as processes that are highly interdependent and interactive. Thus, the statement "cognition leads to emotion" tends to accentuate a false picture of psychological separatism. In the famous "ABCs" of REBT, *A* has traditionally stood for an *activating* event; *B* for the way that this inferred event is evaluated (i.e., a person's *beliefs*); and *C* for the emotional, behavioral, and cognitive *consequences* that stem from *B*. As stated, however, this model does not emphasize the interactive nature of the psychological processes contained within it . . . thus it should be underscored that REBT theory sees the person as having overlapping intrapsychic processes and as being in constant interaction with his or her social and material environment.
>
> (Dryden & Ellis, 2001, p. 299)

We might nevertheless agree with Ellis, that the simplified ABC model is often sufficient, for practical purposes, as a working model presented to clients to explain the rationale for therapy. Though it fails to express the complexity of the processes involved, it perhaps emphasizes those factors that are most important in the clinical practise of psychotherapy as seen from the client's perspective.

If thoughts, somehow or other, determine emotions then it seems natural to view them not only as the *cause* but perhaps also the *cure* of our troubles.

> If what has been hypothesized so far is true, and human emotions are largely a form of thinking or result from thinking, it would appear that one may appreciably control one's emotion by controlling one's thoughts. Or, more concretely, one may control one's emotions by changing the internalized sentences, or self-talk, with which one largely created these emotions in the first place.
>
> (Ellis, 1962, p. 52)

However, arguably, this clinical observation may hold equally true if we regard cognitions as constituting part of the structure of emotions, rather than as their causal antecedents. In fact, if by changing our thoughts we are not merely changing the "cause" of emotion, but directly changing the structure of the emotion itself, the clinical significance of cognitive restructuring, changing thoughts, is probably even greater.

One of the most fundamental premises of Stoicism is, of course, the notion that our judgements influence our emotional responses.

> Very fortunately, however, as Epictetus showed two thousand years ago – it is not *only* the undesirable and uninvited things that happen to you that disturb you – it is *also* your view of them. Aristotle, too, wisely indicated that you could take unfortunate events lightly, moderately, or catastrophically. To a considerable degree, it's your *choice*.
>
> (Ellis, 2004, p. 97)

The ability to separate thoughts from things, and to see the emotive value which we attribute to events as a product of our own perspective upon them, provides us with a fundamental basis for self-control over our desires and emotions. Epictetus goes so far as to propose this model of cognitive-emotional self-control (*sophrosune*) as defining the very essence of what it means to be a philosopher, Philosophizing is virtually this – enquiry into how it is possible to employ desire and aversion without hindrance (*Discourses*, 3.14.10).

The ability to see that certain habitual and thoughtless *decisions*, long ago made by us, have already determined whether we like or dislike, approve or disapprove, love or hate, and continue to do so, provides us with the means to revise our position and make conscious decisions which reformulate our desires, inclinations, and emotional responses.

The cognitive mediation model in Stoicism

The aspect of Stoicism most familiar to practitioners of CBT is therefore the oft-quoted principle from Epictetus that we are disturbed not by things but by our judgement *about* things. Ellis cites this repeatedly as an illustration of the ABC model. However, the underlying concept can, arguably, be traced back to Socrates himself, who expresses essentially the same view, albeit less succinctly than the Stoic philosophers who came after him.

> So, to sum up, Clinias, I said, it seems likely that with respect to all the things we called good in the beginning, the correct account is not that in themselves they are good by nature, but rather as follows: if ignorance controls them, they are greater evils than their opposites, to the extent that they are more capable of complying with a bad master; but if good sense and wisdom are in control, they are greater goods. In themselves, however, neither sort is of any value. . . . Then what is the result of our conversations? Isn't it that, of the other [external] things, no one of them is either good or bad, but of these two, wisdom is good and ignorance is bad?
>
> (*Euthydemus*, 281e)

In other words, the possessions and external events which men conventionally consider to be good or bad are actually not worth getting upset about ("indifferent") in themselves. They are the fruits of fortune and only rendered good or bad by our attitude toward them, the *use* we make of them. By definition, wisdom is the state of mind which makes good use of whatever events befall us, so wisdom and *only* wisdom is truly good, and its opposite, folly, is truly bad. All of which is not entirely unlike the saying, "Life is what we make of it". Similar remarks about cognitive mediation are found throughout the Socratic dialogues of both Plato and Xenophon. For example, in Book One of Plato's *Republic*, Socrates discusses the idea that old-age isn't inherently good or bad but that our *attitude* determines whether or not we complain about it and suffer.

If our emotions are not ultimately determined by external events alone but by our own beliefs and value judgements, then the habit of making healthy and rational judgements is more valuable to us than anything else. By contrast, the habit of making unhealthy and irrational judgements is a recipe for disaster, regardless of our material circumstances. In an exchange with his Stoic students, Epictetus emphasizes that this basic Stoic principle should be written down each day, in different forms, memorized, and stubbornly applied to every challenging situation.

> What, then, should we have at hand upon such occasions? Why, what else than to know what is mine, and what is not mine, what is within my power, and what is not? – I must die: and must I die groaning too? – Exiled. Can anyone prevent me, then, from going with a smile and good cheer and serenity? – "Betray the secret". – I will not betray it; for this is my own power. – "Then I will fetter you". – What are you saying, Man? Fetter me? You will fetter my leg; but not even Zeus himself can get the better of my choice. "I will cast you into prison". My wretched body, rather. "I will behead you". Did I ever tell you, that I alone had a head that cannot be cut off? – These are the things that philosophers ought to study; it is these that they should write about each day; and it is in these that they should exercise themselves.
>
> (*Discourses*, 1.1.21–25)

Although continual practise, including written, contemplative, and behavioural exercises, is required to apply these rational principles to every situation, the Stoics clearly felt that grasping the basic truths of their philosophy in a more general sense also has a liberating and therapeutic effect. Using the metaphor of the mind (*nous*) as a ship (*naus*) on the troubled seas of life, common in ancient literature, Marcus Aurelius reminds himself to take the helm firmly, become the captain (or pilot) of his soul, and steer himself to safe harbour. "It's all in how you perceive it. You're in control. You can dispense with misperception at will, like rounding the point. Serenity, total calm, safe anchorage" (*Meditations*, 12.22).

Ironically, what perhaps is missing from the REBT and CBT appropriations of this Stoic precept is full recognition of the corresponding *positive value* which it implies should be attached to the development and exercise of one's psychological strengths, i.e., the role of *love* in Stoicism, the love of wisdom. The Stoics never tire of reminding themselves how valuable wisdom and insight are, the kind of practical wisdom that comes from understanding precisely what it means to say that it is not things which upset us, but, rather, our judgements, and that this should be the fundamental goal of life rather than the pursuit of wealth or reputation. If CBT were to take this additional step, and encourage clients to place greater personal *value* on the cultivation of their positive cognitive skills ("virtues"), it would close the gap between modern psychotherapy and classical philosophy even further. Doing so does not mean turning all clients into extreme sages, like Socrates or Epictetus, but merely helping them to appreciate the value of their cognitive skills and insights, and to overcome the natural tendency to discount or forget how important it is for one's quality of life to continually develop the mind in this respect. As we'll see, though, third-wave approaches to CBT have moved further in this direction by placing greater emphasis on the process of clarifying one's personal values and actively living in accord with them.

REBT demands and Stoic value judgements

Ellis' approach differs from other modalities of CBT in that he places most emphasis upon the role of irrational or "absolute" demands imposed by the subject upon himself, other people, or his environment. According to Ellis, REBT is based on the assumption that the tendency to make "devout, absolutistic evaluations" of events in life is at the core of emotional disturbance and that these *value judgements* are typically framed in terms of dogmatic "must", "should", "have to", "got to", "ought to" statements, that is, unconditional imperatives (Dryden & Ellis, 2001, p. 301). These are called "irrational beliefs" because they are viewed as cognitions, spoken or unspoken, which embody rigid and unrealistic demands and conflict with the goals of enlightened self-interest. By being "rational", in other words, Ellis often appears to mean something akin to being pragmatic in our pursuit of long-term happiness.

Other types of irrational thought, such as overgeneralizations, or unfounded assumptions, are emphasized throughout other schools of CBT, most notably Beck's cognitive therapy. Ellis concedes that these can contribute to human suffering, and that it can be useful to target them in therapy. However, he insists that fundamentally rigid demands are the pre-eminent *underlying* cause of emotional disturbance, and even that they are a necessary condition of it. Even if I falsely concluded that everyone hated me, an irrational overgeneralization, in principle, I could still say "So what?" to myself and dismiss it without becoming upset. The unconditional demand that people *must* like me, when combined with the belief that they do not, according to REBT, inevitably generates emotional distress. However, other people's attitudes and behaviour, like other external events, are not under my direct control. Ellis makes this point, again by reference to Stoicism, when he advises those using REBT for self-help as follows:

> As Epictetus pointed out two thousand years ago, although you do have considerable power to change and control yourself, you rarely can control the behavior of others. No matter how wisely you may counsel people, they are independent persons and may – and, indeed, have the right to – ignore you completely. If, therefore, you unduly arouse yourself over the way others act, instead of taking responsibility for how you respond to them, you often will upset yourself over an uncontrollable event.
>
> (Ellis & Harper, 1997, p. 198)

The irrationally rigid demands which REBT warns against, which are similar to the "rules" and "assumptions" in Beck's cognitive therapy, also bear a notable resemblance to the unconditional *value judgements* which Stoics believe are at the root of emotional distress. For the Stoic, it is the tendency to judge things as being inherently or absolutely good or bad which leads to irrational craving (*epithumia*) or fear (*phobos*), respectively. In Stoic psychology, irrational desire, or craving, which places too much value on external things and other people's opinions, is the root cause of anxiety. Believing that "I have to" have (or avoid) something, or that other people "must" behave (or not behave) in a certain way, as REBT would put it, is tantamount to saying that these things are of overriding importance in themselves, or absolute external values, as Stoicism would put it. Sometimes the Stoics also articulate these irrational value judgements as demands.

As is often the case, the Stoics give clear examples that would not seem out of place in a modern psychotherapy text; for example, in this striking passage, Epictetus describes the relationship between desire and social anxiety, or stage fright, as follows:

> When I see somebody in a state of anxiety, I say, "What can this man want?" Unless he wanted something or other which is not in his own power, how could he still be anxious? That is why a person who sings to the lyre feels no anxiety while he is singing by himself, but is anxious when he enters the theatre, even if he has a very fine voice and plays his instrument beautifully. For he wants not only to sing well, but to gain applause, and that lies beyond his control. . . .
>
> He does not understand what a crowd is, or the applause of a crowd. He has learned, indeed, how to strike the lowest and highest strings; but what the applause of the multitude is, and what force it has in life, he neither understands, nor has studied. Hence he must necessarily tremble and turn pale. . . .
>
> He does not know that he is wishing to have what is not allowed him, and wishing to avoid what he cannot escape; and he does not know what is his own and what is not his own [i.e., his value-judgements]; for if he did know, he would never feel hindered, never feel restrained, never feel anxious. . . .

If, then, things outside the sphere of choice are neither good nor bad, and all things within the sphere of choice are in our power, and can neither be taken away from us, nor given to us, unless we please, what room is there left for anxiety? But we are anxious about this paltry body or estate of ours, or about what Caesar will think [i.e., about health, wealth, or reputation] and not at all about what is within us. Are we ever anxious not to take up a false opinion? No, for this is in our own power. Or about following an impulse, contrary to nature? No, nor this either. When, therefore, you see any one pale with anxiety, just as the physician pronounces from a person's complexion that this patient is affected in his spleen, and that in his liver, so you likewise should say: this man is affected in his desires and aversions, he is out of sorts, he is feverish. For nothing else changes the complexion or makes a man tremble or sets his teeth a-chattering, or "Shift from leg to leg and squat on one foot then the other".

(*Discourses*, 2.13.1–13)

Instead of attaching too much value to other people's opinions, absolutely *demanding* their approval and *fearing* their rebuke, the musician should patiently train himself, over time, to put value primarily upon his own intentions and judgements and to take the audience's praise or leave it with equanimity. For the Stoics, to strongly value something positively or negatively is to try to control it, and we have more control over our own judgements and intentions than over external events or other people, so we should shift the focus of our value judgements inwards, within the here and now, and focus on the importance of our own mental activity and responses more than other people's opinions. The example of stage fright is extended by Epictetus to oratory and any similar social anxiety. Anyone who anxiously *demands*, rather than merely *preferring*, that others praise him is being unphilosophical, and has failed to understand the nature of things in relation to his sphere of control. He blames his nerves on the situation, neglecting the importance of his own misplaced value judgements in determining his emotional disturbance.

Nor does he even know what anxiety itself is, whether it be our own responsibility or outside it, or whether it be possible to suppress it or not. Because of this, if he is praised, he leaves the stage puffed up with pride: but if he is laughed at, his poor bubble is pricked and collapses.

We too experience something of this kind. What do we admire? Externals. What do we strive for? Externals. Are we then at a loss to know how fear and anxiety overcome us? Why what else is possible when we regard impending events as evils? We cannot help being fearful we cannot help being anxious.

(*Discourses*, 2.16.10)

Catastrophic predictions in Stoicism

By now, it should be obvious that one needs to make certain allowances for the language used in traditional translations of classical texts. Hard's translation in the previously quoted passage alludes to "regarding impending events as evils" here, as elsewhere, when describing something which modern CBT would undoubtedly describe as "making catastrophic predictions about anticipated events". Epictetus, therefore, observed that when we place too much value upon external events we are not only prone to distress but to exaggeration of the kind Ellis called "awfulizing", and which other cognitive therapists call "catastrophizing", or "magnification", a concept already known in classical philosophy by reference to the rhetorical figure of speech called "hyperbole".

> Because of our lack of [Stoic] practice, we are always piling up worries and fancying things to be worse than they really are. Whenever I go to sea, as soon as I gaze down into the depths or look at the waters around me and see no land, I am beside myself, and imagine that if I am wrecked that I must swallow all that sea; nor does it once enter my head that three pints [of water] are enough [to drown me]. What is it then that alarms me? The sea? No, my own judgement. Again, in an earthquake, I imagine the city is going to fall on me; but is not one little stone enough to knock my brains out?
>
> (*Discourses*, 2.16.21–23)

We have a tendency, when anxious, to dramatically inflate certain risks. However, there is something odd about this, because the same risk could be perceived in less hyperbolic terms; a single stone could kill me, but that image is not necessarily as dramatic and frightening as the whole city caving in upon me. Viewing things in this exaggerated way also makes it harder for us to envisage ways of coping. More fundamentally, though, we use rhetorical hyperbole to irrationally inflate our fears as a result of placing too much importance on external events, or as Ellis puts it, irrational demands are often associated with exaggerated "awfulizing".

Cognitive therapists refer to the process of correcting (downgrading) catastrophic predictions as "decatastrophizing", which could be seen as capturing a fundamental aspect of Stoic practise. Epictetus told his students that one of the heroic members of the Stoic Opposition, Paconius Agrippinus, would write letters to himself praising misfortunes as opportunities to copy by exhibiting greater wisdom and virtue.

> And he was such a man that he would write in praise of anything disagreeable that befell him; if it was a fever, he would write of a fever; if he was disgraced, he would write of disgrace; if he were banished, of banishment.
>
> (*Fragment* 56)

Agrippinus, in a sense, was acting as his own therapist, apparently writing what ancient philosophers called "consolation letters" to himself, reframing the situations he faced in less threatening terms and highlighting his capacity for coping with them.

Relative value in Stoicism

However, even the Stoics concede that external things such as health, wealth, and reputation can have conferred upon them a kind of *conditional* or pragmatic value, insofar as they may contribute toward genuine flourishing, one's enlightened self-interest and happiness. The Stoics were very keen to emphasize that *absolute* (primary) value can only be ascribed to the virtues that form essential aspects of living a rational and fulfilled life. However, this is not necessarily incompatible with saying that wealth, for example, might be of value conditionally, *insofar* as it contributes to genuine wisdom and happiness. Perhaps there is a natural human tendency to forget why we pursue external things, as a means to long-term happiness, and to see them as ends in themselves, which would explain why the Stoics are often so wary of ascribing value to them.

There is some debate among academics regarding the interpretation of Stoic doctrine on this point, and there were probably also differences among different branches of ancient Stoicism. The Stoics, particularly Epictetus, do often *sound* as if they're implying that "externals" are completely worthless and devoid of any real value. However, this may be a misinterpretation caused by their use of rhetoric to motivate themselves and their students. Indeed, in many places they explicitly acknowledge that certain "preferred indifferents" have a kind of derivative or conditional value, insofar as they contribute to the pursuit of wisdom and happiness. For example, in one key passage, Epictetus says that those philosophers who go so far as to deny any difference between beauty and ugliness, between the desirable and undesirable, do so out of foolish anxiety, assuming that anyone who acknowledges one external thing to be better than another is bound to be "carried away and overcome" by desire and aversion. He uses the example of the philosopher taking care of his health, looking after his own eyesight, etc.

Epictetus makes it clear that the most important thing is to put externals in perspective by valuing them according to their function and, ultimately, the extent to which they serve the fundamental goal of seeking wisdom and happiness. Everything else is trivial by comparison, but we should, nevertheless, avoid neglecting things which are to be rationally preferred as being of conditional value insofar as they serve reason and the supreme goal of life. We ought, for example, to take care of our eyesight and such things, but only insofar as doing so helps us to live wisely (*Discourses*, 2.23.34–35). Likewise, it is not even straightforwardly true that health is good and sickness is bad but rather that the health of the body is good when used well and bad when used badly (*Discourses*, 3.20.4). Perhaps a more difficult example relates to the well-being of others. As the distress of other people is not entirely under our command, it is right that we should prefer to alleviate it, but wrong that we should absolutely demand that it does not occur, because it is not in our power to do so.

"But my mother grieves when she does not see me". So why has she not learnt these doctrines? I am not saying that it is wrong to take care that she should not lament; but that we are not to wish absolutely what is not in our own power. Now, the grief of another is not in my power; but my own grief is. I will, therefore, absolutely oppose my own grief, for that is in my power; and I will endeavour to prevent another's grief as far as I am able: but not absolutely.

(*Discourses*, 3.24.22–23, modified)

To absolutely demand that others should not grieve is to require something ultimately beyond my power as a mortal, and makes me feel resentful of life for being unfair, when, in fact, it is my own judgement that has become warped and unreasonable, transgressing the natural boundary set by my limited sphere of control.

In the modern military, James Stockdale tried to explain the value Stoicism places on external things to his students as follows:

I know the difficulties of gulping this down right away. You keep thinking of practical problems. Everybody has to play the game of life. You can't just walk around saying, "I don't give a damn about health or wealth or whether I'm sent to prison or not". Epictetus took time to explain better what he meant. He says everybody should play the game of life – that the best play it with "skill, form, speed, and grace". But, like most games, you play it with a ball. Your team devotes all its energies to getting the ball across the line. But after the game, what do you do with the ball? Nobody much cares. It's not worth anything. The competition, the game, was the thing. The ball was "used" to make the game possible, but in itself is not of any value that would justify falling on your sword for it. Once the game is over, the ball is properly a matter of indifference.

(Stockdale, 1995, pp. 191–192)

He means the "externals" – health, wealth, sensory pleasure, and reputation – are neither good nor bad in themselves, but according to the use we make of them in playing the game of life, and should be seen as a means to an end, rather than ends in themselves.

As we have seen, Ellis also clearly recommends that we should substitute rational *desires* or *preferences* for irrational and "absolutistic" *demands*. He terms this his "philosophy of relativism", apparently because the value of many things is seen as relative rather than absolute.

REBT theory argues that a philosophy of relativism or "desiring" is a central feature of psychologically healthy humans. This philosophy acknowledges that humans have a large variety of desires, wishes, wants, preferences, and so on, but that if they refuse to transform these non-absolute values into grandiose dogmas and demands, they will not become psychologically disturbed. They will, however, experience healthy negative emotions (e.g., sadness, regret, disappointment, healthy anger or annoyance) whenever their desires are not fulfilled.

(Dryden & Ellis, 2001, p. 305)

Ellis points to the fact that desires, of course, have positive motivational qualities, essential to human life, which they can retain when made conditional rather than absolute. He also suggests that we should place *less* importance on non-essential things in life, like wealth or fame. At first, Ellis does not seem to follow the Stoics in offering an alternative *unconditional* value judgement. However, elsewhere in his writings, he does speak of *unconditional self-acceptance* (USA), which could perhaps be developed into part of a theory of psychological virtues in REBT, having some kind of more fundamental value comparable to the role of "wisdom" in Stoicism.

Shame-attacking exercises

In certain concrete *practical* respects, REBT also contains therapy interventions that resemble techniques familiar within ancient philosophical therapy. Ellis was known for what he described as REBT's "trademark" use of various "shame-attacking exercises". In order to help clients overcome self-consciousness, social embarrassment, and inhibition, Ellis would prescribe changes in behaviour that were designed to forcefully and directly challenge their sense of shame. For example, he refers to the technique of asking clients to repeatedly stop a bus without getting off, or asking strangers in the street to give them money, etc.

> I realised, soon after I started REBT in 1955, that what we call "shame" is the essence of a great deal of our emotional disturbance. . . .
> Seeing this, I created my now famous shame-attacking exercise in 1968; and perhaps millions of people, especially psychotherapy clients, have done this exercise and trained themselves to feel shamed or sorry about what they did, and about the public disapproval that often went with it, but *not* to put themselves down and not to feel humiliated about their personhood.
>
> (Ellis & MacLaren, 2005, p. 95)

Ellis further explains the exercise as follows:

> Here clients deliberately seek to act "shamefully" in public in order to accept themselves and to tolerate the ensuing discomfort. Since clients do best to harm neither themselves nor other people, minor infractions of social rules often serve as suitable shame-attacking exercises (e.g., calling out the time in a crowded department store, wearing bizarre clothes designed to attract public attention, and going into a hardware store and asking the clerks whether they sell tobacco).
>
> (Dryden & Ellis, 2001, p. 329)

This aspect of Ellis' work is strikingly reminiscent of the practises of the ancient Cynic philosophers, who appear to have adopted, albeit in a more extreme manner, controversial lifestyles and behaviours in order to liberate themselves from social conventions. As Hadot puts it, the Cynics broke with the conventional world in a radical manner by rejecting what the majority of people take for granted as the social norms by which we live, including "cleanliness, pleasant appearance, and courtesy" (Hadot, 2002, p. 109). Cynics reputedly masturbated in public, like Diogenes, or made love in public, like Crates and his wife Hipparchia. They were totally indifferent to social conventions and normal standards of propriety. They viewed money with contempt, were encouraged to beg, and to avoid positions of responsibility, despite living in the city. They were portrayed as viewing even great rulers such as Alexander the Great as their equals, or perhaps inferiors, and did not hesitate to express themselves with absolute candour and freedom of speech (parrhesia), even in the presence of the powerful.

Ellis seems unaware of this precursor to his "shame-attacking" exercises. However, the Cynics themselves specifically refer to the deliberate practise of "shamelessness" (*anaideia*) as a psychotherapeutic exercise. In the case of Diogenes, this was referred to metaphorically as his "defacing the coinage" of social conventions, which inevitably shocked others. So notorious were the shameless acts of Diogenes that Plato allegedly called him "Socrates gone mad".

According to Diogenes Laertius, the famous Cynic, Crates, who trained Zeno, the founder of the Stoic school, was nicknamed "Door-opener" because of his habit of inviting himself into people's houses to lecture them somewhat abrasively on philosophy (*Lives*, 6.5). He also mentions another practise of Crates, which sounds like an even more provocative version of Ellis' shame-attacking exercises, "He used to [verbally] abuse prostitutes designedly, for the purpose of practising himself in enduring reproaches" (*Lives*, 6.5). Epictetus seems to imply that Diogenes and the other Cynics, whom he greatly admired, deliberately broke wind in front of people, presumably also as part of their practise of shamelessness (*Discourses*, 3.22.80). Indeed, I am indebted to Still and Dryden for the following illustration from Montaigne's account of a quite surprising Stoic anecdote:

> In the midst of a discussion, and in the presence of his followers, Metrocles let off a fart. To hide his embarrassment he stayed at home until, eventually, Crates came to pay him a visit; to his consolations and arguments Crates added the example of his own licence: he began a farting match with him, thereby removing his scruples and, into the bargain, converting him to the freer stoic school from the more socially oriented Peripatetics whom he had formerly followed.
>
> (Montaigne, in Still & Dryden, 1999, p. 157)

Crates' exercises in shamelessness, or the overcoming of social anxiety and inhibition, can be seen as a practical training in his maxim, "That a man ought to study philosophy, up to the point of looking on generals and donkey-drivers in the same light" (*Lives*, 6.5). Zeno appears to have assimilated some aspects of his mentor's philosophy into Stoic therapeutics, although moderated by a greater respect for society than the Cynics allegedly displayed.

Like Crates, Diogenes the Cynic, who was revered as a sage by some Stoics, reputedly tested prospective students by instructing them to follow him around carrying a salted fish, or a piece of cheese, in their hands. When some refused, out of embarrassment, he would chide them: "See how a piece of salted fish was enough to dissolve our friendship!" (*Lives*, 6.2). However, one of Diogenes' exercises in shamelessness is even more remarkably similar to REBT shame-attacking. Ellis liked to suggest that, as a shame-attacking exercise, clients might try walking a banana tied to a piece of string through a busy public area, such as a shopping mall, as if they were walking a dog. Compare that with the following anecdote about Diogenes the Cynic:

> Some one dropped a loaf of bread and was ashamed to pick it up; whereupon Diogenes, wishing to give him a lesson, tied a rope to the neck of a wine-bottle and proceeded to drag it across the Ceramicus.
>
> (*Lives*, 6.2)

The Ceramicus was the busy potters' district in the centre of Athens. His behaviour would presumably have especially shocked the potters there who laboured to make delicate ceramic wine-jars just like the one he was dragging through the streets.

Diogenes once asked the Athenians to erect a statue to him, and when asked why he had done so, replied, "I am practising disappointment" (*Lives*, 6.2). These and many similar popular philosophical anecdotes illustrate the striking parallel between the ancient Cynics' psychotherapeutic technique of *anaideia*, or shamelessness, and the modern "shame-attacking" exercises characteristic of Ellis' REBT, which were precursors of "behavioural experiments" used to challenge social anxiety and inhibition in subsequent CBT. Indeed, Beck and his colleagues also refer to "anti-shame exercises", and observe that cognitive therapy provides opportunities for clients to deliberately expose themselves to feelings of shame in order to conquer them (Beck, Emery, & Greenberg, 2005, p. 282).

Philosophical principles in REBT

In *Reason and Emotion in Psychotherapy* (1962), Ellis outlined a list of 11 "irrational ideas which cause emotional disturbance". He also provided a list of several rational objections to each one, and several alternative ways of thinking. The issues covered in this list clearly resemble Stoic themes. Moreover, the very act of listing written objections and alternative ways of thinking in this manner also resembles a corresponding Stoic practise, as can be seen from the list of attitudes to counteract anger listed by Marcus Aurelius, which we can compare with a shorter list drawn up by Ellis. The similarity between

REBT and Stoicism can be well illustrated by concluding this chapter with these passages, which provide typical examples from both REBT and Stoic literature, respectively.

Principles for coping with anger: Albert Ellis

Ellis says that as an alternative to becoming upset over wrongdoing on our own part or that of others, we might apply rational strategies instead (Ellis, 1962, pp. 68–69). We can paraphrase his examples as follows:

1   Rather than criticise or blame others for their behaviour realize that people invariably commit such acts out of either stupidity, ignorance, or emotional disturbance. We would therefore do better to accept the fact that people often act stupidly and try to help them overcome their ignorance or emotional disturbance. (This resembles the well-known Socratic paradox that no man does evil knowingly, or willingly, mentioned by Marcus in point #3 in what follows.)
2   When people blame you, first pause to ask yourself whether you have actually done anything wrong. If you have then try to improve your behaviour whereas if you haven't, remember that other people's criticisms often just reflect their own problems, such as defensiveness or emotional disturbance on their part. (These correspond to aspects of Marcus' points #2 and #3 in what follows.)
3   We should attempt to understand the reasons for the other person's actions, trying first to empathize and see things from their point of view. If we can stop their bad behaviour we should try do so appropriately and calmly. If not we should adopt a philosophical attitude by saying something like: "It's too bad they keep acting that way but it's not the end of the world – it's not a catastrophe as far as I'm concerned!" (Similar advice is found in Marcus' points #2, #3, #5, #6, and #7 in what follows.)
4   We should try to remember that our own mistakes, like those of others, are usually due to ignorance or emotional disturbance and not blame ourselves for wrongdoing that results in this manner. (Compare with Marcus' points #3 and #4 in what follows.)

Principles for coping with anger: Marcus Aurelius
(Marcus Aurelius, *Meditations*, 11.18, my translation.)

When offended by other people's actions:

1   Remember the close bond between yourself and the rest of mankind. . . .
2   Think of the characters of those who offend you at the table, in their beds, and so on. In particular, remember the effect their negative way of thinking has on them, and the misplaced confidence it gives them in their actions.

3   If what they're doing is right, you've no reason to complain; and if it's not right, then it must have been involuntary and unintentional. Because just as "no-one ever deliberately denies the truth", according to Socrates, so nobody ever intentionally treats another person badly. That's why these negative people are themselves insulted if anyone accuses them of injustice, ingratitude, meanness, or any other sort of offence against their neighbours – they just don't realize they're doing wrong.

4   You yourself are no different from them, and upset people in various ways. You might avoid making some mistakes, but the thought and inclination is still there, even if cowardice or egotism or some other negative motive has held you back you from copying their mistakes.

5   Remember, you've got no guarantee they're doing the wrong thing anyway, people's motives aren't always what they seem. There's usually a lot to learn before any sure-footed moral judgements can be made about other people's actions.

6   Tell yourself, when you feel upset and fed up, that human life is transient and only lasts a moment; it won't be long before we'll all have been laid to rest.

7   It's not the actions of these men that upsets us that's their own problem but the colour we put on them ourselves. Get rid of this, make a decision to quit thinking of things as insulting, and your anger immediately disappears. How do you get rid of these thoughts? By realizing that you've not really been harmed by their actions. Moreover, unless genuine harm to your soul is all that worries you, you'll wind up being guilty of all sorts of offences against other people yourself.

8   Anger and frustration hurt us more than the things we're annoyed about hurt us.

9   Kindness is an irresistible force, so long as it's genuine and without any fake smiles or two-facedness. Even the most stubborn bad attitude is nothing, if you just keep being nice to the person concerned. Politely comment on his behaviour when you get the chance and, just when he's about to have another go at you, gently make him mindful of his actions by saying "No, my son; we're not meant for this. I'll not be hurt; you're just hurting yourself". Subtly draw his attention to this general fact; even bees and other animals that live in groups do not act like he does. Do it without any hint of sarcasm or nitpicking, though; do it with real affection and with your heart free from resentment. Do not talk to him harshly like a schoolteacher or try to impress bystanders but, even though other people may be around, talk as if you are alone together in private.

      Keep these nine pieces of advice in mind, like nine gifts from the Muses; and while there is still life in you, begin at last to be a man. While guarding yourself against being angry with others, though, be just as careful to avoid the opposite extreme, of toadying. One is just as bad as the other, and both cause problems. With bouts of rage, always remind yourself that losing your temper is no sign of manhood. On the contrary, there is more strength, as well as more natural humanity, in someone capable of remaining calm and gentle. He proves he has got strength and nerve and guts, unlike his angry, complaining friend. Anger is just as much a sign of weakness as bubbling with tears; in both cases we are giving in to suffering.

Finally, a tenth idea, this time from the very leader of the Muses, Apollo himself. To expect bad men never to do bad things is just madness; it is asking the impossible. And to let them abuse other people, and expect them to leave you alone, that is arrogance.

The Stoic armamentarium

Chapter 7

Contemplation of the ideal sage

Ancient philosophers used an extensive armamentarium, or toolbox, of practical exercises for specific therapeutic purposes, including mental imagery (visualization) and verbal cognitive techniques resembling those found in both modern self-help and psychotherapy. Hadot was probably the first modern writer to fully expose the extent to which classical philosophy entailed practises of this kind. Hadot refers to these philosophical-therapeutic techniques as "spiritual exercises" (*exercitia spiritualia*), borrowing the phrase from St Ignatius of Loyola, the founder of the Jesuit order. As he notes, although no systematic treatise has come down to us containing instructions for the "spiritual exercises" found in ancient schools of philosophy, allusions to such practises abound in the works of various Roman and Hellenistic authors (Hadot, 1995, pp. 83–84). It appears therefore that these exercises were fairly well known as it's taken for granted by these authors that allusions to them will be familiar enough for most readers to understand. Hadot believes that they would have constituted daily practises within the philosophical schools and part of a "traditional course of oral instruction" (*ibid.*).

As we have seen, it is important to grasp just how much classical philosophy differs in this respect from the *modern* conception of philosophy as a purely "academic" subject. Philosophy was originally a way of life, first and foremost, and philosophers were identified as such primarily in terms of their behaviour and not on the basis of abstract debate, indeed the Pythagorean philosophers reputedly observed a vow of *silence* which lasted many years.

From Pythagoras, in the sixth century BC, the first major historical figure to found a philosophical-therapeutic community, to the closure of the Athenian Academy in 529 AD by the Christian Emperor Justinian I, the practise of philosophy as a broadly *psychotherapeutic* "art of living" seemed to endure for just over a thousand years, during which a widespread European tradition of formal training in meditative and philosophical-psychotherapeutic practises were fairly well-known and widely practised. However, notoriously little is known about the actual practise of philosophy before the time of Socrates in the fifth century BC. Although the practical techniques in question probably existed before the time of Socrates, it is largely following his example that they entered Western consciousness, because his story was to become a "living call", as Hadot puts it, an exhortation to embrace the philosophical lifestyle (*ibid.*, p. 89).

Ancient philosophers typically revered the founder of their school as an exemplary role model, the closest mortal approximation to the ideal of the perfect philosophical sage. In particular, one finds the semi-mythical figure of Pythagoras, Socrates himself, Zeno the founder of Stoicism, Diogenes the Cynic, and the Stoics' great rival, Epicurus, held in such esteem. Sometimes, legendary figures such as Hercules or Orpheus were viewed in a similar light. In one of his most striking epistles, Seneca asks:

> If you come across a man who is never alarmed by dangers, never affected by cravings, happy in adversity, calm in the midst of storm, viewing mankind from a higher level, and the gods from their own, is it not likely that a feeling will find its way into you of veneration for him?
>
> (*Letters*, 41)

For the Stoics, in principle, wise men could be found in any walk of life. Undoubtedly, however, Socrates was the pre-eminent example of the incarnate philosophical sage.

Introducing the ideal sage

"Begin with the end in mind", is one of the *Seven Habits* recommended in recent decades by the bestselling self-help author Stephen Covey (Covey, 1989). It is not a trivial matter to observe that, unlike Stoicism and most classical philosophies, CBT lacks any clear account of the ideal toward which it aims. If asked to point to a specific human being who embodies the principles of CBT in their life, most therapists would probably be at a loss for words. I do not know of any detailed discussion of the goal of optimum functioning implicit in CBT either, although one should clearly follow from its principles. By contrast, one of the most fundamental techniques of ancient philosophical therapy was the public discussion and private contemplation of the perfect sage and his virtues, the imaginary embodiment, ideal role model, and ultimate "end", or goal, of philosophical practise.

> Since the dawn of Greek thought, the sage has functioned as a living, concrete model. Aristotle testifies to this in a passage from his *Protrepticus*: "What more accurate standard or measure of good things do we have than the Sage?"
>
> (Hadot, 1995, p. 147)

Indeed, Epictetus argued that in any walk of life we need some kind of ideal or standard against which to measure ourselves as human beings, and that the sage provides a standard for the "art of living" as a whole. If we do not refer our actions to a single, unifying standard, then we risk acting at random, or following an irrational standard (*Discourses*, 3.23.1).

However, some ancient philosophers appear to have been sceptical as to whether any mortal could ever be elevated to the level of a perfect sage and the concept was, therefore, treated as an imaginary ideal. The Stoic Chrysippus claimed never to have known one in real life. However, later Stoics seem more willing to point to historical individuals who approximate to the ideal. Epictetus' students, rather impudently perhaps, asked him whether he was himself a sage. He replied, "By the gods, I wish and pray to be, but I am not yet". He continues, "I can, however, show you one, so that you no longer have to search for an example", and he refers them first to Diogenes the Cynic and then to Socrates (*Discourses*, 4.1.151–152). Indeed, he frequently refers to Diogenes and Socrates as role models who are both wise and morally good, and sometimes also to the pre-Socratic philosopher Heraclitus. Marcus Aurelius appears to name the same three examples opposing them to three ultimately tragic military and political figures. "Alexander and Caesar and Pompey. Compared with Diogenes, Heraclitus, Socrates? The philosophers knew the what, the why, the how. Their minds were their own. The others? Nothing but anxiety and enslavement" (*Meditations*, 8.3).

This is particularly striking, of course, coming from a Roman emperor, who would be expected to emulate the great leaders of the past rather than some penniless philosophers who went around barefoot and dressed in rags. Seneca was willing to consider famous statesmen from the Roman republic such as Laelius the Wise and Cato of Utica as role models. Epictetus recommends that his students contemplate the example set by members of the Stoic Opposition, Roman politicians such as Paconius Agrippinus and Helvidius Priscus who opposed autocratic rule of certain emperors.

> The image of the Stoic sage was thus not a hypothetical ideal, but rather based upon an idealized image of actual individuals, an image that functioned as an exemplar or role model. Names often cited include [the Cynics] Antisthenes and Diogenes, but ultimately the Stoic sage is based upon the figure of Socrates.
>
> (Sellars, 2003, p. 62)

The concept of the ideal sage was also linked with that of various gods, or their mortal incarnations. The Stoics often refer to the divine figure of Hercules in this respect, as an iconic representation of moral fortitude.

However, although real people, or mythic characters, provided concrete examples for the ideal of the sage, it seems that it was most often understood by philosophers to be an abstraction. Hadot believed that historians of philosophy had possibly neglected the importance placed on discourses describing the ideal sage in the philosophical schools of antiquity (Hadot, 2002, p. 224). They placed more emphasis, he says, on defining the ideal behaviour of the perfect sage than upon tracing the features of real historical role models, although this was also a fairly common topic of study. The key question became "What would the Sage do in such-and-such circumstances?" (*ibid.*). This question provided Stoics with a specific cognitive strategy to help them cope with adversity, in many guises. For example, Epictetus offers precisely this advice in his *Handbook*.

> When you are about to meet someone, especially one of the people enjoying high esteem, ask yourself what Socrates or Zeno would have done in such circumstances, and you will not be at a loss to deal with the situation properly.
>
> (*Encheiridion*, 3)

Elsewhere, he says that following contemplation of the lives and actions of wise men, living or dead, that "If you set these thoughts against your impression, you will overpower it, and not be swept away by it" (*Discourses*, 2.18.23). This, like modern cognitive therapy, appears to contain a recommendation to monitor specific irrational thoughts and immediately challenge them by focusing on an alternative perspective, in this case derived from a cognitive model.

Marcus Aurelius is quite possibly employing the same technique in his own contemplations, when he writes a reminder to himself to "Look into their minds, at what the wise do and what they don't" (*Meditations*, 4.38). Over a thousand years later, the Neostoic Justus Lipsius wrote that the examples of the wise serve as "mirrors or precedents". "For that the Constancy and Patience of good men in miseries is as a clear light to this obscure world. They provoke others by their example, and tread the path in which they should walk" (Lipsius, 2006, p. 91).

In CBT, it is common practise to help clients re-evaluate their judgements by considering whether someone else would necessarily share the same perspective. Aaron Beck refers to this as "alternate therapy", the generation of alternative, or more rational, viewpoints (Beck, 1976). In the *Handbook*, Epictetus likewise speaks of everything having two alternative "handles", a good one by which it can be picked up and carried, and a broken one by which it cannot (*Encheiridion*, 42). He means that for each incident that we face in life, there are alternative perspectives, helpful and unhelpful ways of looking at things, which allow us to cope with or "handle" adversity well or badly. To borrow the example given by Epictetus, if my brother wrongs me, I can focus on the fact that he has offended me, and pick up the injustice of the incident, which may lead me to handle things badly. Alternatively, one may look it from another viewpoint, and focus on the fact that he is after all my brother. Reminding myself first and foremost of the bond between us may be a better "handle" to pick things up by if I want to cope well with events. There are two sides to every coin, we might say. There are alternative perspectives to be taken upon every event in life.

It is noteworthy that the passage from Epictetus' *Handbook* so widely cited in CBT literature, which reminds us that we are not upset by things themselves, but by our judgements about them, is immediately followed by the advice to consider the fact that events which seem awful to one person may be indifferent to another. Epictetus deliberately employs the most fundamental example in the Stoic canon, the fact that even death itself is not a catastrophe in the eyes of all men. He specifically refers to the example of Socrates, who faced his own execution with equanimity and resignation. "Death, for instance, is nothing terrible, or else it would have appeared so to Socrates too. But the terror lies in our own judgements about death, that death is terrible" (*Encheiridion*, 5).

The fact that other people, especially the wise and good, perceive events differently should be a constant reminder to us that our own judgements colour our emotional responses to our fortune. There is always an alternative perspective we can adopt. We can always ask ourselves how the sage would handle any given situation, and how he would view our own actions.

Being observed by the sage

The Epicureans were less ambiguous than the Stoics about the sage, whom they explicitly identified with the founder of their own school. They repeatedly refer to practises involving Epicurus himself as a supreme role model. The Stoics appear to recognize this as one of many practical techniques that they basically shared with their rival school. "This advice from Epicurean writings: to think continually of one of the men of old who lived a virtuous life" (*Meditations*, 11.26). Although the Stoics had at first named themselves "Zenonians" after their founder, they changed their name to the place where they met because they did not consider Zeno, or any other mortal, to be *perfectly* wise. Nevertheless, they considered it helpful to model the traits in others that they considered admirable and worthy of emulation.

This basic method allows a surprising number of variations to be developed. One interesting modification was the practise of imagining oneself actually to be in the physical presence of the sage, that is, being observed by them. Like Marcus Aurelius, Seneca was happy to import contemplative techniques into Stoicism from its rival school, Epicureanism, which emphasized the technique of students' imagining that Epicurus was always present, observing both their thoughts and actions.

> "We need to set our affections on some good man and keep him constantly before our eyes, so that we may live as if he were watching us and do everything as if he saw what we were doing". This, my dear Lucilius, is Epicurus' advice, and in giving it he has given us a guardian and a moral tutor – and not without reason, either: misdeeds are greatly diminished if a witness is always standing near intending doers. The personality should be provided with someone it can revere, someone whose influence can make even its private, inner life more pure. Happy the man who improves other people not merely when he is in their presence but even when he is in their thoughts! And happy, too, is the person who can so revere another as to adjust and shape his own personality in the light of recollections, even, of that other.
>
> (*Letters*, 11)

According to Hadot, this practise may explain the importance placed by followers of Epicurus on the possession of his portrait or rings bearing his image (Hadot, 2002, p. 124). The Stoics were more flexible in their approach, being willing to consider a number of exemplary figures. Seneca, therefore, adds the following advice on choosing a sage or hero to model one's behaviour upon:

> Choose someone whose way of life as well as words, and whose very face as mirroring the character that lies behind it, have won your approval. Be always pointing him out to yourself either as your guardian or as your model. There is a need, in my view, for someone as a standard against which our characters can measure themselves. Without a ruler to do it against you won't make the crooked straight.
>
> (*Letters*, 11)

In this approach, the sage can be viewed as a kind of internal critic, or *rational conscience*, for the philosophical student. A similar function is performed in Christianity by the notion of God being able to see into one's heart and mind. However, for the Hellenistic schools of philosophy, self-evaluation was not based on moral dogmas derived from theological scripture, but from their own critical reflection upon the ideal philosophical viewpoint and way of life. Self-criticism is therefore intended to be therapeutic and *philosophical* rather than simply moralizing. Perhaps a better analogy, therefore, would be the *daimonion* of Socrates, the inner voice or sign that was said to guide him by warning him against certain courses of action. In modern psychotherapy, it is frequently observed that the client may internalize an impression of the therapist that comes to mind in relation to certain events between sessions. Beck and his colleagues report having observed on many occasions that the client will tend to internalize and replay the kinds of questions posed by the cognitive therapist, and the discussions had with him, and even to hear his voice or picture him spontaneously between sessions, modelling and replaying events from the sessions (Beck, Rush, Shaw, & Emery, 1979, p. 71).

The example of Socrates

Elsewhere, regarding an array of role models for coping with adversity, Seneca advises his friend Lucilius:

> If you still need an example, take Socrates, an old man who had known his full share of suffering, who had taken every blow life could inflict, and still remained unbeaten either by poverty, a burden for him aggravated by domestic worries, or by constant hardships, including those endured on military service.
>
> (*Letters*, 104)

Seneca proceeds to recount in detail the various hardships that Socrates faced with equanimity, ranging from his notoriously troublesome wife, Xanthippe, to his unjust trial and execution at the hands of tyrants.

In addition to the famous Platonic *dialogues* featuring Socrates, various anecdotes regarding both his wisdom and self-mastery were circulated in the ancient world and served as a means of moral education. For example, in his popular account of the lives of philosophers, Diogenes Laertius relates the following anecdote about Socrates.

> And often, when he beheld the multitude of things which were being sold, he would say to himself, "How many things are there which I do not want". And he was continually repeating these iambics: "For silver plate and purple [robes] useful are, for actors on the stage but not for men".
>
> (*Lives*, 2.5)

Seneca advises that personal contact with a philosophical mentor is more valuable than the written word, adding, "the road is a long one if one proceeds by way of precepts but short and effectual if by way of personal example" (*Letters*, 6).

> Cleanthes would never have been the image of Zeno if he had merely heard him lecture; he lived with him, studied his private life, watched him to see if he lived in accordance with his own principle. Plato, Aristotle and a host of other philosophers all destined to take different paths, derived more from Socrates' character than from his words.
>
> (*ibid.*)

Epictetus repeatedly reminds his students that the life of Socrates is always available to them, ready to hand, as a model of excellence in various areas of life (*Discourses*, 4.5.2–4). He even goes so far as to state:

> And now that Socrates is dead, the memory of him is of no less benefit to mankind (and perhaps even greater benefit) than what he did or said when still alive. Study these points, these judgements, these arguments, contemplate these examples, if you wish to be free, if you desire freedom in accordance with its true value.
>
> (*Discourses*, 4.1.169)

The example of Socrates' life provides a compass for novice Stoics to navigate their lives by. Hence, Epictetus dubs the aspiring Stoics "emulators of Socrates" (*Discourses*, 2.6.26).

> Socrates fulfilled himself by attending to nothing except reason in everything that he encountered. And you, although you are not yet a Socrates, should live as someone who at least wants to be a Socrates.
>
> (*Encheiridion*, 51)

For those reading the Platonic dialogues for the first time, one of the most striking characteristics of Socrates is his peculiarly light-hearted and even mischievous character, known as "Socratic irony".

Socrates' lack of gravity or seriousness about himself, despite being absolutely engaged with the most serious questions, provides an ideal example of the paradoxically *light-hearted* philosopher. Socrates' ironic refusal to think of himself as wise, his insistence that he was ignorant, was clearly not intended to be self-demeaning but rather psychologically empowering. It obviously served an important purpose and allowed him to exercise tremendous freedom and flexibility in his thinking. It prevented him from taking himself too seriously and becoming rigid in his thinking or trapped in a particular viewpoint. Ellis, likewise, considered it essential that his clients should learn to let go of those unreasonable demands that they imposed upon *themselves* and to accept themselves instead as *fallible* and *imperfect* human beings. I think Ellis might have seen Socrates, in his famous "irony" or professed ignorance, as someone who was able to laugh at himself and to pursue the most serious things in life in an admirably casual and light-hearted manner.

Some of his own contemporaries apparently perceived Socrates' irony as a mere façade, assuming that he considered himself wise, at least on some matters, but pretended otherwise in order to wrong-foot his opponents in debate. However, there are a number of reasons to believe that he may have been sincere. It is as though, by thoroughly accepting himself as flawed and unwise at the outset, he was prepared in advance for refutation and unafraid of being proved wrong on the most important matters. As Ellis recognized, when we truly accept ourselves as fallible and stop demanding perfection, stop demanding that we are always right, it liberates us from a rigid attitude that inevitably leads to emotional tension.

Perfectionism tends to be self-defeating; it leads to performance anxiety. It is all too easy for philosophers, who deal in absolutes, and in the most heady, serious issues, to take themselves *too* seriously in a way that leads to intellectual *rigidity* and paralysis. Socrates is, undoubtedly, an *unusual* philosopher in this respect. He is surprisingly comfortable, for instance, with incomplete arguments and fragmentary conclusions. He is more interested in the *process* of philosophizing than the notion of producing a philosophical *theory*, let alone organizing a formal *school* or writing a *book*. Most of what we know of Socrates, of course, comes from the writings of his students, Plato and Xenophon, in which he is usually portrayed in semi-dramatic form as the main protagonist in various philosophical dialogues.

> It must be admitted that this ironic, often ludic [playful] presence of Socrates makes reading the dialogues rather disconcerting for the modern reader, who reads them looking for Plato's theoretical "system". Compounding this difficulty are the numerous doctrinal inconsistencies which become evident when the reader moves from one dialogue to another.
>
> (Hadot, 2002, p. 73)

There are certainly very few great thinkers in the history of academic philosophy who could be described as *jovial*, with the possible exception of Socrates. His friends compared him to the mischievous satyrs and to Silenus, a mythological drunkard who served as tutor to the god of wine, Dionysus.

On the one hand, it is easy to see that Socrates' light-heartedness helps to balance what could be an imposing subject and, thereby, reassures novice philosophers that they might be able to join the otherwise daunting debate. However, it highlights a more profound matter of concern. The sage would presumably be *happy*, if only because he must be mentally healthy to maintain his contemplations to the best of his ability, but it is difficult to imagine how to reconcile this with the incredible demands seemingly placed upon him by commitment to the ideal of enlightenment. By accepting that he was only mortal, finite, and fallible, and that no mortal could truly aspire to absolute wisdom, Socrates lifted a tremendous burden from his mind that allowed him to function more freely. As Nietzsche observes:

> If all goes well, the time will come when one will take up [Xenophon's] memorabilia of Socrates rather than the Bible as a guide to morals and reason. . . . The pathways of the most various philosophical modes of life lead back to him. . . . Socrates excels the founder of Christianity in being able to be serious cheerfully and in possessing that wisdom full of roguishness that constitutes the finest state of the human soul. And he also possessed the finer intellect.
>
> (Nietzsche, 1996, p. 332)

Though the figure of Socrates provides the most celebrated living example of the Socratic ideal, however, the philosophers appear to have made a practise of seeking virtue in everyone around them. We can learn from others, even if they are not always as *near* to wisdom as Socrates.

The sage within everyone

We have seen that the attitude of contemplation toward the virtues of the ideal sage extended to great men such as Socrates. However, a similar attitude was to be applied even to more "ordinary" people, such as one's friends and family, and even one's enemies. Traces of this contemplative practise may even be found in the ancient Pythagorean doctrines, supposed to antedate the time of Socrates, which advise us to contemplate and model the words and actions of others.

> First honour the immortal gods, as the law demands;
> Then reverence thy oath, and then the illustrious heroes;
> Then venerate the divinities under the earth, due rites performing;
> Then honour your parents, and all of your kindred.
> Among others make the most virtuous thy friend!
> Love to make use of his soft speeches, and learn from his deeds that are useful.
> (*Golden Verses of Pythagoras*)

Insofar as everyone is *capable* of rationality, the philosopher seeks the spark of wisdom or virtue in other people, including his own knowledge of his friends, teachers, and ancestors. In particular, though, those who offer examples of having coped well with life's ups and downs, the ever-turning wheel of fortune, can serve as Stoic role models. Hence, Plutarch, in his essay *On Contentment*, recommends that "another thing that is important for contentment is to reflect on famous men, and how they have not been affected at all by circumstances identical to one's own".

Perhaps the most thorough illustration of this exercise in Stoicism comes from a source that has often been overlooked. Many readers of *The Meditations* of Marcus Aurelius find themselves flicking through the first chapter, which seems to some to be little more than a preface to the "real" meditations. However, this opening chapter can be read as a detailed example of a Stoic therapy exercise. Marcus Aurelius appears, on close inspection, to be attempting to review the most significant individuals in his life, and, in the majority of cases, to summarize their respective virtues in carefully condensed statements, sometimes in one or two key words. By far the longest section of this chapter is dedicated to reviewing the virtues of his adoptive father, the Emperor Antoninus Pius. It begins with the following words:

> Compassion. Unwavering adherence to decisions, once he'd reached them. Indifference to superficial honours. Hard work. Persistence. Listening to any-one who could contribute to the public good. His dogged determination to treat people as they deserved.
>
> (*Meditations*, 1.16)

Marcus continues to recount in patient detail the lessons to be learnt from his adoptive father and predecessor as emperor, whom he obviously holds dear as a role model. He finally concludes with the words:

> You could have said of him (as they say of Socrates) that he knew how to enjoy and abstain from things that most people find it hard to abstain from and all too easy to enjoy. Strength, perseverance, self-control in both areas: the mark of a soul in readiness – indomitable.
>
> (*Meditations*, 1.16)

We have seen that Antoninus Pius provided an example of how a Stoic can enjoy things in life, preferring them without becoming attached to them. Marcus Aure-lius' recollections regarding his friends and family members provides an example of deliberate cognitive-behavioural modelling. He begins by carefully analyzing the lessons he can learn from the significant people in his life. Even if they are not perfect, he can identify certain strengths and learn to imitate them. The first step to doing so, however, is putting them into words. By naming the virtues of others, Marcus helped himself to memorize and try to emulate them.

Role modelling in CBT

We might compare the "ideal sage" of antiquity to the Jungian notion of an archetype of the "wise man". However, a more relevant analogy for our present purpose would be with certain techniques in modern CBT. The concept of modelling behaviour evolved within later approaches to behaviour therapy, and modelling of attitudes, etc. is now an established CBT technique.

> Basically, modelling consists of learning by observation. The therapist serves as a model or provides [another] role model for a particular behavior the client is encouraged to imitate. For example, the therapist may invite the client to accompany him or her to a store to observe the assertive return of faulty merchandise. Some people (especially in group therapy) respond better to peer-modelling and imitation.
>
> (Lazarus, 1981, p. 247)

There are a variety of ways in which modelling can be employed in therapy. Lazarus refers to the therapist acting as a direct behavioural model, a function performed by the philosopher as teacher in ancient Stoicism. He also mentions asking the client to select behavioural models from their peers, a tactic Ellis and MacLaren also recommend.

> Modelling can be effective in aiding your client to "get out of her own navel". You can ask her to pick out someone she knows personally or a person or character she may have read or heard about who she admires and would like to emulate. Ask your client to be specific about the person or character's qualities she would like to possess and use the identified person as a reference in sessions.
>
> (Ellis & MacLaren, 2005, p. 68)

Lazarus described an early modelling technique, derived from REBT, which he calls "rational imagery":

> Whenever a person feels extremely upset (angry, anxious, or depressed) he should imagine himself confronting a group of his peers (objective onlookers) with a question: "What would you consider a reasonable response under the circumstances?"
>
> (Lazarus, 1971, p. 179)

Lazarus explains that he instructs his clients to systematically question their beliefs, in any imaginary conversation, either with one or a whole panel of "rational observers". Sometimes, if appropriate, the client may choose to imagine their therapist taking the role of inner "rational adviser".

These and other cognitive-behavioural modelling techniques clearly resemble the advice mentioned previously, from the Stoic *Handbook*, to "ask yourself what

Socrates or Zeno would have done in such circumstances". In short, the various therapeutic uses of contemplating the sage can perhaps be listed as follows:

1   The image of the sage can provide a general goal to aim toward.
2   One can ask oneself what the sage would do when faced with specific challenges.
3   One can imagine being observed by a sage and how one would act in their presence.
4   The sage can be imagined challenging or proposing alternatives to one's current beliefs and ways of acting.
5   Verbally describing, or writing down, the virtues of one's peers and heroes may make it easier to remember and assimilate them.

It is possible to see contemplation of the sage as one of the most fundamental meditative practises of ancient philosophy, from which several others derive. The sage may provide a concrete example from which specific principles of living, and verbal precepts or maxims, may be deduced. Moreover, the very notion of being observed by the sage appears to be a tool that can help the philosopher to heighten self-awareness, circumspection, and mindfulness, virtues that may facilitate many other aspects of therapeutic change.

Chapter 8

Stoic mindfulness of the "here and now"

Think, before you act, that nothing stupid results; to act inconsiderately is part of a fool.

– (The Golden Verses of Pythagoras)

The *Golden Verses of Pythagoras* thereby reminded ancient philosophers to be *cautious* and *circumspect* at all times. In recent decades, the "third-wave" of modern CBT, also known as "mindfulness and acceptance-based" CBT, has incorporated a range of interventions based upon "mindfulness" meditation practises, particularly in the treatment of depression (Segal, Teasdale, & Williams, 2002). These techniques are designed to heighten self-awareness of one's body, feelings, and thoughts through periods of meditative contemplation and the ongoing practise of self-awareness during the day. One of the major influences behind this approach was the stress reduction programme run by Jon Kabat-Zinn at the University of Massachusetts Medical Centre, which is explicitly based on Buddhist mindfulness meditation practises (Kabat-Zinn, 1990).

Cognitive-behavioural therapists have enthusiastically pointed out the relevance of Eastern mindfulness-based meditation techniques to modern psychotherapy, and the connection with certain aspects of established CBT. However, the notion of "mindfulness", which is popular in modern Buddhist and psychotherapeutic literature, clearly bears comparison to certain European philosophical concepts. In a recent article on Stoicism's relationship with CBT, McGlinchey rightly observes that the similarities between Stoic and Buddhist thought should be of interest to CBT practitioners "in light of the field's increasing attention to approaches grounded in the Buddhist tradition (e.g., mindfulness meditation), and suggest a greater affinity between Eastern and Western systems of thought than one might initially realize" (McGlinchey, 2004, p. 52).

Mindfulness in Stoicism

Ironically, although neither Ellis nor Beck appears to have mentioned this fact, similar self-awareness practises were an essential part of the Stoic philosophy, which Beck, as we've seen, described as constituting the "philosophical origins" of CBT (Beck, Rush, Shaw, & Emery, 1979, p. 8). Indeed, the emphasis upon "mindfulness" is one of the most notable aspects of Stoicism to have been *omitted* by early proponents of CBT. It's therefore somewhat surprising that third-wave therapists have largely ignored the Stoic approach to mindfulness. It would seem natural to look to Stoicism in this regard because CBT originally derived its central premise, the cognitive model of emotion, in part from Stoicism and had already assimilated many other Stoic influences. Moreover, Stoicism has the advantage of already being part of European culture in a way that Eastern meditative practises are not. Many ideas derived from the Stoics are already familiar to Westerners, albeit in a somewhat vague and fragmentary manner.

The exotic appeal of Eastern meditation is often mitigated by the fact that much of the symbolism and terminology surrounding Buddhist and Taoist practises remains fairly inscrutable to Westerners with a superficial knowledge of the history of the tradition and the language in which it is formulated. For all the obstacles surrounding the interpretation of ancient Graeco-Roman philosophy, and there are many, there is no doubt that modern Westerners are more familiar with this tradition from their own culture, although they may be unaware of this until they are introduced to some of the main themes. Modern readers frequently translate Eastern philosophical ideas *into* Graeco-Roman philosophical concepts in order to understand them, oblivious of the fact that the very things that appeal to them are largely half-remembered fragments of their own cultural heritage. For example, Stoicism is a "here and now" philosophy that centres upon the concept of *prosoche*, "attention to oneself", which can also be translated as "mindfulness". When we read about Buddhism being a "here and now" (*hic et nunc*) philosophy we are unwittingly viewing it through the lens of a Latin figure of speech which seems so familiar because our dimly-recollected European philosophical heritage made such extensive use of this concept. Although other Western philosophical schools advocated living in a manner grounded in the present moment, the Stoics arguably placed most emphasis on this practise and it's with *Stoic mindfulness* that we'll be mostly concerned in this chapter.

Seneca provides a wonderful account of the here and now orientation based upon the saying of the Stoic philosopher Hecato, "Cease to hope and you will cease to fear" (*Letters*, 5). Seneca interprets this with reference to the basic Stoic discipline of desire and aversion, which sees emotional disturbance as the result of over-attachment, or, rather, over-concern with external things. According to Seneca, hope and fear "march in unison like a prisoner and the escort he is handcuffed to" and both embroil us in anticipated, and therefore imagined, events.

> Fear keeps pace with hope. Nor does their so moving together surprise me;
> both belong to a mind in suspense, to a mind in a state of anxiety through

looking into the future. Both are mainly due to projecting our thoughts far ahead of us instead of adapting ourselves to the present. Thus it is that foresight, the greatest blessing humanity has been given, is transformed into a curse. Wild animals run from the dangers they actually see, and once they have escaped them worry no more. We however are tormented alike by what is past and what is to come. A number of our blessings do us harm, for memory brings back the agony of fear while foresight brings it on prematurely. No one confines his unhappiness to the present.

(*Letters*, 5)

In this remarkable passage, Seneca makes observations that would not be out of place in modern psychotherapy, but in his uniquely powerful literary style. Indeed, Beck and his colleagues say something very similar with regard to the cognitive therapy of anxiety, "Anxiety is a result of projecting oneself into a dangerous situation in the future. As long as the person is in the present, there is no danger" (Beck, Emery, & Greenberg, 2005, p. 243).

The gift that allows us to contemplate the future and the past, and distinguishes us from other animals, becomes a curse when it allows us to dwell upon troubles that are not present and may not even be real. When such projection of our thoughts across time runs amok, planning and problem-solving for the future can easily turn into *anxious* worrying, whereas reflecting on what we can learn from the past may be replaced by *depressive* rumination. The only true reality is the present moment, where our ability to take action is centred. Elsewhere, Seneca quotes the Epicurean maxim: "The life of folly is empty of gratitude, full of anxiety: it is focused wholly on the future" (*Letters*, 15).

Another aspect of this "here and now" orientation is brought out beautifully by the Epicureans. When we find ourselves, for the first time, in the presence of something completely and utterly new, we are filled with wonder. We might imagine the world looking this way to a small child, or to a blind man who suddenly regains his sight. Over time, we become jaded and habituated to the world, though, and mundane things cease to excite us. However, by immersing ourselves more fully in the present moment, and thereby ceasing to compare it to the past, in a sense, we recapture something of its novelty. The Epicurean philosopher and poet Lucretius writes, "there is nothing so mighty or so marvellous that the wonder it evokes does not tend to diminish in time".

Take first the pure and undimmed lustre of the sky and all that it enshrines: the stars that roam across its surface, the moon and the surpassing splendour of the sunlight. If all these sights were now displayed to mortal view for the first time by a swift unforeseen revelation, what miracle could be recounted greater than this? What would men before the revelation have been less prone to conceive as possible?

(*On the Nature of Things*, 2)

This contemplative technique also appears in Stoicism: for example, when Seneca writes:

> In my own case, at any rate the very contemplation of wisdom takes much of my time; I gaze upon her with bewilderment, just as I sometimes gaze upon the firmament itself, which I often behold as if I saw it for the first time.
>
> (*Letters*, 64)

Philosophy, according to Socrates, begins with the sense of wonder, and wonder is, therefore, the hallmark of the philosopher (Plato, *Theaetetus*, 155d3). The sense of wonder, in this way, is intimately related to consciousness of the here and now.

However, the philosophical sage is not merely wide-eyed but also circumspect and self-possessed. The Chinese Taoist sage, Lao Tzu, said that the wise man was as cautious as someone crossing a winter stream. Epictetus says something virtually identical, when he writes that the Stoic should walk about *cautiously*, like someone wary of treading on a nail or twisting his ankle on rocky ground (*Encheiridion*, 38). Rather than literally being careful of every footstep, of course, he means that one should mind one's own *thinking*. Elsewhere, he says that one who is making good progress in Stoicism keeps watch continually over himself, his thoughts, and judgements, as he would his own deadliest enemy, "and one lying in wait for him" (*Encheiridion*, 48). Hence, "you should turn all your attention to the care of your mind" (*Encheiridion*, 41). As he says repeatedly elsewhere, the aversions we normally experience concerning external things should be transposed on to our inner thoughts and feelings about them instead.

The sage does not so much as lift a finger without guarding against the tendency to error in what the Stoics refer to as man's "ruling faculty" (*hegemonikon*), the helmsman of the soul. This unwavering attention to one's self, one's faculty of judgement, was a central feature of Stoicism.

> Attention (*prosoche*) is the fundamental Stoic spiritual attitude. It is continuous vigilance and presence of mind, self-consciousness which never sleeps, and a constant tension of the spirit. Thanks to this attitude, the philosopher is fully aware of what he does at each instant, and he wills his actions fully.
>
> (Hadot, 1995, p. 84)

For student of Stoicism, mindfulness meditation and cognitive psychotherapy are already fully integrated because the "self" which he identifies with, and in which his "self-interest" is invested, is precisely his "ruling faculty", i.e., his judgement and cognition. Self-awareness, therefore, is especially awareness that centres upon the constant stream of interaction between the activity of consciousness and its objects. To put it another way, from moment to moment, the Stoic is particularly mindful of how he uses his mind, particularly his desires and value judgements. "Attend to your impressions", says Epictetus, "watch over them without sleeping, for it is no small thing that you are guarding" (*Discourses*, 4.3.7). He warns students that if they allow their attention to slip, or delay it until another time, they risk fostering a habit of complacency in their actions, lapsing into inattention (*Discourses*, 4.12.1–2).

Attention, self-awareness, can be developed in any activity, hence Epictetus asks the rhetorical question whether there is anything in life which is not better performed by attentive individuals, and whether any task is improved by a lack of awareness (*Discourses*, 4.12.4–5). Marcus Aurelius continually provokes himself to contemplate his current state of mind by posing such questions to himself as:

> What am I doing with my soul? Interrogate yourself, to find out what inhabits your so-called mind and what kind of soul you have now. A child's soul, and adolescent's, a woman's? A tyrant's soul? The soul of a predator – or its prey?
>
> (*Meditations*, 5.11)

It is as though a Stoic technique might consist in asking oneself periodically, "*Quo vadis?*" Where are you going? Where is your current judgement leading you, toward happiness or ruin? This conception of mindfulness is especially well suited to integration within modern CBT, perhaps more so than the kind of self-awareness exercises practised in Buddhism. It has sometimes been observed that the standard CBT practises, such as self-monitoring of negative automatic thoughts, inevitably contribute to an increase in self-awareness. Stoicism embraces this psychological fact and deliberately amplifies it, asking that we watch over our thoughts *at all times*, without interruption, constantly on the lookout for the thinking errors which cause emotional disturbance.

> So is it possible to be altogether faultless? No, that is impracticable; but it is possible to strive continuously not to commit faults. For we shall have cause to be satisfied if, by never relaxing our attention, we shall escape at least a few faults.
>
> (*Discourses*, 4.12.19)

The basic guiding principle in this contemplative practise is the central dogma of Stoicism: that some things belong to us and others do not. Hence, one of the first exercises recommended by Epictetus in his philosophical *Handbook* recommends that, from the outset, we should practise questioning every one of our subjective impressions, examining it, testing it, and applying the Stoic principles to evaluating it. In particular, he stresses, we should ask ourselves whether each impression attributes importance to things under our control or to external events. If it relates to external things, outside of our direct control, we should constantly affirm in our minds, "It is nothing to me", focusing instead upon our own sphere of control, primarily our responsibility for our own thoughts and judgements. This resembles the concept of "distancing" in cognitive therapy, whereby the client, through monitoring his or her automatic thoughts, learns to take a step back from them and treat them less literally, distinguishing mere thoughts from facts.

The Stoic, therefore, continually reminds himself to mind his own business, and to be concerned with his own judgements more than external events or other people's opinions (*Encheiridion*, 1). He is, thereby, mindful precisely of the inter-action of thought with perception. To borrow Korzybski's terminology from gen-eral semantics, one of the major influences on REBT, he cultivates an ongoing "consciousness of abstraction" and continually reminds himself of the maxim, "The map is not the terrain", that is, thoughts are not things. By contrast, when we are forgetful of ourselves, *mindless* instead of *mindful*, our thoughts and judge-ments merge imperceptibly with our experiences so that we lose track of the role of our opinions in shaping our perceptions, blinded to the distortions we impose on things. James Stockdale could relate this way of thinking to the challenges of being a modern fighter pilot:

> There is nothing old fashioned or out of date about [Epictetus]; you find as many applications for what he says while in a dogfight in a supersonic jet as you can in a classroom talking about the nature of evil in the world. But he urges us to acquire a constancy of character that will *make it impossible for another to do you wrong*. And to get that invulnerability, that inner invulner-ability, requires mastering the ability to be continually conscious of whether you are dealing with something you control or something that in the last instance you do not control.
>
> (Stockdale, 1995, pp. 240–241)

"Cognitive" or "philosophical" katharsis

The Stoic must perpetually separate his own mental activity from his perception of the outside world. This is the original philosophical-therapeutic meaning of the term *katharsis* ("purification"), which Plato used to refer to the careful separation of opinion and perception, and which Freud ultimately turned into something with an entirely different meaning. Epictetus explicitly discusses the Stoic theory of *katharsis*, which literally means "cleanliness", or "purification", in the following passage:

> The first and highest purity [*katharotes*], or impurity, then, is that which develops in the psyche. But you would not find the impurity of the mind and the body to be alike. For what other kind of impurity could you find in the mind than that which renders it unclean with regard to its own func-tions? Now the functions of the mind are its impulse to act or not to act, its desires and aversions, preparations, intentions, assents. What can it be, then that renders it unclean and impure in these functions? Nothing other than its false judgements. So the impurity of the psyche consists accordingly in bad judgements, and its purification [*katharsis*] in the production within itself of judgements of the kind that it ought to have; and a pure [*kathara*] psyche is

one that has judgements of the right kind, for this alone is free from confusion and defilement of its own functions.

(*Discourses*, 4.11.5–8, modified)

This kind of distinctively philosophical *katharsis*, consisting in the purification of judgements from certain errors, could perhaps be referred to as "cognitive *katharsis*" or "cognitive hygiene". This was the original meaning of the term in classical philosophical therapy, long prior to Freudianism, from which it perhaps deserves to be reclaimed.

Indeed, *katharsis*, in this sense, can be better compared to the concept of "distancing" in Beckian cognitive therapy. Beck states quite clearly, "The process of regarding thoughts objectively is labeled distancing" (Beck, 1976, p. 243). He further explains that what he means by "distance", in this sense, is the ability to regard one's position in terms of "I believe" rather than "I know". He likewise describes distancing as the client's ability to treat their own thoughts as hypotheses, and distancing or separating our thoughts from the external reality to which they refer.

> In an analogous way, a person who can examine his automatic thoughts as psychological phenomena rather than as identical to reality is exercising the capacity for distancing. Take, for example, a patient who, for no justifiable reason, has the thought, "That man is my enemy". If he automatically equates the thought with reality, his distancing is poor. If he can regard the idea as a hypothesis or inference, rather than accept it as fact, he is distancing well.
>
> (*ibid.*)

This technique of "distancing" in cognitive therapy is very much like the practise of *katharsis* in classical philosophy and also the closely related Stoic method known as "objective representation" (*phantasia kataleptike*). By continually monitoring their own judgements, the Stoics learned to carefully suspend their judgements regarding external events, purifying what was previously mingled, which, essentially, means distinguishing between *subjective* opinion and *objective* reality.

Cognitive *katharsis* is, therefore, the natural product of Stoic mindfulness. Moreover, this formula is so fundamental that it applies to every conceivable situation. This fact contributes to the famously *self-possessed* and *constant* character of the ideal Stoic sage, always the same, always aware of himself and in control. Every situation, from this point of view, presents just another instance in an infinite series of variations on the same fundamental question, in the terms of Epictetus, "What use am I making of my impressions right now?"

> Thanks to his spiritual vigilance, the Stoic always has "at hand" (*procheiron*) the fundamental rule of life: that is, the distinction between what depends on us and what does not.
>
> (Hadot, 1995, p. 84)

Self-awareness seems like the natural basis of any psychological exercise what-soever, and *continual* self-awareness the natural development of therapeutic techniques into the broader sphere of a philosophical *way of life* and, perhaps, even consciousness of one's place in relation to the whole universe. According to Hadot, attention to the present moment is, in some respects, the essence of the spiritual exercises found in Stoicism and other Hellenistic schools of philosophy (Hadot, 1995, pp. 84–85). He says that by its very nature, remaining grounded in the here and now frees us from the grip of unhealthy passions "which are always caused by the past or the future – two areas which do *not* depend on us" (*ibid.*). The present moment is where our locus of control is situated and by taking each moment one step at a time, each instant becomes more bearable. Moreover, atten-tion to the present moment makes us more conscious of its value in relation to the whole of cosmic Nature (*ibid.*).

Once again, modern CBT seems to fall short of explicitly endorsing a system of positive values of the kind found in Stoicism, although they are clearly assumed in its prescriptions. If focusing on the present moment in this way is therapeutic, and to be recommended, as Hadot states, this may perhaps imply some kind of positive value judgement regarding the "here and now".

Self-awareness and impulse control

A corollary of the emphasis upon self-awareness in philosophical therapeutics was the recommendation that extreme emotions should be handled with care. This often consisted of the incredibly sound and common sense advice that no important decision should be taken when in the grip of rage, depression, or other irrational emotions, but that time should be taken to calm down and recover one's composure before acting. Iamblichus attributed the origin of this practise to the ancient Pythagorean sect.

> If however at any time any one of them fell into a rage, or into despond-ency, he would withdraw from his associates' company, and seeking solitude, endeavour to digest and heal the passion.
>
> Of the Pythagoreans it is also reported that none of them punished a serv-ant or admonished a free man during anger, but waited until he had recovered his wonted serenity. They use a special word, *paidartan*, to signify such [self-controlled] rebukes, effecting this calming by silence and quiet.
>
> (Iamblichus, *Life of Pythagoras*)

Epictetus, likewise, discusses the example of a man temporarily assailed by impressions of irrational avarice or inappropriate sexual impulses and emphasizes that, although these initial impressions may occur to almost anyone, we are imme-diately presented with a choice as to whether we indulge or challenge them. He makes it clear that his students must remind themselves that to give in once to an unhealthy impulse is to weaken ourselves so that we become more vulnerable to it again in the future, whereas to question it forcefully is to strengthen ourselves by forming a stronger habit of resistance to it in the future. This strategy of focusing upon the longer-term consequences of an action is often found in CBT.

Epictetus gives various specific examples of how such an impulse might be counteracted and controlled, including praising oneself for seeing that it is merely an impression of desirability and not a thing good in itself, and reminding oneself of the example of Socrates' behaviour, as a role model in respect of similar situations.

> If you set these thoughts against your impression, you will over-power it, and not be swept away by it. But, in the first place, do not allow yourself to be carried away by its intensity: but say, "Impression, wait for me a little. Let me see what you are, and what you represent. Let me test you". Then, afterwards, do not allow it to draw you on by picturing what may come next, for if you do, it will lead you wherever it pleases. But rather, you should introduce some fair and noble impression to replace it, and banish this base and sordid one. If you become habituated to this kind of exercise, you will see what shoulders, what sinews and what vigour you will come to have. But now you have mere trifling talk, and nothing more.
>
> (*Discourses*, 2.18.22–6)

First, the Stoic must learn to pause for thought and observe his situation, an aspect of mindfulness that is essential to most remedial action. The Stoics believed that although irrational ideas could always impose themselves upon the mind, especially in adversity, nevertheless, by maintaining emotional calm and self-awareness, the sage could choose either to grant or to withhold his assent to his initial impressions. A similar notion is found in Dubois' rational psychotherapy.

> We should react briskly, act enthusiastically for good, obey the impulse of our better feelings. But however spontaneous this reaction may be, we must nevertheless leave time for calm reason to exercise a rapid control. Our reason is that which as an arbiter judges finally the value of the emotions of sensibility which make us act. It is a sentiment of goodness, of pity, which carries us away, reason very quickly gives its approval. But when we are about to give way to a feeling of anger, envy, vexation, reason should intervene to correct the first impression and modify the final decision.
>
> (Dubois & Gallatin, 1908, p. 56)

Similar "stop and think" techniques are employed in modern CBT to control impulses by "nipping them in the bud" before they have a chance to grow out of control.

Stoic meditations on impermanence

The Stoic emphasis upon the here and now is closely associated with a sense of mortality, transience, and urgency. From moment to moment, life slips away from us, unless we take time to "smell the roses", enjoy the present, and take action to progress toward wisdom. This sense of urgency is shared with the Epicureans: for example, in this passage from Epicurus:

> We have been born once and cannot be born a second time; for all eternity we shall no longer exist. But you, although you are not in control of tomorrow, are postponing your happiness. Life is wasted by delaying, and each one of us dies without enjoying leisure.
>
> (*Vatican Sayings*, 14)

By placing too much value upon externals, we place all of our hopes upon the future, and lose track of the true source of happiness right under our nose, our attitude toward living.

The transience of things and the importance of valuing the here and now is a common theme in classical poetry, for example, in the *carpe diem* of Horace, who studied and was influenced by both Stoic and Epicurean thought. Horace advises us, in his 11th *Ode*, to "seize the day", while time relentlessly flies away from us, and put no trust in tomorrow. Indeed, he makes many similar remarks throughout the *Odes*:

> Let the soul be happy in the present, and refuse to worry about what will come later.
>
> (Horace, *Odes*, 2.16.35, in Hadot, 2002, p. 196)

> Think about arranging the present as best you can, with serene mind. All else is carried away as by a river.
>
> (Horace, *Odes*, 3.29.33, *ibid.*)

Horace expresses a similar notion in the *Epistles*, which he attributes to the philosophy of Epicurus. A similar motif is found in a well-known poem attributed either to Virgil or Ausonius, which begins "Gather ye rosebuds while ye may, remembering that thy bloom as swift does fade" (*Idyllia*, 19.49). This topic is found in many Greek and Roman poems and indeed subsequent poetry influenced by them. The refrain, *ubi sunt*, "Where are they now?" is a common poetic theme that reminds us of the transience of life by emphasizing how many things have passed away before us. Where are they now, the great philosophers and heroes of the Greek and Roman world? They are all gone. Where are those who worried and complained about their misfortunes in life?

> In the face of everything that happens to you, keep before your eyes those who, when the same things happened to them, were at once distressed, bewildered, and resentful. And where are they now? Nowhere!
>
> (*Meditations*, 7.58)

As the ancient pre-Socratic philosopher Heraclitus famously said, *panto rhei*, everything flows, and nothing is permanent.

Christianity

The influence of Hellenistic philosophy upon the authors of the *New Testament* has long been noted, and there are some well-known illustrations of this "here and now" theme in Christianity. In the Gospel of Luke, Jesus visits a village and speaks to several would-be disciples; one hesitates, saying:

> I will follow thee; but let me first go bid them farewell, which are at home at my house. And Jesus said unto him, No man, having put his hand to the plough, and looking back, is fit for the kingdom of God.
>
> (*Luke*, 9: 62)

This can be read as an admonition to attend to the business of the present moment and not be distracted by the past. However, the most famous allegory upon this theme in Christian literature is undoubtedly the following:

> And why take ye thought for raiment? Consider the lilies of the field, how they grow; they toil not, neither do they spin: And yet I say unto you, that even Solomon in all his glory was not arrayed like one of these. Wherefore, if God so clothe the grass of the field, which to day is, and to morrow is cast into the oven, shall he not much more clothe you, O ye of little faith? Therefore take no thought, saying, What shall we eat? or, What shall we drink? or, Wherewithal shall we be clothed? (For after all these things do the Gentiles seek:) for your heavenly Father knoweth that ye have need of all these things. But seek ye first the kingdom of God, and his righteousness; and all these things shall be added unto you. Take therefore no thought for the morrow: for the morrow shall take thought for the things of itself. Sufficient unto the day is the evil thereof.
>
> (*Matthew*, 6: 28–34)

The expression "Eat, drink and be merry, for tomorrow we die", also derives from Biblical passages, such as *Isaiah* 22: 13. Indeed, as we shall see, contemplation of the here and now is closely bound up in classical literature with the meditation upon death, another of the cardinal methods of ancient philosophical psychotherapy.

The meditation on death

The meditation on death (*melete thanatou*) is one of the most enduring and influential contemplative practises in the whole of classical Greek and Roman literature. The theme is central to the legendary drama surrounding the last days, trial, and execution of Socrates, and, therefore, to all subsequent Socratic schools of philosophy. The noble death of Socrates, a truly historic event, served as the ultimate model of a sage remaining philosophical and serene in the face of adversity. The example of Socrates' death as a kind of philosophical martyr, though paralleled by many famous stories regarding the deaths of great heroes and sages, was only really superseded in cultural importance, four centuries later, by the Christian myth of the crucifixion of Jesus. However, whereas Jesus was the Son of God, according to the Christian faith, and soon rose from his tomb and ascended to Heaven, Socrates was a mortal and his story therefore maintains a special poignancy for philosophers.

In a famously striking passage, Seneca draws once again upon the rival Epicurean philosophy to express the importance of contemplating one's own death:

> Epicurus will oblige me with the following saying: "Rehearse death", or – the idea may come across to us rather more satisfactorily if we put it in this form – "It is a very good thing to familiarize oneself with death". . . . To say this is to tell a person to rehearse his freedom. A person who has learned how to die has unlearned how to be a slave.
>
> (*Letters*, 26.8)

This is not a morbid rumination. As Seneca elsewhere states, we should imitate the sage as one who both *enjoys life* and yet is unafraid of death. Again, the Pythagoreans hint at a similar contemplation:

> Then make the habit, never inconsiderately to act;
> Neither forget that death is appointed to all;
> That possessions here gladly gathered, here must be left.
>
> (*Golden Verses of Pythagoras*)

The Stoics return to this theme time and time again, with Epictetus' handbook clearly advising the contemplation of one's own mortality as a therapeutic exercise to be repeated daily. "Let death and exile, and all other things which appear dreadful be set before your eyes each day, but mainly death, and you will never experience any base thought, nor too readily crave anything" (*Encheiridion*, 21). Elsewhere, he elaborates on the Stoic theory that the fear of death is absolutely fundamental to human anxiety and that it maintains other fears in life.

> Why, do you not reflect, then, that the source of all human evils, and of mean-spiritedness and cowardice, is not death, but rather the fear of death? Discipline yourself, therefore, against this. To this let all your discourses, readings, exercises, tend. And you will know that in this way alone are men made free.
>
> (*Discourses*, 3.25.38)

The meditation on death is closely intertwined with the meditation upon the here and now, because remembering our mortality, and the uncertainty of our future, increases the value of the present moment. Following the recommendations of Epictetus, Marcus Aurelius repeatedly reminds himself to embrace the present moment, with his own mortality constantly in mind.

> You could leave [your life] right now. Let that determine what you do and say and think.
>
> (*Meditations*, 2.11)

> Do everything as if it were the last thing you were doing in your life.
>
> (*Meditations*, 2.5, modified)

> Perfection of character: to live your last day, every day, without frenzy, or sloth, or pretence.
>
> (*Meditations*, 7.69)

Epictetus alludes to the practise by which a slave would reputedly whisper *memento mori*, "Remember you must die", in the ear of Roman generals during their victory celebrations, or "triumph".

This notion spawned one of the most enduring and influential genres in the history of art, with countless references to be found scattered throughout European culture. From the iconic image of Hamlet, the young philosophy student, holding the skull of Yorick, to the preserved shark's carcass displayed by Damien Hirst, images of death and the transience of human life pervade our art, each one reminding us to stop and contemplate the implications of the inescapable fact that we must die. For centuries, clocks, watches, and sundials have borne inscriptions such as *hora fugit*, "the hour flies", an Epicurean maxim derived from Horace. It is only in recent centuries that widespread awareness of this traditional contemplative practise has waned as we have gradually lost touch, collectively, with the philosophical practises that preceded modern forms of psychotherapy and self-help.

The Phaedo of Plato

One of the most important sources regarding this theme in philosophy, the contemplation of death, is Plato's dialogue the *Phaedo* in which Socrates calmly contemplates his imminent death in discussion with his friends. Socrates, of course, had been condemned by the Athenian court for impiety and corrupting the youth. He was forced to kill himself by drinking a poisonous concoction based on hemlock. The portrayal of Socrates in the *Phaedo*, along with the *Apology* and *Crito*, served as a model for the ideal "good death" to subsequent generations of philosophers. One of the themes of the dialogue that ensues in the *Phaedo* is the notion that philosophy itself is a "preparation for death". Socrates boldly asserts that "those who practice philosophy in the right way are in training for dying and they fear death least of all men" (*Phaedo*, 67e).

This makes the whole discourse peculiarly self-referential because by read-ing about Socrates preparing himself for death we are ourselves entering into a contemplative process of philosophical preparation for death. The *Phaedo* itself, in a sense, is therefore a *memento mori*, a verbal reminder of our philosophical relationship with death. For many centuries, study of the *Phaedo*, and probably reading it aloud, would have contributed to the psychological formation of noviti-ate philosophers. Perhaps we could even consider it a kind of Socratic "book of the dead", a text meant to be read to prepare one for dying, like the Egyptian or Tibetan books of the dead, although in this case preparation was lifelong. Plu-tarch, for instance, says that the Stoic Cato of Utica began reading the *Phaedo* as he was preparing to take his own life (*Life of Cato the Younger*, 68). This notion of philosophy as preparation for death was quite familiar until recent centuries. Michel de Montaigne composed a Stoic-influenced essay entitled, "That philoso-phising is learning how to die", in which he borrows Seneca's provocative saying, "He who has learned how to meet death, has unlearned how to be a slave".

In the *Phaedo*, Socrates suggests that the purpose of philosophy, and espe-cially the meditation upon death, is the "separation" (*khorismos*) of the soul from the body, which constitutes a kind of metaphysical "purification" (*katharsis*). He appears to have in mind something comparable to the concept of "cognitive distancing", which we discussed earlier. By certain philosophical practises it is possible to become more aware of the distinction between consciousness and its objects: that is, to separate our thoughts from external things. The philosopher separates himself from his body in the sense that he ceases to *identify* himself with it, but "purifies" his sense of self by focusing it instead purely upon his own faculty of judgement and volition. Socrates is clear that this training contributes to the acquisition of self-control over one's irrational passions and impulses, which suggests that it involves a form of self-awareness and cognitive restructuring.

In the legend of Socrates' last days, therefore, we have not only the contem-plation of the ideal sage but also of death and transience. We discover the basis of the philosophers' emphasis upon the here and now, and the purification of his mind from irrational emotional attachments which lead him to confuse his own thought with external facts. These attitudes form the basis of continual Stoic self-reflection and mindfulness, from moment to moment, and the systematic analysis and disputation of irrational thoughts and attitudes to which we will now turn.

Chapter 9

Self-analysis and disputation

The central method of cognitive therapy consists of monitoring one's own thoughts, challenging certain ones that are irrational and unhelpful, and progressively modifying the beliefs that underlie them. One of the most fundamental practises of Stoic therapy likewise entails challenging certain erroneous impressions and beliefs.

Cognitive self-monitoring in Stoicism

At the outset, it should be emphasized that the Stoic term for a mental "impression" (*phantasia*) might refer to a feeling, dream, intuition, memory, anticipation, notion, or anything we might now call a mental "representation". As Epictetus observed, the practise of examining and questioning one's impressions can be seen as a derivative of the famous maxim of Socrates, "The unexamined life is not worth living" (Plato, *The Apology*, 38a).

> For, just as Socrates used to say that we are not to live an unexamined life, so neither are we to accept an unexamined impression, but to say, "Stop, let me see what you are, and where you come from", just as the nightwatch[men] say, "Show me your token". Have you that token from nature, which every impression must have if it is to be accepted?
>
> (*Discourses*, 3.12.15)

One of the slogans of Epictetus' teaching was, "Make the right use of impressions". In other words, the Stoic should continually examine his thoughts and ruthlessly challenge any which may be irrational and unhealthy. Indeed, as an aid or reminder in this, Epictetus recommends that the Stoic student imagines that each impression poses the question, "What do you think of that?" (*Discourses*, 3.8.1). The philosopher must respond by considering whether his response is rational or irrational, whether it sticks to the facts or distorts them emotively. This was technically part of the Stoic discipline, which they termed "Logic", and which seems to refer to something more pragmatic than the word would imply to a modern reader. As Hadot puts it, ancient Logic was "not limited to the abstract theory of reasoning", or formal syllogisms, but rather it was part of a daily practise involving the application of reason to problems of life (Hadot, 2002, p. 135). Logic in this ancient sense refers very broadly to the mastery of our inner discourse and use of reason. Hadot notes that this was so important for the Stoics because they inherited the Socratic doctrine of moral intellectualism, which holds that our unhealthy passions are based upon irrational discourse or reasoning.

> In other words, they are the result of errors in judgement and in reasoning. We must therefore monitor our inner discourse to see whether erroneous value judgements have crept into it, for this would add something foreign to the comprehensive representation [*phantasia kataleptike*].
>
> (*ibid.*)

Our impressions should be true, which means for Stoics that impressions of external events should be relatively neutral, i.e., free from strong value judgements of the sort that cause intense desire or emotional distress.

Epictetus describes the discipline of logic or "assent", as we've seen, by explaining that the philosopher should treat every impression as a night watchman or a border guard might treat a stranger, demanding they show proof of their identity before allowing them to pass. It is as if the Stoic challenges each impression with the words, "Friend or foe?" (*Discourses*, 3.12.15).

> "Consciousness of our errors is the first step to salvation". This remark of Epicurus' is to me a very good one. For a person who is not aware that he is doing anything wrong has no desire to be put right. You have to catch yourself doing it before you can reform.
>
> (*Letters*, 28)

Seneca encourages his friend Lucilius to closely monitor his own judgements for important errors and to dispute them vigorously, in a manner that resembles the use of "automatic thought records" to self-monitor cognitive errors in modern CBT. Psychological self-examination was also encouraged by dialogue with a philosophical teacher. However, the use of personal journals appears to have provided another tool in the philosophical armamentarium through which such detailed and systematic scrutiny of one's thoughts and behaviour could be accomplished. The Stoic discipline of *assent* was therefore a discipline of *cognition*, which can be directly compared with the use of cognitive therapy techniques in modern CBT.

The Stoic therapy journal (hypomnemata)

In a style clearly pre-empting the use of self-monitoring records in cognitive therapy, Epictetus observes how "diseases of the soul" grow stronger with repetition of the symptoms and exhibit the typical "practice effect" found in habit formation. However, he also prescribes that his students keep note of the frequency of these lapses into unhealthy emotions, such as excessive rage, and self-monitor their progress as follows.

> If then, you do not wish to be ill-tempered, do not feed the habit. Give it nothing to promote its growth. Keep quiet to begin with, and count the days on which you have not been angry. I used to be angry every day; now every other day; then every third and fourth day; and, if you avoid it as many as thirty days, offer a sacrifice of thanksgiving to god. For habit is first weakened, and then entirely destroyed. "I was not distressed today; nor the next day; nor for three or four months after; but took due care when things happened that might have caused me distress". Be assured that you are in a fine way.
>
> (*Discourses*, 2.18.12–14)

Epictetus continues by emphasizing that this psychotherapeutic exercise should be repeated regularly in a manner resembling the physical training of an athlete, so it was clearly meant to be a systematic technique of therapeutic self-monitoring.

The use of daily records of negative emotions or behavioural habits is common today as part of self-monitoring in CBT. In traditional behaviour therapy, a client might be asked to write down in their diary how many times they felt like biting their fingernails each day, for instance (Azrin & Nunn, 1977). However, modern CBT practitioners also make considerable use of more thorough self-monitoring exercises involving daily "automatic thought records" and other structured homework assignments. These cognitive self-monitoring techniques might entail not only recording the frequency or intensity of a feeling or behaviour but also recording problematic thoughts and writing down one's rational responses to them. By monitoring and recording his thoughts, the client often spontaneously develops more insight, objectivity, and distance from his faulty thinking (Beck, Emery, & Greenberg, 2005, p. 190).

A similar type of method is twice prescribed by Epictetus in the *Discourses*, who also advises Stoic novices to write down their precepts, or rational responses to irrational passions, every day and to repeatedly rehearse them in contemplative practise until they are memorized and "ready to hand" in the face of adversity. After providing some examples of specific rational responses to adversity, Epictetus tells his students, "These are the things that philosophers ought to meditate upon; it is these that they should write down each day; and it is in these that they should exercise themselves" (*Discourses*, 1.1.25, modified). Elsewhere he says:

> Have these reflections "ready to hand" by night and day. Write them down, read them, talk about them, both to yourself, and to somebody else when you say, "Is there any help that you can give me in this?"
>
> (*Discourses*, 3.24.103, modified)

In ancient Greek, personal notes and philosophical reflections recorded on an ongoing daily basis were known as *hypomnemata*. Many people take for granted the therapeutic value of keeping a diary. However, philosophical *hypomnemata* were not intended merely to be "cathartic writing" in the modern sense, a way of venting one's feelings in private, etc. The primary therapeutic use in ancient times appears to have been to aid the formulation and *memorization* of philosophical maxims. According to Diogenes Laertius, the Cynic Antisthenes was famous for rebuking a student who complained about losing his notebook, "You ought to have written them on your mind and not on paper" (*Lives*, 6.1). Ideas were written down in order to work them over and memorize them, not merely to record them and forget about them. This "cognitive" therapy use of the journal, to aid memorization of rational responses to adversity and other maxims, resembles certain aspects of modern CBT.

By far the most influential and most important example of a Stoic therapeutic journal is, of course, provided by the famous *Meditations* of Marcus Aurelius. In his book, *The Inner Citadel*, Hadot carried out a comprehensive analysis of *The Meditations*, concluding that these particular *hypomnemata* contain many instances of specific "spiritual exercises", apparently derived mainly from the teachings of Epictetus (Hadot, 1998). Many people assume *The Meditations* are merely a collection of random musings. However, Hadot showed that they are the record of a personal regime of specific verbal and cognitive exercises designed, a programme of psychological self-help and spiritual development. It seems likely that Marcus Aurelius had studied the teachings of Epictetus since his youth, and was directly following the instructions quoted previously from Epictetus' *Discourses* to "write down and reread" his own Stoic precepts and reflections on a daily basis. If that is the case, we have both the teacher's recommendations for these cognitive exercises in Stoicism and many specific examples of it being put into practise decades later, by someone following his branch of Stoicism.

Throughout *The Meditations* we witness Marcus repeatedly reformulating basic Stoic principles in different ways, presumably in an attempt to clarify the doctrines in his own mind and help to engrave them meaning more and more deeply in his memory until they become ready to hand in the face of challenging situations in daily life. According to Epictetus, these notes were meant to be reread repeatedly, and Marcus shows great care in his choice of words; invariably he seems to be condensing as much *rhetorical* power as he can into the fewest words possible. Of course, this practise also resembles the classical rhetorical strategy of formulating concise *aphorisms* for greater persuasive effect. However, another verbal strategy occurs throughout Stoic literature, which may be equally important and can be seen, paradoxically, as the philosophical *opposite* or *inversion* of conventional rhetorical strategies: the deliberate stripping away of emotive figures of speech and corresponding value judgements.

Phantasia kataleptike and "counter rhetoric"

One of the central and most characteristic techniques of Stoicism is a philosophical and rhetorical exercise that involves re-describing external events in more objective language, sometimes in writing, in order to moderate one's emotional responses. As Marcus Aurelius puts it, "Nothing is so conducive to spiritual growth as this capacity for logical and accurate analysis of everything that happens to us" (*Meditations*, 3.11).

> Thus the task of the Stoic analysis of impressions and judgements is to examine impressions and to reject any value judgements they might contain. Its aim is to develop an experience of the world as it is in itself, that is, an experience that presents things as neither god nor bad in themselves.
>
> (Sellars, 2003, p. 158)

In part, this is what Epictetus means by his repeated assertion that the essence of philosophy is the correct use of one's impressions, arrived at by continually challenging and testing their validity. Indeed, one of the first exercises described in the *Handbook* requires the Stoic to describe things to which he feels emotionally attached in plain language, starting with lowly items like a jug, but working up in graduated steps and stages toward more emotionally significant items, like one's wife or child (*Encheiridion*, 3). Ellis directly borrowed this Stoic practise from the *Handbook* in his advice to those using REBT for self-help:

> Try not to exaggerate the importance or significance of things. Your favourite cup, as Epictetus noted many centuries ago, merely represents a cup that you like. Your wife and children, however delightful, remain mortals. Don't take a defensive "so-what" attitude and falsely tell yourself, "So what if I break my cup, or my wife and children die? Who cares?" For you'd better care for your cup and your wife and children, in order to lead a more zestful life. But if you exaggeratedly convince yourself that this is the *only* cup in the world or that your life would be completely empty without your wife and children, you will overestimate their value and make yourself needlessly vulnerable to their possible loss.
>
> (Ellis & Harper, 1997, p. 174)

Similar advice is given by Beck and his colleagues to clients in cognitive therapy, whose interpretation of their problem has become "too far removed from reality":

> When you become too remote from what you can perceive with your five senses, it's easy to enter in to the world of fantasy and nonreality. When you stick with what you can perceive, you're usually on much safer ground.
>
> (Beck, Emery, & Greenberg, 2005, p. 197)

This exercise seems to have been done in ancient Stoicism by running through the description verbally in one's mind, or by carefully writing it down and revising it, as in many passages of *The Meditations*. In any case, it constitutes an important recurring theme in Stoic therapeutics. For example, to a list of other principles and exercises, Marcus Aurelius adds the following:

> Always make a sketch or plan of whatever presents itself to your mind, so as to see what sort of thing it is when stripped down to its essence, as a whole and in its separate parts; and tell yourself its proper name, and the names of the elements from which it has been put together and into which it will finally be resolved. For nothing is as effective in creating greatness of mind as being able to examine methodically and truthfully everything that presents itself in life.
>
> (*Meditations*, 3.11)

Elsewhere he reminds himself to look deeper into things, stripped down to their essence (*Meditations*, 12.8). This method seems to admit of several variations, the simplest of which is to suspend the use of value judgements or emotive language in our descriptions of things, which amounts, in a sense, to sticking to our initial impression of the bare facts, devoid of value judgements.

> Say nothing more to yourself than what the first impressions* report. You have been told that some person is speaking ill of you? That is what you have been told: as to the further point, that he has harmed you, that you have not been told. I see that my little child is ill? I see just that; I do not see that his life is at risk. And so, in this way, always keep to first impressions and add nothing of your own from within, and then nothing bad will befall you. Or rather, add that you are well acquainted with everything that comes to pass in the world.
>
> (*Meditations*, 8.49)

Marcus, once again, seems clearly to have been influenced by reading Epictetus, who gave many similar examples, including the following:

> He was carried off to prison.
> What happened?
> He was carried off to prison.
> The remark [i.e., the judgement] "He has fared ill", is an addition that each man must make for himself.
>
> (*Discourses*, 3.8.4)

> Does someone take his bath quickly? Do not say that he does it badly, but that he does it quickly. Does any one drink a great quantity of wine? Do not say that he drinks badly, but that he drinks a great quantity. For, unless you understand the judgement from which he acts, how should you know that he is acting badly? And thus it will not come to pass that you receive convincing

impressions [*phantasia kataleptike*] of some things, but give your assent to different ones.

(*Encheiridion*, 45)

This method is similar to the technique known as "extensional" thinking, or "orientation by facts" rather than mere words, from Korzybski's system of general semantics, which was an important precursor of REBT and CBT. Indeed, in a preface to his *Science and Sanity*, first published in 1933, Korzybski specifically wrote of the relationship between semantics and psychotherapy.

> I may add that all existing psychotherapy, no matter of what school, is based on the partial and particular extensionalization of a given patient, depending upon the good luck and personal skill of the psychiatrist.
>
> (Korzybski, 1958, p. xlvii)

Korzybski claimed that although most psychotherapists in his day were unaware of this semantic perspective on their work, psychological improvement typically consists in a form of semantic reorientation, based upon a more objective grasp of events. Korzybski would probably have seen modern CBT as more akin to his own philosophy than was the Freudian psychoanalysis of his day, and what he means by "semantic disturbance" is comparable, in some respects, to what modern CBT practitioners would call "cognitive distortion".

This technique of "objective representation", though eminently Stoic, was probably shared with other Hellenistic schools. Even the Epicureans remind their students:

> Most of this illusion is due to the mental assumptions which we ourselves superimpose, so that things not perceived by the senses pass for perceptions. There is nothing harder than to separate the facts as revealed from the questionable interpretations promptly imposed on them by the mind.
>
> (Lucretius, *On the Nature of Things*, 4)

There are many other instances in the modern literature of self-help and psychotherapy where clients are advised to stick to the essential facts and avoid excessive emotional embellishments in their internal dialogue. However, this formula originated as one of the pre-eminent techniques of Stoic psychotherapy.

This method is quintessentially Stoic: it consists in refusing to add subjective value-judgements – such as "this object is unpleasant", "that one is good", "this one is bad", "that one is beautiful", "this is ugly" – to the "objective" representation of things which do not depend on us, and therefore have no moral value. The Stoics' notorious *phantasia kataleptike* – which we have translated as "objective representation" – takes place precisely when we refrain from adding any judgement value to naked reality. In the words of

Epictetus: "we shall never give our assent to anything but that of which we have an objective representation".

(Hadot, 1995, pp. 187–188)

The basic notion of pausing to re-describe things to ourselves in more objective and less emotive terms, or more concretely and less abstractly, can be seen as a kind of *counter* rhetoric. Language contains a whole armamentarium of rhetorical devices intended to arouse emotion in others and often to distort their perception of things. We all make irrational overgeneralizations, employ colourful metaphors, insinuate, apply emotive terms, etc., for rhetorical effect. We do it so habitually that the majority of us are caught off guard when attention is drawn to the fact. More crucially, however, we often use the same kind of language in our own internal chatter, turning rhetoric against ourselves.

To give a contemporary example, suppose at a meeting I say to myself, "I can't believe it! They just shot me down in flames; everyone always treats me like dirt!" This is an unwitting blast of rhetoric, which condenses a whole host of verbal and intellectual distortions. What is its purpose? It seems designed to provoke exaggerated anxiety and hostility, but why would I want to do that to *myself*? We are often the unwitting victims of our own *internal* rhetoric run amok, though. This bewitchment of our intelligence by means of language, as Wittgenstein once put it, can also be seen as a kind of ongoing, conscious but unintentional, process of negative self-hypnosis or autosuggestion. We simply do not pay enough attention to our stream of consciousness, in most cases, to stop and realize what effect it is having upon our emotional state and perspective on things.

This is perhaps most strikingly illustrated when we attempt to reverse the process, peeling back the layers of emotive language and other rhetorical flourishes, in an attempt to be more objective. I might translate the previous exclamation quite simply as follows, in more objective language: "Somebody disagreed with something that I said". Perhaps adding, "Though other people seemed indifferent, or agreed with parts of what I'd said" for clarity". Clearly, that way of looking at things is less upsetting, and yet it may also be more grounded in reality.

Hadot refers to the process of analysis and re-description in Stoicism as "physical definition" or "objective representation", which is one possible translation of the difficult-to-translate Stoic technical term *phantasia kataleptike*. A more literal translation would perhaps be "a mental representation that grasps (things)", an orientation to the facts, getting to grips with the reality of the situation.

The concept of physical or objective description is also bound up with the Stoic discipline of Physics (or metaphysics), insofar as it attempts to describe things as if seen from an absolutely impersonal perspective, the View from Above, rather than in terms that confuse the bare facts with personal emotional reactions. Therefore, it also requires, as far as possible, placing things within their true context, the *whole* context of the universe in its entirety. That means acknowledging the relative transience of things by reminding oneself of their lifespan, from origin to demise. It also means thinking of them as part of the total framework of universal determinism: that is, either as the Will of God or as simply part of the vast causal machinery of Nature. For instance, Marcus contemplates things as follows:

> What this object is that presently makes an impression on me, and what it is composed of, and how long it will naturally persist, and what virtue is needed in the face of it, such as gentleness, courage, truthfulness, good faith, simplicity, self-sufficiency, and so forth. So, as each case presents itself, you should say: this has come from God, this from the coordination and interweaving of the threads of fate and similar kinds of coincidence and chance.
>
> (*Meditations*, 3.11)

Baudouin and Lestchinsky refer to the practise of analysis into constituent parts, as follows:

> The principle that underlies the [Stoic] method may be described as depreciation by analysis. When we decompose into its constituent parts the object which has been of so much concern to us, we shall realise that it is a matter of no moment (much as a child which has pulled a toy to pieces is disillusioned, and says, "Is that all it is?").
>
> (Baudouin & Lestchinsky, 1924, p. 48)

The most striking illustration of this is found in *The Meditations*, where Emperor Marcus Aurelius goes so far as to "decompose" his own imperial robes of office. "This purple robe is sheepskin dyed in shellfish gore" (*Meditations*, 6.13). This is a particularly striking example because, in the ancient world, it was a well-known irony that the regal "Tyrian purple" dye of the emperor's robes came from the rancid-smelling mucus glands of the *murex* sea snail. The job of extracting the rare and priceless *purpura* dye was considered notoriously unpleasant. According to Pliny the Elder, the innards of many molluscs were boiled, skimmed, and filtered for at least 14 days, during which the stench produced was legendary. Marcus recounts this amid a series of other examples in his notebook, apparently recording his daily practise in the Stoic method of objective representation.

> When you have savouries and fine dishes set before you, you will gain an idea of their nature if you tell yourself that this is the corpse of a fish, and that the corpse of a bird or a pig; or again, that fine Falernian wine is merely grape-juice, and this purple robe some sheep's wool dipped in the blood of a shellfish; and as for sexual intercourse, it is the friction of a piece of gut and, following a sort of convulsion, the expulsion of some mucus. Thoughts such as these reach through to the things themselves and strike to the heart of them, allowing us to see them as they truly are. So follow this practice throughout your life, and where things seem most worthy of your approval, lay them

naked, and see how cheap they are, and strip them of the pretences of which they are so vain.

(*Meditations*, 6.13)

Again, the example of meat is notable. We often use more *euphemistic* names for meat on the plate: cow becomes "beef", pig becomes "pork", sheep becomes "mutton", deer becomes "venison", molluscs become "seafood", etc. Scottish "haggis" is made from the lungs of a sheep boiled inside its stomach. People today are often quite disturbed when reminded exactly how their meat is produced. They sometimes say things like, "I wouldn't be able to eat it if I thought about where it came from". Of course, these distressing images can easily be put out of mind by most people. The Stoic considers this self-deception and would rather know and remember the truth about his food. The same strategy is employed across the board in Stoicism, with any number of different objects, events, and even people.

Socratic disputation (elenchus)

The term "Socratic disputation" or "Socratic questioning" is used in most modern textbooks on CBT, although there is little discussion to be found therein regarding its historical provenance. Although they perhaps construe the term loosely, Beck and his colleagues clearly state that "Cognitive therapy uses primarily the Socratic method" (Beck, Emery, & Greenberg, 2005, p. 167). Every cognitive therapist therefore realizes that the method of questioning used by them derives ultimately from the philosopher Socrates. However, there's no discussion of the role the Socratic method actually played in ancient philosophical approaches to psychotherapy, including Stoicism, and how this might be of interest to modern CBT.

In philosophy, the Socratic method of questioning is referred to as the *elenchus*, meaning literally "testing" or "refutation". This was the term used to describe cross-examination of a witness in an ancient Greek court of law, such as during the trial of Socrates himself. The *elenchus* is the central technique used by Socrates himself in the dialogues written by Plato and Xenophon. He is portrayed as engaging in discussion with experts in different fields whom he taxes with penetrating questions, seeking a definition of the key practical virtues of interest to them. For instance, in Plato's *Laches*, Socrates questions several Athenian generals about how courage should be defined. Socrates professed his own ignorance, the famous "Socratic irony", and focused on pressing his interlocutor with difficult questions about their value judgements, etc. Typically he'll begin by asking for a concise verbal definition of a virtue from his interlocutor and then cross-examine them to expose contradictions in their thinking. Often the initial definition is shown to be too narrow or too broad. For instance, courage is initially defined as standing one's ground in the face of the enemy – something that would make sense when thinking of heavy infantry (hoplites). Socrates quickly points out that this definition is too narrow, though. It wouldn't apply to cavalry who charge the enemy or to courage exhibited in non-military settings. Plato's dialogues are often inconclusive;

nevertheless through persistent questioning Socrates usually appears to get significantly closer to a workable definition of the virtue being examined.

Socrates also described himself, metaphorically, as following in his mother's profession of *midwifery*, or *maieutics*. He was a midwife to his interlocutors' opinions and tried to help them to give birth to insight into philosophical truth. Although modern cognitive therapists have surprisingly little to say about one of their favourite pieces of terminology, the behaviourist B. F. Skinner was well aware of the historical meaning of Socratic questioning as a form of "midwifery" and its relevance to psychotherapy.

> The metaphor appears also in theories of psychotherapy. The patient is not to be told how to behave more effectively or given directions for solving his problems; a solution is already within him and has only to be drawn out with the help of the midwife-therapist.
>
> (Skinner, 1971, p. 85)

Skinner acknowledged that maieutic practises "have their place" in behaviour therapy. In his view, the main advantage of Socratic questioning is that the client might be gently induced to develop insights that were almost within his grasp to begin with, or on the tip of his tongue, as it were.

> We read books which help us say things we are on the verge of saying anyway but cannot quite say without help. We understand the author, although we could not have formulated what we understand before he put it into words. There are similar advantages for the patient in psychotherapy.
>
> (*ibid.*, p. 86)

Sometimes, these incipient insights are the result of a process of working through unresolved *intellectual conflicts*. As we've seen, Socrates himself typically employed his trademark method of questioning to expose internal contradictions in the thinking of those claiming expertise, employing a strategy known as the *reductio ad absurdum*. He then left his interlocutors in a state of mental confusion, known as philosophical *aporia* or disorientation. People often find themselves in contradiction because their underlying values subtly conflict with the life they actually find themselves pursuing. To persuade people to change their philosophy of life, fundamentally, they must be shown that their ways of acting or thinking are inconsistent with their true values.

Socrates himself viewed his method of questioning as a form of moral and psychological therapy, which attempted to cure a form of philosophical arrogance or conceit. He believed that we often behave as though we were certain about what is good or virtuous in different areas of life, when in fact our beliefs are contradictory and therefore *cannot* be true. (At least not *completely* true, when combined with one another.) If we can tolerate the discomfort and confusion caused by having our cherished beliefs questioned then we potentially become more open-minded as a result and capable of genuine learning, with regard to the most important things in life.

Five hundred years after Socrates' execution, but still long before the advent of cognitive therapy, Epictetus describes the therapeutic use of the Socratic method in Stoicism.

> Every error implies a contradiction: for, since the man who errs does not wish to err, but to act rightly, it is evident that he is not doing what he wishes. For what does a thief wish to achieve? His own interest. If, then, thieving is against his interest, he is not doing what he wishes. Now every rational soul is naturally averse to contradiction: but so long as a person fails to understand that he is involved in a contradiction, there is nothing to prevent him from performing contradictory actions, but when he has come to understand it, he must necessarily renounce and avoid the contradiction, just as bitter necessity makes a man renounce what is false as soon as he perceives that it is false, though as long as he does not have that impression, he assents to it as true.
>
> (*Discourses*, 2.26.1–3)

Epictetus concludes that just as surely as a heavy weight will throw a set of finely balanced scales decisively in one direction, the human mind must be swayed when it perceives an indisputable contradiction in its own behaviour.

We all accept that what is contradictory *cannot* be completely true. However, it often requires considerable patience and effort, as Socrates' dialogues show, to bring someone fixed in their ways to the realization that they are contradicting their own better wisdom (*Discourses*, 2.26.7). Some people responded to having their contradictions pointed out by becoming inspired to seek further insight, others seem to have been offended, and it may even have been his habit of exposing the ignorance of professed experts, including some influential figures, that led to Socrates' execution by the Athenian court. However, when Socrates was successful, he claimed to be able to bring others to a point of deep moral and philosophical insight of direct practical relevance to their way of life.

These tactics clearly resemble certain aspects of the modern therapeutic relationship, and even Freudian psychoanalysis has been compared to Socratic *elenchus*. However, the cognitive therapists are probably more justified in adopting the terminology because of the obvious resemblance between the Socratic method of questioning and their own approach to cognitive disputation. Although it often seems that Socrates actually exerts considerable influence over his interlocutors, and his professions of ignorance may appear something of a ruse, nevertheless, the notion of helping others to achieve deep personal insight by encouraging them to think for themselves is clearly one shared by modern psychotherapy. The methods of Socratic questioning, of course, have changed over the intervening two and a half millennia. However, a number of additional parallels, of a more *specific* nature, can be drawn between Socratic and Stoic methods, on the one hand, and the cognitive disputation methods employed in modern REBT and CBT on the other.

Selective thinking/generalization

The Platonic philosopher Plutarch draws on certain aspects of Stoicism in his writings. He provides an excellent account of the role of cognition in mediating our response to external events, which begins by referring to the beneficial effect of modelling other people's rational responses to adversity.

> When we have a fever, everything tastes bitter and unpleasant, but once we have seen other people taking the same food without revulsion, we stop blaming the food and drink, and start to blame ourselves and our illness. In the same way, we will stop blaming and being disgruntled at circumstances if we see other people cheerfully accepting identical situations without getting upset.
>
> (*On Contentment*, 468f)

Plutarch continues, by noting a morbid tendency for people to dwell on the negative aspects of their situation, or their own character, and to selectively ignore or discount the positive:

> So when unwelcome incidents occur, it is also good for contentment not to ignore all the gratifying and nice things we have, but to use a process of blending to make the better aspects of our lives obscure the glare of the worse ones. But what happens at the moment is that, although when our eyes are harmed by excessively brilliant things we look away and soothe them with the colours that flowers and grapes provide, we treat the mind differently: we strain it to glimpse the aspects that hurt it, and we force it to occupy itself with thoughts of the things that irritate it, by tearing it almost violently away from the better aspects. And yet the question addressed to the busybody can be transferred to this context and fit in nicely: "You spiteful man, why are you so quick to spot someone else's weakness, but overlook your own?" So we might ask: why, my friend, do you obsessively contemplate your own weakness and constantly clarify it and revivify it, but fail to apply your mind to the good things you have? Cupping-glasses extract from flesh anything particularly bad, and likewise you are attracting to yourself the very worst of your attributes. You are making yourself no better at all than the Chian [from Chios, the ancient wine-making capital] who used to sell plenty of quality wine to other people, but for his own meal used to taste wines until he found a vinegary one; and when someone asked one of his servants what he had left his master doing, the servant replied, "Looking for bad when surrounded by good".
>
> (*On Contentment*, 468f-469c)

Closer to our own age, the Renaissance Neostoic, Justus Lipsius, wrote something similar about the human tendency to focus upon and magnify the negative.

> It is a thing naturally given to men to cast their eyes narrowly upon all things that are grievous, but to wink at such as be pleasant. As flies and such like

vile creatures do never rest long upon smooth and fine polished places, but do stick fast to rough and filthy corners, so the murmuring mind does lightly pass over the consideration of all good fortune but never forgets the adverse or evil. It handles and pries into that, and often augments it with great wit. Like as lovers do always behold something in their mistress by which they think her to excel all others, even so do men that mourn in their miseries.

(Lipsius, 2006, p. 116)

In cognitive therapy, the tendency to discount the positive or simply to ignore it by engaging in a kind of inattention known as "selective thinking" or "tunnel vision" is a well-known maintaining factor in emotional disturbance. This thinking error is closely bound up with the tendency to overgeneralization, that negative things "always" happen and positive ones "never" do, and to the labelling of things, people, or events as completely bad or worthless.

In Stoicism, the importance of the context of events is taken to philosophical extremes. All things are to be considered within the ultimate context of the totality of all space and time, as part of the whole universe, rather than isolated events. The calling of a philosopher, according to Epictetus, is:

never to deliberate on anything as though detached from the whole, but be like our hand or foot, which, if they had reason, and understood the constitution of nature, would never exercise any impulse or desire, except by reference to the whole.

(*Discourses*, 2.10.4)

We shall return to this theme in connection to the contemplative exercise that scholars have called, "the View from Above"; however, a corollary of this broad perspective can also be found in another cognitive therapy practise.

Contrasting consequences

Another strategy common to both cognitive therapy and Stoicism is the practise of pausing to contemplate the consequences of different courses of action, or different attitudes of mind. Prior to the advent of cognitive therapy, Skinner recognized that describing the consequences of a course of action could shape people's behaviour.

Another way to change a mind is to point to reasons why a person should behave in a given way, and the reasons are almost always consequences which are likely to be contingent on behavior.

(Skinner, 1971, p. 95)

Considering the positive and negative consequences of different courses of action obviously influences our decision-making. It is common, for instance, for smokers to be asked to picture the long-term consequences of continuing to smoke, and to compare them with an alternative vision of their future as a *non*-smoker. Clients can be asked to view the consequences of holding on to an irrational belief, and weigh that against the advantages of abandoning it in favour of a more rational and constructive way of thinking about things. Epictetus gives a clear description of a similar strategy in the *Handbook*. As elsewhere, he emphasizes the value of postponing action, to "stop and think", allowing oneself time to cool off, and consider things philosophically.

> When you are struck by the impression of some [hedonistic or egotistical] pleasure, guard yourself, as with impressions generally, against being carried away by it; rather, let the matter await your leisure, and allow yourself a measure of delay. Then bring to mind both of these moments in time: that in which you will enjoy the pleasure, and that in which you will regret it and criticise yourself after you have enjoyed it; and set against these how you will rejoice and praise yourself if you abstain. But if you feel that it is the right moment to embark upon the action, take heed that you are not overcome by its enticements and its seductions and attractions; but set against this how much better it is to be conscious of having gained a victory over it.
>
> (*Encheiridion*, 34)

This notion was symbolized in ancient literature by the so-called Pythagorean Fork, the choice of either the path of vice (*kakia*) or the path of virtue (*arête*). In his *Memorabilia*, Xenophon portrays Socrates as recounting a famous parable regarding Hercules, which is attributed to the Sophist, Prodicus. Hercules, a Stoic role model, who was forced to choose between the paths of vice and virtue early on in his life, and, of course, chose the initially hard but ultimately rewarding path of virtue or excellence, which led to his undertaking the famous *Twelve Labours*. Epictetus explicitly makes the analogy between the effort of self-mastery in Stoicism and the mythic labours of Hercules.

> Pray, what figure do you think Hercules would have made if there had not been a lion like the one they tell of, and a hydra, and a stag, and unjust and brutal men, whom he drove off and cleared away? And what would he have done if nothing like these had existed? Is it not plain that he would have wrapped himself up and slept? In the first place, then, he would never have become a Hercules by slumbering his whole life away in such delicacy and ease; or if he had, what good would it have been? What have been the use of those arms of his, and his strength overall; of his endurance, and greatness of mind, if such circumstances and opportunities had not stirred him to action and exercised him?
>
> (*Discourses*, 1.6.32, modified)

Likewise, the great Pythagorean sage, Apollonius of Tyana, reputedly said:

> If you were to choose like Hercules, showing an iron will and not disregarding the truth or shunning a humble life according to nature, you will be able to say that you have captured many lions and slain many hydras, giants, centaurs, and all the creatures that fell before Hercules.
>
> (Philostratus, *The Life of Philostratus*)

The following ancient epigram on the Pythagorean Fork was designed to remind us to consider the consequences of our actions, by stopping to think of the choices that we make.

> The Pythagoric Letter two ways spread, Shows the two paths in which
>   Man's life is led.
> The right hand track to sacred Virtue tends, Though steep and rough at first,
>   in rest it ends;
> The other [Vice] broad and smooth, but from its Crown On rocks the
>   Traveller is tumbled down. He who to Virtue by harsh toils aspires,
> Subduing pains, worth and renown acquires:
> But who seeks slothful luxury, and flies,
> The labour of great acts, dishonour'd dies.
>
> (Pseudo-Virgil (Maximinus), in Guthrie, 1988, p. 158)

Indeed, the image of the twin paths of Error and Excellence, or Death (*Via Mortis*) and Life (*Via Vitae*), finds expression in the Greek poet Hesiod's *Works and Days* as far back as the eighth century BC, in a passage quoted by Xenophon in his *Memorabilia* of Socrates.

> Error it is possible to find in abundance and with ease; for the way to it is smooth, and lies very near. But before the temple of Excellence the immortal gods have placed labour, and the way to it is long and steep, and at the commencement rough; but when the traveller has arrived at the summit, it then becomes easy, however difficult it was at first.

The recurring theme in Graeco-Roman thought is that man is repeatedly presented with a choice between diverging paths in life: one represents the easy option, but ultimately leads to moral decay; the other requires considerable effort but leads to the prize of self-realization and personal fulfilment (*eudaimonia*). This is the proverbial "road less travelled" alluded to by M. Scott Peck in his book of the same name, which famously opens with the line, "Life is difficult", itself a Stoic theme (Peck, 1978). Personal improvement requires patience and effort but laziness, as Peck puts it, continually tempts us to throw the towel in and revert back to our old habits of thought and behaviour.

By contemplating the longer-term consequences of our actions, we help to reinforce and maintain our motivation to work toward change. The technique, of mentally reviewing the consequences of our actions, is found therefore in both Stoicism and modern CBT.

Double standards method

Indeed, many of the specific tactics employed by the Stoics in disputing irrational beliefs resemble the therapeutic interventions used in different forms of CBT. For example, one of the favoured techniques of the Beckian cognitive therapy approach is known as the "double standards" method.

> When patients consider *other* people's beliefs, they often get psychological distance from their own dysfunctional beliefs. They begin to see an inconsistency between what they believe is true or right for themselves and what they more objectively believe is true about other people.
>
> (Beck, 1995, p. 160)

Judith Beck explains that common variations involve asking the client to imagine whether they would be happy to apply the same harsh standards they apply to themselves to a small child, or to imagine whether they would think someone else who shared similar beliefs and acted accordingly was being reasonable.

This is actually a recurring strategy in the Socratic dialogues of both Plato and Xenophon. The same strategy is also found, very clearly described, in Epictetus' Stoic approach. In the *Handbook*, he says that we can learn how to adapt to nature by considering how our judgements apply to other people's misfortunes. Epictetus says that if a neighbour's slave breaks a valuable drinking cup, we are ready to say, quite rightly, "Oh well, these things happen!" However, we should be just as ready to view things philosophically when our own property is damaged or destroyed. As elsewhere, Epictetus begins with trivial examples, petty valuables, but extrapolates the same principle to far more sensitive issues. He reminds us that if the child or wife of another man dies, we say things like, "Such is the human lot", that is, "It's a tragedy, but these things happen in life". Even in the face of such adversity, when our own loved ones die, we should remind ourselves how philosophically we would view the misfortune befalling others (*Encheiridion*, 26). We view other people's setbacks philosophically and should view our own in the same rational light; to think otherwise is to apply a double standard. Yet again, Stoicism can be seen to employ strategies in common with modern CBT but elevated from the field of therapy to the level of a more general, and more fundamental, philosophy of life. We should continually train ourselves to view things from this philosophical perspective, according to the Stoics. The ideal Stoic sage regards his own misfortune as dispassionately and objectively as the fate of others.

In the *Discourses*, Epictetus' follower Arrian provides a transcript of Stoic therapy with a somewhat neurotic-sounding government official, who complains:

> But I am so very miserable about my poor children, that the other day, when my little daughter was sick and was considered to be in danger, I could not bear even to be with her, but ran away, until somebody told me she had recovered.
>
> (*Discourses*, 1.11.4)

Epictetus engages in a penetrating discussion with the man. He exposes the underlying irrational belief that to run away from her bedside in panic, though it might be unreasonable, was a *natural* expression of his feelings of intense love for his sick daughter. The man assumes, in other words, that if he loves his daughter he should be so distressed by her illness that he will run away consumed by grief. Epictetus exposes the contradiction, the double standard, in his beliefs, as follows.

> So it was right for you, when you were affectionately disposed towards your child, to run off and leave her? And has the child's mother no affection for her?
> Yes; surely she has.
> Would it have been right, then, that her mother too should have left her, or would it not?
> It would not.
> What of the nurse? Does she love the child?
> She does.
> Ought she then to have left her?
> By no means.
> And her attendant? Does he not love her?
> He does.
> Should he not also, then have gone away and left her, so that in consequence the child would have been left all alone and helpless because of the great affection of you her parents and those around her, or would have died, perhaps, in the hands of people who neither loved her nor cared for her?
> Heaven forbid!
> But is it not unreasonable and unfair, that what you think right in yourself, on account of your affection, should not be allowed to others, who have the very same affection as you?
> It is absurd.
> Pray, if you were sick yourself, should you be willing to have your relatives, and children themselves and your wife, so very affectionate as to leave you alone and desolate?
> By no means.
>
> (*Discourses*, 1.11.21–24)

Epictetus concludes that the man did not act out of genuine "affection" at all but because he (mistakenly) believed that acting in accord with his raw emotions of anxiety was somehow the natural right thing to do, although contrary to reason and common sense. Here, Epictetus is clearly employing the Socratic *elenchus* for therapeutic purposes, to expose a contradiction in the form of a double standard. However, this discussion would not look out of place in a cognitive therapy text-book. It provides yet another good example of common factors in Stoicism and modern CBT.

Having recorded, analyzed, and disputed his irrational judgements, the Stoic proceeded to defend himself by more proactive means, rehearsing the positive dogmas of his philosophy of life. This constitutes a means of protecting himself against future relapse, through mental rehearsal, and also generalizing improvement by changing his underlying philosophical attitude to reflect the goals of enlightenment (*sophia*) and mental health (*eudaimonia*), as we shall see.

Chapter 10

Autosuggestion, premeditation, and retrospection

One of the most fundamental techniques common to many of the philosophical-therapeutic systems of antiquity appears to have been the repetition, rehearsal, and memorization of key statements or philosophical principles of living (*dogmata*). From the Socratic "know thyself" (*gnothi seauton*) and "nothing in excess" (*meden agan*) inscribed at the Delphic shrine of Apollo, enshrining the cardinal philosophical virtues of wisdom and self-mastery, respectively, to the *memento mori* ("remember thou must die") of the Roman Stoics' meditation upon death, classical literature is replete with pithy sayings, proverbs, and aphorisms designed to be instantly memorable and to help instil enlightened philosophical attitudes.

Autosuggestions, affirmations, and coping statements

Seneca made a habit of including many philosophical maxims from poetry and literature in his letters to his Stoic student Lucilius. He saw them not as random sayings but as constituting a closely interconnected and continuous stream, a coherent system of thought, although drawn from many sources, all illustrating basic Stoic tenets.

> They do not drip forth occasionally; they flow continuously. They are unbroken and are closely connected. Doubtless they would be of much benefit to those who are still novices and worshipping outside the shrine; for single maxims sink in more easily when they are marked off and bounded like a line of verse.
>
> (*Letters*, 33)

However, he also states that they are a beginner's tool and should not become a substitute for behaviour change. Seneca compares such sayings to the proverbs and apophthegms taught to children for rote memorization. Elsewhere, he says that philosophical maxims are like seeds: they are small in size and yet grow to produce impressive results as long as they are planted in fertile soil (*Letters*, 38).

This Stoic use of short precepts and sayings clearly bears comparison to many modern psychotherapeutic practises, such as the use of autosuggestions or affirmations in hypnotherapy or of "coping statements" and "self-instructions" in CBT. According to Sellars, the main function of psychological ("spiritual") training in Stoicism was the "incorporation of philosophical doctrines into one's everyday habits" (Sellars, 2003, p. 121). This process of philosophical "habituation", as he puts it, transforms one's character, changing underlying beliefs, which, in turn, transforms one's behaviour. Likewise, Ellis describes the forceful rehearsal of "coping statements" in REBT in a manner resembling certain forms of autosuggestion but notably designed to reinforce underlying philosophical principles and attitudes.

> Keep thinking, thinking, and thinking Rational Beliefs (RBs) or coping statements, such as: "It's great to succeed but I can fully accept myself as a person and have enjoyable experiences even when I fail!" Don't merely parrot these statements but go over them carefully many times and think them through until you really begin to believe and feel that they are true.
>
> (Ellis & MacLaren, 2005, p. 124)

One of the central principles of CBT is that negative judgements and bad habits of thinking should be repeatedly counteracted by means of direct disputation and the cultivation of alternative, more realistic and helpful thoughts and attitudes. However, Epictetus also clearly recommends throughout his writings that irrational judgements should be repeatedly and forcefully counteracted by opposing, rational beliefs, which must acquire the force of habit (*Discourses*, 1.27.3–4).

The Stoics were well aware that engrained habits of negative thought, emotion, and behaviour would require patient effort, and skilful use of technique, to overturn. The metaphor of athletic training was important in this regard, as we have seen, but so also the analogy with military themes. The verbal principles of the Stoic are thought of as "weapons" of the mind, which he uses to fight against emotional disturbance. Hence, the Justus Lipsius speaks of sowing in his heart the "seed of good thought", thereby to "lay up some wholesome lessons in my mind, as it were weapons in an armoury, which are always ready with me at hand against the force and mutability of fortune" (Lipsius, 2006, p. 80). The recollection of these weapons, the precepts of Stoicism, may perhaps have been symbolized by the physical act of clenching one's fist. For example:

> The student as boxer, not fencer.
> The fencer's weapon is picked up and put down again.
> The boxer's is part of him. All he has to do is clench his fist.
> (*Meditations*, 12.9)

Or, in keeping with the medical metaphor, they are like the instruments of a physician:

> Doctors keep their scalpels and other instruments handy, for emergencies. Keep your philosophy ready too.
> (*Meditations*, 3.13)

Both of these metaphors make it clear that the Stoics thought of their precepts as more than just ideas tossed around in idle debate. These are the weapons used in the lifelong battle for happiness and mental health.

Memorization and affirmation

As Hadot observes, the formulation of Stoic principles into short sentences is not arbitrary, it reflects the Greek and Roman preoccupation with the art of *memorization* and the training of recall is here being turned to a specific therapeutic purpose. For both the Epicureans and Stoics, it was essential that students be provided with fundamental principles that could be expressed in a few words (Hadot, 1995, p. 84). They must be clear and simple enough to be recalled with ease in a variety of situations, becoming like a reflex with continual practise.

The psychology of memorization, among other things, requires that we utilize (positive) rhetoric in the service of philosophy and employ our imaginations in as vivid and concrete a manner as possible, turning what might seem at first to be an abstract intellectual principle into a fully-fledged "visualization technique" of the kind found in modern psychotherapy. Hadot says that in order to benefit from the spiritual exercises of ancient philosophy, we must train our imagination and emotions as well as reason, bringing into play "all the psychagogic techniques and rhetorical methods of amplification" (Hadot, 1995, p. 85).

> We must formulate the rule of life to ourselves in the most striking and concrete way. We must keep life's events "before our eyes", and see them in the light of the fundamental rule. This is known as the exercise of memorisation (*mneme*) and meditation (*melete*).
>
> (*ibid.*)

The Stoics believed that their precepts were useful for the novice as a way of concentrating their attention and memory and could serve as a substitute for observing the role model of a living sage or hero in person.

Xenophon had earlier implied that memorization of philosophical precepts required constant practise and repetition, comparable to the memorization of stanzas from epic poems.

> No doubt many professed philosophers would say that a good man can never become bad, nor a self-disciplined man a bully, just as one who has learned any other subject can never become ignorant of it. But this is not my view of the matter. It seems clear to me that just as those who do not exercise their bodies cannot carry out their physical duties, so those who do not exercise their characters cannot carry out their moral duties: they can neither do what they ought to do nor avoid what they ought to avoid. . . .
>
> For I observe that just as epic poetry fades from the minds of those who fail to rehearse it, so those who neglect what their teachers tell them are liable to

forget it. Now when a person forgets the advice he has been given, it means that he has also forgotten the influences that set his heart on self-discipline; and when he has forgotten these it is not surprising that he should forget self-discipline too.

(Memorabilia, 1.2)

Xenophon believes that constant practise of philosophical principles is one way to keep alive the influence of the teacher as role model, the example of Socrates. It may well be that Stoics actually derived some of their precepts from systematic contemplation of the actions of the sage, in imagination. These subsequently provided a mnemonic device to help them recall what a sage would do under various circumstances. These sorts of practises would become particularly important in the absence of a real teacher, e.g., if a student travelled or their teacher passed away.

The Stoics' great rival, the Epicurean school, made use of many identical methods. However, whereas the Stoics appear to have employed a great many formulaic statements, followers of Epicurus condensed the essence of their philosophy into a single *general purpose* therapeutic affirmation, known as the *tetrapharmakos*, or "fourfold remedy".

> There is no need to fear God,
> Nor worry about death.
> What is good is readily attainable,
> And what is bad is easily endured.

The Stoics borrowed the related Epicurean maxim that pain is usually either chronic and mild *or* acute and severe. Seldom is it *both* genuinely intense *and* long-lasting, if only because we would probably die before long. For instance, Marcus Aurelius writes:

> With regard to most pains, furthermore, let this saying of Epicurus come to your aid, that "pain is neither unendurable nor everlasting, if you keep its limits in mind and do not add to it through your own imagination".

(Meditations, 7.64)

Beck and his colleagues appear to be alluding to this passage from *The Meditations* when they write "Pain is never unbearable or unending, so long as you remember its limitations and do not indulge in fanciful exaggeration", in relation to the role of increasing attitudes of anxiety tolerance in cognitive therapy (Beck, Emery, & Greenberg, 2005, p. 242). What is bad is, therefore, easily endured. Likewise, pleasure can be found in the simplest things in life, and the Epicurean sage even learns to enjoy the mere sense of his own existence. The best things in life are free; what is good is readily attainable.

Good and bad in Epicureanism are merely equated with sensing pleasure and pain. However, in Stoicism they are equated with acting rationally or irrationally.

Stoic happiness (*eudaimonia*) comes not from pleasure (*hedone*) but from the sense of moral and intellectual fulfilment that derives from acting in complete accord with our own higher nature as thinking beings, from one's sense of purpose and integrity. Nevertheless, the two competing schools of thought have a great deal in common, especially from our modern point of view. Their mutual emphasis upon the benefit of memorizing key formulas, in the form of affirmations or rational statements of belief, until they are integrated into one's character and easily recalled in the face of adversity, can easily be compared to modern CBT.

Epictetus repeatedly exhorts his students to commit their precepts to memory, to rehearse them in private, and to continually train themselves in their use in daily life. "Having these thoughts always at hand, and engrossing yourself in them when you are by yourself, and making them ready for use, you will never need any one to comfort and strengthen you" (*Discourses*, 3.24.115). Galen, physician to the Stoic emperor Marcus Aurelius, explains that the principles of Stoicism were meant to be combined with regular rehearsal of the type of actions associated with them, that is, that one should recall certain therapeutic cognitions while behaving accordingly.

> All we must do is keep the doctrine [*dogma*] regarding insatiability and self-sufficiency constantly at hand, and commit ourselves to the daily exercise of the particular actions which follow from these doctrines.
>
> (Galen, quoted in Sellars, 2003, p. 119)

Marcus Aurelius himself refers to the gradual process of habitual conditioning through exercise, repeating verbal formulae and mental images, as similar to progressively dyeing an object with a different colour. In a similar manner, both Epictetus and Seneca use the metaphor of *digestion* to illustrate the slow internalization and assimilation of precepts through repetition. The *Handbook* insists that one should never claim to be a philosopher or talk about philosophical principles before laymen, but, rather, exhibit one's philosophy through one's actions.

> For sheep do not bring their fodder to the shepherds to show how much they have eaten, but digest their food internally, and produce wool and milk externally. And so you likewise should not display your principles to laymen, but rather show them the actions that result from these principles once they have been digested.
>
> (*Encheiridion*, 46)

Epictetus, in his typically outspoken manner, accuses his students of "vomiting" forth undigested philosophical precepts rather than taking time to assimilate them fully into their character. The maxims of the Stoic were, therefore, not merely verbal formulae but were intended to be memorized, internalized, and manifested in behaviour change.

Prospective meditation

Certain sects of philosophers appear to have started the day by calmly exercising their imagination in contemplative reflection to tone their minds in preparation for the day ahead. According to the Neoplatonist, Iamblichus, morning meditation was a practise that existed in ancient therapeutic philosophy as far back as the time of Pythagoras.

> They took solitary morning walks to places which happened to be appropriately quiet, to temples or groves, or other suitable places. They thought it inadvisable to converse with anyone until they had gained inner serenity, focusing on their reasoning powers. They considered it turbulent to mingle in a crowd as soon as they rose from bed, and that is the reason why these Pythagoreans always selected the most sacred spots to walk.
>
> (Iamblichus, *Life of Pythagoras*)

Elsewhere, also says, "They were to adore the rising sun". Marcus Aurelius likewise describes how the Pythagoreans prepared for the day ahead by taking time, first thing in the morning, to gaze upon the stars at daybreak and contemplate the vastness of the cosmos and their place within it (*Meditations*, 11.27). This suggests that they may have begun the day by doing something akin to the contemplative method dubbed "the View from Above" by modern scholars, which we shall examine in due course.

The rational psychotherapists Baudouin and Lestchinsky allude to this practise of morning meditation, commenting on the relevant excerpts from Marcus Aurelius (*Meditations*, 11.27) as follows:

> Consequently, one who has learned how to control his mind has thereby also learned, to a certain extent, how to control his body. . . .
>
> Such mastery can only be acquired by daily training. Moreover, day after day, the first hour especially demands our attention, for the attitude we adopt at this time sets the course for the day. Pythagoras was well aware of the fact, for he recommended silence and meditation during the first hour after waking:
>
> "The Pythagoreans would have us lift our eyes heavenward on rising in the morning".
>
> Marcus Aurelius, in his turn, tells us that the opening hour of the day is the one in which good resolutions can be made with the best effect. . . .
>
> He also tells us that it is good, at this hour, to dwell upon the thoughts that may help us to overcome slothful inclinations. . . .
>
> This initial victory will pave the way for the victories of subsequent hours. Through such minor daily conquests we shall be enabled to acquire good

habits. A number of these good habits must be acquired; our energies must be ever on the watch; all our moral faculties must be duly exercised. . . .

Thanks to the suppleness acquired by this course of moral gymnastics, the mind will be enabled to overcome all obstacles.

(Baudouin & Lestchinsky, 1924, p. 58)

The Stoics therefore, following the Pythagoreans, appear to have specifically set aside time in the mornings for rehearsal of verbal affirmations in preparation for the day ahead.

If any of you, withdrawing himself from externals, turns to his own faculty of choice, working at it and perfecting it, so as to bring it fully into harmony with nature; elevated, free, unrestrained, unhindered, faithful, self-respecting: if he has learned too, that whoever desires, or is averse to, things outside his own power can neither be trustworthy nor free, but must necessarily be changed and tossed back and forth with them; must necessarily subject himself to others, who can cause or prevent what he desires or wants to avoid: if, finally, *when he rises in the morning,* he observes to keep these rules; bathes and eats as a man of integrity and honour; and thus, in every matter that befalls him, puts his guiding principles to work, just as the runner does in the business of running, or the voice-trainer in the training of voices: this is the man who is truly making progress [in Stoicism], this is the man who has not travelled in vain.

(*Discourses*, 1.4.18–21, modified; *italics added*)

Elsewhere, referring to the Pythagorean exercise, Epictetus provides examples of the kind of questions that should be rehearsed in contemplative inner dialogue each morning upon awakening. In order to follow the Stoic precept to make the right use of one's impressions, and cognitions, one should meditate upon such questions as: "What do I need in order to be free from irrational emotions, and to enjoy peace of mind?" One should also meditate each morning upon the existential question "What am I?", apparently following the precept to "know thyself". Each morning, Stoic students should remind themselves of the evidence that they are not merely to be identified with their property or reputation, but, rather, that their nature is essentially that of a "rational animal" (*Discourses*, 4.6.34).

Having reviewed the virtues of his friends and family, and paid homage to the gods, Marcus Aurelius opens his *The Meditations* with the following advice to himself. It seems not only that this is the start of the book but also the type of contemplation with which he started each day:

When you wake up in the morning, tell yourself: The people I deal with today will be meddling, ungrateful, arrogant, dishonest, jealous, and surly. They are like this because they can't tell good from bad. But I have seen the beauty of good, and the ugliness of evil, and have recognised that the wrongdoer has a nature related to my own – not of the same blood or birth, but the same mind, and possessing a share of the divine. And so none of them can hurt me. No one can implicate me in ugliness. Nor can I feel angry at my relative, or hate him. We were born to work together like feet, hands, and eyes, like the two rows of teeth, upper and lower. To obstruct each other is unnatural.

(*Meditations*, 2.1)

Marcus is talking about rehearsing both the basic dogma of Stoicism, "follow nature", and the prospect of encountering the most challenging individuals imaginable, the worst-case scenario. This kind of mental exercise might be compared to the boxer who trains for a fight by punching a heavy bag. The philosopher exerts himself against something *resistant*, against the mental image of impending misfortune. The specific practise of mentally rehearsing philosophical principles in the face of anticipated *adversity*, in the imagination, is one of the cardinal techniques of classical philosophical-therapy, as we shall see.

Hence, philosophers of different schools seem to have employed a variety of practises designed to coincide with awakening in the morning and also upon retiring to bed in the evening. It seems that in the morning, in addition to isolated meditation, the Pythagoreans also practised some kind of mental rehearsal of the day ahead in which they prepared for challenges by rehearsing appropriate philosophical precepts. This was complemented by a practise employed before going to sleep, which involved reviewing the whole preceding day from beginning to end, three times, in order to improve the memory but also to provide an opportunity for contemplative self-analysis. We may, therefore, discern two complementary periods of contemplation in ancient philosophical therapy, which might be termed "*prospective*" and "*retrospective*" meditation.

Retrospective meditation

Indeed, Marcus Aurelius, Epictetus, and Seneca all refer to a second Pythagorean meditation that was practised before retiring to sleep. Seneca describes the method as taught by a philosopher called Quintus Sextius who founded a philosophical sect at Rome around 50 BC known as the School of the Sextii, which combined elements of Stoicism and Neopythagoreanism.

Our soul ought to be brought up for examination daily. It was the custom of Sextius when the day was over, and he had betaken himself to rest, to inquire of his spirit: "What bad habit of yours have you cured today? what vice have you checked? in what respect are you better?" Anger will cease, and become more gentle, if it knows that every day it will have to appear before the judgment seat. What can be more admirable than this fashion of discussing the whole of the day's events? how sweet is the sleep which follows this self-examination? how calm, how sound, and careless is it when our spirit has either received praise or reprimand, and when our secret inquisitor and censor has made his report about our morals? I make use of this privilege, and daily plead my cause before myself: when the lamp is taken out of my sight, and my wife, who knows my habit, has ceased to talk, I pass the whole day in review before myself, and repeat all that I have said and done: I conceal nothing from myself, and omit nothing: for why should I be afraid of any of my shortcomings, when it is in my power to say, "I pardon you this time: see that you never do that anymore?"

(*On Anger*, 3.36, modified)

Some scholars claim that the Pythagoreans, who believed in reincarnation, employed this method to improve memory and thereby aid the recollection of past lives. Cicero mentions it as a training exercise for improving memory in old age:

after the manner of the Pythagoreans – to keep my memory in working order – I repeat in the evening whatever I have said, heard, or done in the course of each day. These are the exercises of the intellect, these the training-grounds of the mind.

(Cicero, *On Old Age*, 11, modified)

In any case, the Stoics clearly employed retrospective contemplation primarily as a method of daily self-analysis, similar to the kind found in modern CBT. Presumably, therefore, if a philosopher concluded that he had acted badly or failed to follow his principles, on awakening the next morning he would take account of this and redouble his efforts to prepare for similar challenges ahead. Iamblichus describes these Pythagorean exercises as follows:

Pythagoras ordered them never to do anything without previous deliberation and discussion, in the morning forming a plan of what was to be done later, and at night to review the day's actions, which served the double purpose of strengthening the memory, and considering their conduct.

(Iamblichus, *Life of Pythagoras*)

Moreover, the Pythagoreans' mental preparation took account of any possible catastrophes which might befall them, in order to cultivate a Stoic-like sense of being "ready for anything". "It was a precept of theirs that no human casualties ought to be unexpected by the intelligent, expecting everything which is not in their power to prevent", Iamblichus adds. His own philosophical teacher, Porphyry, provides a more detailed description:

He [Pythagoras] advised that special regard should be given to two times of the day: the one when we go to sleep, and the other when we awake. At each of these we should consider [respectively] our past actions, and those that are to come. We ought to require of ourselves an account of our past deeds, while of the future we should have a providential care.

Therefore he advised everybody to repeat to himself the following verses before he fell asleep,

> Nor suffer sleep to close thine eyes
> Till thrice thy acts that day thou has run o'er;
> How slip? What deeds? What duty left undone?
> And on rising, the following:
> As soon as ere thou wakest, in order lay The actions to be done that fol-
> lowing day.

(Porphyry, Life of Pythagoras, 40)

A few lines earlier, the *Golden Verses* clearly state that "The highest duty is honour to self", from which it seems logically to follow that each evening the Pythagorean examined primarily whether he had let *himself* down in any respect that day, and how he could better fulfil his duty to care for himself in the future. This suggests that self-analysis centred on asking whether one's actions contributed toward one's "peace of mind", or happiness, mental health (*eudaimonia*), and enlightenment (*sophia*).

The Stoic Epictetus also quotes these lines approvingly (*Discourses*, 3.10.3). Elsewhere, he comments on the actions of the philosopher throughout his day, saying that they should be reviewed at night, and he interprets the Pythagorean prescription as follows:

> To these he transfers the Pythagorean precept "Let not sleep approach thy weary eyes . . . " "*Where did I transgress*: in matters of flattery? *What did I do*? Could it be that I acted as a free man, as a noble-spirited man?" If he discovers any such action, he rebukes and accuses himself. "What business did you have to say that? For could you not have lied? Even the philosophers say there is nothing to stop one telling a lie". . . . Go over your actions. "*Where did I transgress*: in relation to peace of mind? *What did I do* that was unfriendly, or unsociable, or inconsiderate? *What have I failed to do that I ought to have done* with regard to these matters?"

(Discourses, 4.6.32–33)

To clarify, according to this passage and others, before falling asleep each night, the Pythagorean philosopher mentally reviews his acts from the preceding day three times. In doing so, he repeatedly asks himself, with reference to his peace of mind and ultimate well-being, what errors he has made in his behaviour, what he has done well, and what he has neglected or avoided doing. Following this, on awakening the next morning at daybreak, he first gives praise to the rising Sun, the symbol of Apollo, a patron god of philosophy. He then mentally rehearses the day ahead, carefully planning his actions in advance, presumably taking account of any lessons learned from the previous night's mental review and preparing himself in advance to face adversity.

The line from the famous *Golden Verses of Pythagoras*, used by Porphry and translated by Guthrie as "How slip? What deeds? What duty left undone?", seems to describe a process of self-analysis falling into three, quite logical, categories:

1   The philosopher mentally reviews errors that he has made during the day, disputing his own actions.
2   He recounts things done well and praises himself for them, reinforcing his own constructive behaviour.
3   Alternative behaviour is planned, that is, what should have been done instead.

One might regard this as resembling modern problem-solving methods in CBT, as the Pythagoreans and Stoics could also be said, in modern jargon, to be reviewing the pros and cons of their own behaviour and generating alternative solutions to be implemented the following day.

If it really originated with Pythagoras and his followers, that would suggest a living tradition of European philosophers employing this contemplative strategy as part of a daily self-help regime which may have spanned many centuries, perhaps even a thousand years. However, of these two practises, morning and evening, it is the premeditation of future events, typically conducted at daybreak, which seems to hold both the most interest for ancient philosophers and the most pertinence for modern CBT.

Chapter 11

Praemeditatio malorum and mental rehearsal

Aequam memento rebus in arduis servare mentem. [Remember to keep a calm and balanced mind in the face of adversity.]

– (Horace, *Odes*, 2.3)

When asked what benefit he had obtained from philosophy, Diogenes the Cynic reputedly said, "If no other, at least this, that I am prepared for every kind of fortune" (Diogenes Laertius, *Lives*, 6.2). The problem of how to prepare oneself in advance to cope with misfortune was something with which all schools of philosophy wrestled and concerning which they all attempted to provide practical guidance.

The Stoic technique of premeditation

One of the most fundamental techniques of classical philosophical therapy was the method known as *praemeditatio malorum*, which means preparing the mind in advance to cope with adversity. For simplicity, we can refer to this notion simply as "philosophical premeditation".

Hadot considers *praemeditatio malorum* to be one of the best-known Stoic spiritual exercises, translating it as the "pre-exercise of evils" (Hadot, 2002, p. 137). He describes it as an exercise intended to "prepare us for facing trials" in life, by imagining in advance various difficulties, reversals of fortune, sufferings, and even death.

> Philo of Alexandria says that those who practice *praemeditatio* do not flinch beneath the blows of Fate, because they have calculated its attacks in advance; for of those things which happen against our will, even the most painful are lessened by foresight, when our thought no longer encounters anything unexpected in events but dulls the perception of them, as if they were, old, worn-out things.
>
> (*ibid.*)

Elsewhere, Hadot provides an overview of the *praemeditatio malorum* technique, which he relates to the practise of morning and evening meditation (Hadot, 1995, p. 85). He describes it as allowing us to be ready whenever unexpected or dramatic circumstances happen. We are to imagine ourselves undergoing poverty, suffering, and even death. "We must confront life's difficulties face to face", says Hadot, "remembering that they are not evils, since they do not depend on us" (*ibid.*). In order to benefit from this exercise, though, we must first "engrave striking maxims in our memory", which will allow us to accept such events, dreaded by the majority of people, as natural and ultimately indifferent. Stoic maxims and sayings must be kept ready "at hand", which remind us of the persuasive arguments (*epilogismoi*) capable of correcting our response to difficult circumstances and checking the passions of fear, anger, sadness, or excessive desire.

> First thing in the morning, we should go over in advance what we have to do during the course of the day, and decide on the principles which will guide and inspire our actions. In the evening, we should examine ourselves again, so as to be aware of the faults we have committed or the progress we have made.
>
> (*ibid.*)

For the Stoic, the central dogma, the distinction between freedom and nature, or that which is our responsibility and that which is not, is the standard by which all specific incidents are judged and the basis for premeditation. However, this core principle can be supported by a wide range of specific verbal arguments defined in relation to any given specific challenge.

As Hadot also observes, the following passage from Book Ten of Plato's *Republic* appears to prefigure later Stoic remedies. In it, Socrates recommends that we prepare ourselves through philosophical training to maintain a calmness in adversity by recalling a number of Stoic-sounding maxims, such as the principle that it does us more harm than good to indulge in complaining to ourselves or others.

> The law [of reason] says, doesn't it, that it is best to keep as quiet as possible in misfortunes and not get excited about them? First, it isn't clear whether such things will turn out to be good or bad in the end; second, it doesn't make the future any better to take them hard; third, human affairs aren't worth taking very seriously; and finally, grief prevents the very thing we most need in such circumstances from coming into play as quickly as possible.
>
> (*Republic*, 604b – d)

When asked what he means by "the thing most needed", Socrates replies:

> Deliberation. We must accept what has happened as we would the fall of the dice, and then arrange our affairs in whatever way reason determines to be

best. We mustn't hug the hurt part and spend our time weeping and wailing like children when they trip. Instead, we should always accustom our souls to turn as quickly as possible to healing the disease and putting the disaster right, replacing lamentation with cure.

(ibid.)

The technique of premeditation essentially consists in visualizing a future catastrophe as if it were happening now and restoring emotional calm by repeating appropriate principles of living, that is, rational arguments and coping statements. These principles are usually called "dogmas", or "precepts", but also referred to as maxims, formulas, sayings, etc., and symbolically described as the "weapons" of the Stoic warrior. The Cynic Antisthenes, an early forerunner of the Stoics, likewise said that "Virtue is a weapon of which man cannot be deprived" (Diogenes Laertius, *Lives*, 6.1). A well-known fable of Aesop, who lived long before the first recorded philosophers in the sixth or seventh century BC, puts the notion beautifully. A wild boar was sharpening his tusks against a tree when a fox came by and asked him why he was doing this. "I don't see the reason", remarked the fox, "there are no hunters nor hounds in sight. In fact, right now I can't see any threat at all". "True", replied the boar, "but when danger does arise, I'll have other things on my mind than sharpening my weapons".

There are countless references to the concept of mental preparation in classical philosophy, poetry, and literature. It is perhaps one of the most characteristic techniques of Stoic psychotherapy, and Seneca expresses it in terms that echo this proverb of Aesop:

> It is in times of security that the spirit should be preparing itself to deal with difficult times; while fortune is bestowing favours on it then is the time for it to be strengthened against her rebuffs. In the midst of peace, the soldier carries out manoeuvres, throws up earthworks against a non-existent enemy and tires himself out with unnecessary toil in order to be equal to it when it is necessary. If you want a man to keep his head when the crisis comes, you must give him some training before it comes.

(Letters, 18)

In time of peace, prepare for war. Here, Seneca is referring to the practise of enduring hardship to prepare oneself for the possibility of a reversal of future, but his words extend to Stoic mental rehearsal as well. This attitude was common to most other schools, including the Epicureans, whose sayings, for example, exclaim:

> I have anticipated you, Fortune, and have barred your means of entry. Neither to you nor to any other circumstance shall we hand ourselves over as captives.

(Vatican Sayings, 47)

Indeed, Epictetus goes so far as to define practical philosophy specifically in terms of this ability, "But what is it to study philosophy? Is it not to prepare yourself for future events?" (*Discourses*, 3.10.6). It is, perhaps, because of the centrality of mental preparation to classical philosophy that, in modern usage, the adjectives, "Stoical" and "philosophical" can both be used to mean the same thing: "calm in the face of adversity".

The twentieth century French philosopher, Foucault, had a great interest in this area and discusses classical philosophical meditation at length in one of his last lectures. He describes the *praemeditatio malorum* of the Stoics as a psychothera-peutic procedure divided into three distinct components:

> *First*, it is not a question of imagining the future as it is likely to turn out but to imagine the worst that can happen, even if there's little chance it will turn out that way – the worst as certainty, as actualising what could happen, not as calculation of probability.
>
> *Second*, one shouldn't envisage things as possibly taking place in the distant future but as already actual and in the process of taking place. For example, imagining not that one might be exiled but rather that one is already exiled, subjected to torture, and dying.
>
> *Third*, one does this not in order to experience inarticulate sufferings but in order to convince oneself that they are not real ills. The reduction of all that is possible, of all the duration and of all the misfortunes, reveals not some-thing bad but what we have to accept. (Foucault, 1988, p. 36)

Through *praemeditatio malorum*, we are able to employ our current mental resources, calmly meditating upon relevant maxims or affirmations, while antici-pating a future event.

As Foucault notes, the Stoics divided their exercises into *meditatio*, a word that can mean both "preparation" and "meditation", and *gymnasia*, practical training through activity. "While *meditatio* is an imaginary experience that trains thought, *gymnasia* is training in a real situation, even if it's been artificially induced" (*ibid.*, p. 37).

The same distinction is found in modern CBT, where exposure to stressful events can be either *in vitro* (in the laboratory of the mind) or *in vivo* (in everyday life), that is, in imagination or through behavioural assignments in the real world. A person can confront a fear of enclosed spaces, for example, first of all by imag-ining themselves in a place such as a lift, and, subsequently, when they are able, by placing themselves in certain confined situations in reality, which is normally done in progressive steps, moving from the least to the most challenging types of situation.

Indeed, on close inspection, the premeditation technique seems to have a num-ber of subtle implications. It allows the Stoic to condition his memory so that he is more likely to recall his rules of life and rational arguments in the right place, at the right time, even in the face of adversity and under stress. It also leads to the contemplation of impermanence, and the transience of the present state of affairs, by anticipation of future changes in fortune.

> When practicing it, philosophers not only wished to dull the shock of reality; they also wanted to steep themselves thoroughly in the truths of Stoicism and restore their inner tranquillity and peace of mind. We must not be afraid to think in advance about events which other people consider unfortunate. On the contrary, we are to think of them often, in order to tell ourselves, above all, that future evils are not evils, because they do not depend on us, and do not pertain to morality. The thought of an imminent death also transforms our way of acting in a radical way, by forcing us to become aware of the infinite value of each instant: "We must accomplish each of life's actions as if it were the last" (*Meditations*, 2.5). With the exercise of foreseeing evils and foreseeing death, we shift almost unnoticeably from practiced philosophy to practiced ethics. Such foresight is intimately linked to action, as practiced by Stoic philosophers. When they act, they foresee all obstacles, and nothing happens contrary to their expectations. Their moral intention remains whole, even if obstacles arise.
>
> (Hadot, 2002, p. 137)

In this dense passage, Hadot alludes to the intersection of premeditation with other Stoic exercises, such as the separation of inner and outer, the contemplation of death, attention to the present moment, and the Stoic "reserve clause".

Indeed, ancient philosophers, unlike most modern therapists, took this notion to the extreme. As Foucault writes, "The meditation on death is the culmination of all these exercises" (1988). The Stoics reasoned that if they could overcome their fear of future events in this way, they should focus upon conquering man's greatest fear. Hence, the philosophical technique of the meditation on death (*melete thanatou*) can be seen as the ultimate form of the *praemeditatio malorum*. As noted earlier, Epictetus mentions the fact that Roman generals had servants who whispered *memento mori* ("remember thou must die") in their ears to help them moderate their pride during the celebration of a triumph. However, the contemplation of one's own mortality is not meant to evoke a morbid or melancholic state. The ideal of the Stoic sage, exemplified by Socrates, was both to love life and yet be unafraid of death. "A person who has learned how to meet his death", writes Seneca, "has unlearned how to be a slave" (*Letters*, 26).

Mental rehearsal in Beck's cognitive therapy

One example of a similar technique in modern cognitive therapy can be found in certain versions of what Beck calls "cognitive rehearsal". For instance, Beck and his colleagues recommended targeting suicidal thoughts directly in some cases by identifying possible stressful situations which require problem-solving and employing what they call "cognitive rehearsal", or "forced fantasy" (Beck, Rush,

Shaw, & Emery, 1979, p. 223). This technique comprises three steps followed by the client:

1   To imagine themselves in a desperate and challenging situation.
2   To allow themselves to experience their typical sense of despair and suicidal thoughts.
3   To combat this by forcefully rehearsing the generation of possible solutions to the problem, despite their negative feelings.

They compare this to the "stress-inoculation" method of Donald Meichenbaum, an earlier cognitive-behavioural approach that also involves anticipating problem situations in imagination and systematically rehearsing better ways of thinking about them and coping behaviourally.

Indeed, Beck and his colleagues describe a variety of different mental imagery techniques that could be compared to those found in classical philosophy (Beck, Emery, & Greenberg, 2005, pp. 210ff.). In particular, they borrow a mental imagery technique called "repeated review", or "emotional review", from an early cognitive psychotherapist, called Victor Raimy, which is similar to the premeditation technique described by the Stoics and others (Raimy, 1975). In this technique, the client is simply asked to repeatedly visualize some distressing event, such as an anticipated catastrophe, as if it is happening now. People who take time to deliberately visualize events in a repetitive manner often report spontaneous reduction in their anxiety and changes in their perspective and attitude.

Beck and his colleagues suggest that, put crudely, the cognitive model of anxiety suggests that the client has the underlying belief that: "Something bad is going to happen that I won't be able to handle" (Beck, Emery, & Greenberg, 2005, p. 201). Patiently reviewing feared events in imagination, when in a "rational mode" of thinking, can lead the client to make repeated spontaneous reality checks, giving an opportunity for anxious thoughts to modify themselves in gradual adaptation to the reality of the situation being envisaged. Often, this may take the form of a gradual realization that risks have been inflated, or one's ability to solve problems has been neglected or under-utilized. Beck and his colleagues are particularly interested in the shift from unrealistic or catastrophic thinking about the future to more realistic appraisals of threat, but they also recognize that anxious feelings (affect) may frequently appear to reduce during this kind of mental rehearsal, often termed "imaginal exposure", without any obvious changes in cognition or the content of the imagery, through a process of "emotional habituation", as behaviour therapists have long observed (Beck, Emery, & Greenberg, 2005, p. 216; Wolpe, 1990).

Raimy saw this method as implicit to many traditional forms of psychotherapy, which, in some shape or form, require clients to repeatedly revisit disturbing events in their imagination, either through visualization, role-play, or verbal discussion. However, he concluded that mental imagery provided the most efficient means of repeated reviewing emotional events, and this is the method adopted by

Beck and his colleagues. They describe, for instance, how one patient was helped to become more Stoical and accepting of old age:

> By reviewing what he fears, the patient is able to start to accept the possibility of the feared event. In the reviewing process, he is counteracting his avoidance tendency. At the start of one review, the patient, who was afraid of growing old, thought, "It's too terrible to face. I can't believe this is happening". Later she was able to imagine directly, with minimal anxiety, what it would be like to be old. The reviewing process gets the patient to face the reality of the situation and makes it easier to accept.
>
> (Beck, Emery, & Greenberg, 2005, p. 250)

Indeed, they observe that this kind of repeated review could easily be confused with morbid rumination or worry, the crucial difference being, however, that in this case it is deliberate and involves concrete imagery rather than abstract verbal discursive thought.

It may be that the most important component of this approach is that it involves facing one's fears systematically, repeatedly, and in concrete visual terms, something that might be described as a kind of "avoidance-reversal" technique in psychotherapy. "One way of approaching the problem of avoidance in anxiety is to encourage the patient to visualize anxiety-producing situations in the office" (*ibid.*, p. 258). Likewise, Beck and his colleagues also observe that repeated review, *à la* Raimy, tends to lead the client to progressively face and accept the reality of certain situations and see it in a larger context (*ibid.*, p. 250). Certainly, that concept would appear close to the heart of the Stoic prescription to calmly meditate upon future adversity. The Stoics appear to have deliberately rehearsed their verbal precepts while contemplating, in imagination, future adversity, in addition to allowing spontaneous changes in cognition and affect to occur. However, cognitive therapists, following Meichenbaum's influential research on "self-instruction" methods, have also assimilated the use of short phrases or instructions, like the Stoic precepts, which may be mentally rehearsed before facing the problematic situations in reality (*ibid.*, pp. 269–270).

Rational emotive imagery (REI) and multimodal therapy (MMT)

In one of the first books on REBT, Ellis provided a detailed account of common irrational ideas that cause emotional disturbance. He listed among them the idea that if something is dangerous or fearsome, then one should be concerned about it and dwell upon it continually (Ellis, 1962, p. 75). Modern CBT, in general, views irrational worry as often motivated and maintained by the implicit assumption, or "metacognition", that it is potentially helpful to dwell upon our fears. We feel that we need to give our attention to our worries but in doing so we often simply become *more* worried and achieve nothing positive. By contrast, the "work of worrying" can be done productively only when we face our fears calmly and systematically, with our focus upon rational problem solving, or at least resigning ourselves to coping as best we can.

Ellis developed an early cognitive-behavioural technique known as rational emotive imagery (REI), which allows the client to face their fears in a more constructive manner and this is the main imagery technique used in his approach to therapy. There are a number of variations; however, the basic formula can be described as follows. REI helps the client to question the validity of negative cognitions. An anticipated activating event (A) is pictured, as if happening now, while the client mentally rehearses changing his negative emotions and behavioural reactions (C) by swapping his negative cognition (B) for a positive one. Ellis describes the technique in the following words in his advice to patients:

> Use rational emotive imagery to vividly imagine unpleasant activating events before they happen; let yourself feel unhealthily upset (anxious, depressed, enraged, or guilty) as you imagine them; then work on your feelings to change them to appropriate emotions (concern, sadness, healthy anger, or remorse) as you keep imagining some of the worst things happening. Don't give up until you actually do change your feelings.
>
> (Ellis & MacLaren, 2005, pp. 125–126)

This is achieved as follows, according to some REBT practitioners:

> the client is instructed to imagine a feared situation and simultaneously repeats very forcefully to herself (either aloud or internally depending upon the situation) a previously negotiated helpful coping statement. This helps clients to experience less anxiety and prepares them for difficult situations or it can be used to help them deal with how they behaved in an earlier situation.
>
> (Curwen, Palmer, & Ruddell, 2000, pp. 119–120)

Arnold Lazarus, the founder of multimodal therapy (MMT), an early form of CBT that combined elements of Ellis' rational therapy and Wolpe's behaviour therapy, described a number of mental imagery techniques that resemble Stoic premeditation. For example, one method, termed "anti-future shock imagery", is described as follows:

> By taking stock of the most probable changes that are likely to occur, and by encouraging the client to *visualise* himself or herself coping with these changes, you facilitate the client's acceptance of the inevitable. These "emotional fire-drills" tend to reduce relapse rates.
>
> (Lazarus, 1981, p. 242)

Lazarus' notion of "emotional fire-drills" to prepare for future shocks echoes many Stoic passages; for example, Seneca responds to a terrible calamity suffered by one of his friends with the following advice to his student, Lucilius:

> What is quite unlooked for is more crushing in its effect, and unexpectedness adds to the weight of a disaster. The fact that it was unforeseen has never failed to intensify a person's grief. This is a reason for ensuring that nothing ever takes us by surprise. We should project our thoughts ahead of us at every turn and have in mind every possible eventuality instead of only the usual course of events. . . . This is why we need to envisage every possibility and to strengthen the spirit to deal with the things which may conceivably come about. Rehearse them in your mind: exile, torture, war, shipwreck.
>
> (*Letters*, 91)

Clearly, the Stoics had wrestled with the problem of sudden, unexpected calamities, and the use of mental rehearsal (premeditation) to systematically envisage coping with a range of setbacks, well in advance, was their main therapeutic strategy in this regard.

The basic underlying notion in most of these mental exposure techniques is sometimes expressed in the acronym "FEAR" by modern psychotherapists: "Face Everything And Recover". By patiently and systematically confronting our fears, and accepting the situation, anxiety and other negative feelings will usually recede. The mere act of confronting fears in reality or in imagination is usually known as "exposure therapy". It naturally leads to "emotional habituation", getting used to the situation and a corresponding reduction in the level of nervous arousal and distress.

However, another benefit of facing fears has been highlighted by cognitive therapists, especially Beck (1976). Doing so provides us with an opportunity to reality-check our preconceptions, and to test new ways of thinking about things in order to cope with them, a process often termed "cognitive restructuring". Hence, a useful variation of the acronym FEAR is "False Evidence Appearing Real", which alludes to the role of thinking errors and unfounded assumptions in emotional disturbance. As most of our fears are mediated by cognitive distortions, it follows that the problem situation itself is seldom as inherently frightening or catastrophic as it first appears.

Spinoza: remedia affectuum (remedies for the emotions)

In the seventeenth century, the Dutch philosopher Spinoza produced a hugely influential work called the *Ethics*. Spinoza was greatly influenced by classical Greek and Roman literature on philosophical therapy and has, with some justification, been called *more* Stoic than the Stoics. He recommended that "precepts", or "rules of living", effectively affirmations similar to the Stoic precepts, should be internalized and associated with challenging events. In the fifth book of the *Ethics*, he describes the use of such verbal precepts in association with mental imagery, to rehearse coping with future adversity.

> The best we can do, therefore, so long as we do not possess a perfect knowledge of our emotions, is to frame a system of right conduct, or fixed practical precepts, to commit it to memory, and to apply it forthwith to the particular circumstances which now and again meet us in life, so that our imagination may become fully imbued therewith, and that it may be always ready to our hand.
>
> (*Ethics*, Prop. 10, note)

Again, like the Stoics, Spinoza suggests that we mentally prepare for the typical problems that people are likely to encounter in life:

> Now, that this precept of reason may be always ready to our hand in time of need, we should often think over and reflect upon the wrongs generally committed by men, and in what manner and way they may be best warded off by [the appropriate rules of living]: we shall thus associate the idea [i.e., the mental image] of wrong with the idea of this precept, which accordingly will always be ready for use when a wrong is done to us.
>
> (*ibid.*)

He first of all addresses the problem of irrational anger, and the principles which help us to moderate it in this way, adding:

> if the anger which springs from a grievous wrong be not overcome easily, it will nevertheless be overcome, though not without an inner conflict, far sooner than if we had not thus reflected on the subject beforehand.
>
> (*ibid.*)

From anger he proceeds to discuss the conquest of fear,

> We should, in the same way, reflect on courage as a means of overcoming fear; the ordinary dangers of life should frequently be brought to mind and imagined, together with the means whereby through readiness of resource and strength of mind we can avoid and overcome them.
>
> (*ibid.*)

He concludes this section on emotional remedies with an encouraging word for the student:

> Whosoever will diligently observe and practice these precepts (which indeed are not difficult) will verily, in a short space of time, be able, for the most part, to direct his actions according to the commandments of reason.
>
> (*ibid.*)

In many ways, Spinoza's great metaphysical endeavour represents a final resurgence of classical antiquity in the realm of psychotherapy. His grand system is difficult to penetrate but may still hold considerable value for a rational modern psychotherapy.

Russell: *The Conquest of Happiness*

The influence of the Stoic tradition can clearly be seen in the writings of Bertrand Russell, one of the most important philosophers of the twentieth century. Russell greatly admired Spinoza and had studied his writings in depth. He subsequently wrote one of the earliest modern self-help books, *The Conquest of Happiness* (1930), which contains ideas that seem influenced by Spinoza and possibly the Stoics. For instance, Russell describes a philosophical method of overcoming anxiety and worry, indistinguishable from the *praemeditatio malorum*, which was noted by Beck and his colleagues in their manual of cognitive therapy for anxiety (Beck, Emery, & Greenberg, 2005, p. 220). Russell also provides, arguably, one of the most lucid explanations of exposure therapy for which one could wish:

> Worry is a form of fear, and all forms of fear produce fatigue. A man who has learnt not to feel fear will find the fatigue of daily life greatly diminished. Now fear, in its most harmful form arises where there is some danger which we are unwilling to face. At odd moments horrible thoughts dart into our minds; what they are depends upon the person, but almost everybody has some kind of lurking fear.
>
> (Russell, 1930, p. 60)

Russell provides his own examples, but he emphasizes that this technique is part of a very general one for overcoming fear of all kinds:

> Probably all these people employ the wrong technique for dealing with their fear; whenever it comes into their mind, they try to think of something else; they distract their thoughts with amusement or work, or what not. Now every kind of fears grows worse by not being looked at. The effort of turning away one's thoughts is a tribute to the horribleness of the spectre from which one is averting one's gaze; the proper course with every kind of fear is to think about it rationally and calmly, but with great concentration, until it becomes completely familiar. In the end familiarity will blunt its terrors; the whole subject will become boring, and our thoughts will turn away from it, not, as formerly, by an effort of will, but through mere lack of interest in the topic. When you find yourself inclined to brood on anything, no matter what, the best plan always is to think about it even more than you naturally would until at last its morbid fascination is worn off.
>
> (*ibid.*)

He provides the following explanation of the technique itself:

> When some misfortune threatens, consider seriously and deliberately what
> is the very worst that could possibly happen. Having looked this possible
> misfortune in the face, give yourself sound reasons for thinking that after all
> it would be no such very terrible disaster. Such reasons always exist, since at
> the worst nothing that happens to oneself has any cosmic importance. When
> you have looked for some time steadily at the worst possibility and have said
> to yourself with real conviction, "Well, after all, that would not matter so
> very much", you will find that your worry diminishes to a quite extraordinary
> extent. It may be necessary to repeat the process a few times, but in the end, if
> you have shirked nothing in facing the worst possible issue, you will find that
> your worry disappears altogether, and is replaced by a kind of exhilaration.
>
> (*ibid.*, pp. 59–60)

This is the basic principle of habituation or extinction of anxiety through repeated
exposure to a feared event. Russell's compellingly articulate comments may well
have had some influence over early behaviour therapists and subsequent cognitive
therapy.

The ancient origins of premeditation

Within the Stoic literature itself, as we have seen, Seneca discusses the exercise
of mental preparation many times in relation to distressing life events. He advises
that we should "rehearse before our mind" every possible calamity, as a kind of
emotional fire-drill, to borrow Lazarus' phrase.

> All the terms of our human lot should be before our eyes; we should be antici-
> pating not merely all that commonly happens but all that is conceivably capa-
> ble of happening, if we do not want to be overwhelmed and struck numb by
> rare events as if they were unprecedented ones; fortune needs envisaging in a
> thoroughly comprehensive way.
>
> (*Letters*, 91)

Perhaps this sounds alarmist, as cognitive therapists also advise their clients to
be careful not to be too much on the outlook for threats, or to inflate the prob-
ability of danger – common thinking errors among the anxious. However, Seneca
immediately proceeds to emphasize that Stoic contemplation of the transience of
things should moderate our anxiety. He is assuming that the Stoic will proceed
calmly and contemplatively, questioning the realism of the perceived threats and
evaluating his ability to cope. "So let us face up to the blows of circumstance and
be aware that whatever happens is never as serious as rumour makes it out to be".
The emphasis throughout Stoic literature is upon rationality and realism, and that
extends to the contemplation of future adversity: "So the spirit must be trained to a

realization and an acceptance of its lot". With regard to such blows of fate, which were common risks during his lifetime, Seneca writes:

Escape them you cannot, scorn them you can. And scorn them you will if by constant reflection you have anticipated future happenings. Everyone faces up more bravely to a thing for which he has long prepared himself, sufferings, even, being withstood if they have been trained for in advance. Those who are unprepared, on the other hand, are panic-stricken by the most insignificant happenings. We must see to it that nothing takes us by surprise. And since it is invariably unfamiliarity that makes a thing more formidable than it really is, this habit of continual reflection will ensure that no form of adversity finds you a complete beginner.

(*Letters*, 107)

The Platonist, Plutarch, writes in his essay *On Contentment*,

Whoever it was who said, "Fortune, I have made a pre-emptive strike against you, and I have deprived you of every single loophole", was not basing his confidence on bolts, locks and fortifications, but on principles and arguments which are available to anyone who wants them. And this kind of argument should not induce any degree of resignation or disbelief, but admiration, emulation, enthusiasm, and investigation and observation of oneself in relatively trivial circumstances, to prepare oneself for the more important matters, so that one does not avoid them or divert one's mind from attention to them or take refuge in excuses like "That's probably the most difficult thing I'll ever come across". For if the mind is self-indulgent, and takes the easiest courses all the time, and retreats from unwelcome matters to what maximizes its pleasure, the consequence is weakness and feebleness born of lack of exertion; but a mind which trains and strains itself to use rationality to conceive an image of illness and pain and exile will find that there is plenty of unreality, superficiality and unsoundness in the apparent problems and horrors each of them has to offer, as detailed rational argument demonstrates.

(*On Contentment*, 476c)

Plutarch seems to point to certain irrational thoughts of surprise as the cause of anxiety:

The point is that, if anything happens which may be unwelcome, but is not unexpected, this kind of preparedness and character leaves no room for "I couldn't have imagined it" and "This isn't what I'd hoped for" and "I didn't expect this", and so stops the heart lurching and beating fast and so on, and quickly settles derangement and disturbance back on to a foundation. Carneades [the sceptical Platonic philosopher] used to remind people who were involved in important affairs that unexpectedness is the be-all and end-all of distress and discontent.

(*ibid.*)

He adds, "distress can be avoided by the beneficial practise of training oneself to gain the ability to look straight at fortune with open eyes".

In a similar vein, Marcus Aurelius opens his *Mediations* with a record of his use of mental preparation:

> When you wake up in the morning, tell yourself: The people I deal with today will be meddling, ungrateful, arrogant, dishonest, jealous and surly. They are like this because they can't tell good from evil.

(*Meditations*, 2.1)

It might be better to say that the people he expects to meet are fallible, and may well be irrational, but that he can better understand their behaviour as being based upon ignorance rather than malice. He also reminds himself to see all mankind as a brotherhood. He proceeds to rehearse his coping strategies, the beliefs which will help him see things more constructively

> And so none of them can hurt me. No one can implicate me in ugliness. Nor can I feel angry at my relative, or hate him. We were born to work together like feet, hands, and eyes, like the two rows of teeth, upper and lower. To obstruct each other is unnatural. To feel anger at someone, to turn your back on him: these are obstructions.

(*Meditations*, 2.1)

He makes it clear that his mental preparation involves having his principles "ready to hand". "Take no enterprise in hand at haphazard, or without regard to the principles governing its proper execution" (*Meditations*, 4.2). These are the Stoic principles discussed elsewhere. As we shall see in the following chapter, however, the Stoics' attitude to the future is also mediated by the special philosophical principle, known as the "reserve clause", which shapes their perception of things by mitigating emotional attachments.

Chapter 12

Stoic fatalism, determinism, and acceptance

> Whatever sorrow the fate of the Gods may here send us Bear, whatever may
> strike you, with patience unmurmuring; To relieve it, so far as you can, is
> permitted, But reflect that not much misfortune has Fate given to the good.
>
> — (*The Golden Verses of Pythagoras*)

Psychotherapists, mainly those influenced by *existential* philosophy, have from
time to time suggested that emphasizing awareness of human free will may be of
therapeutic value (Frankl, 1959). However, by contrast, philosophical therapists
in the Socratic tradition, running from the Stoics all the way down to Spinoza and
Dubois, have argued that contemplating the idea of universal causal determinism
tends to have a more pronounced therapeutic effect upon the emotions.

The contemplation of determinism in rational psychotherapy

Dubois was perhaps the first modern rational psychotherapist to explicitly argue
that emotional problems could be made worse by certain, often unspoken, philosophical assumptions about free will and determinism that prevail in modern
society.

> Patience towards unavoidable events, depending neither upon us nor upon
> others, is synonymous with *fatalism*; it is a virtue, and it is the only stand
> to take in face of the inevitable. . . . The idea of necessity is enough for the
> philosopher. We are all in the same situation towards things as they are, and
> towards things that we cannot change. The advantage will always lie with
> him who, for some reason or other, knows how to resign himself tranquilly.
>
> (Dubois, 1909, pp. 240–241)

This notion is derived from the Stoic literature. In the *Handbook*, Epictetus
boldly asserts that if we merely train ourselves in wishing things to happen as

they do, instead of expecting them to happen as we wish, then our lives will go smoothly (*Encheiridion*, 8). In the *Discourses*, he actually defines the practise of philosophy in terms of such acceptance, when he writes, "Being educated [in Stoic philosophy] is precisely learning to will each thing just as it happens" (*Discourses*, 1.12.15). In an extant fragment from his lost discourses, he says that the man who refuses to accept his fortune is a "layman in the art of life" (*Fragment* 2).

The conceptual and metaphysical problem of free will has been a central *theoretical* concern throughout the entire history of Western philosophy. However, Dubois, the Stoics, and others, have seen confusion over precisely this issue as a central *psychotherapeutic* concern. Dubois dedicates a whole chapter of his textbook on psychotherapy to the issue of determinism, in which he asserts, "My convictions on this subject have been of such help to me in the practise of psychotherapy that I can not pass this question by in silence" (Dubois, 1904, p. 47). In modern society we take certain metaphysical views regarding free will for granted, and seldom examine whether they are well founded, or even logically consistent.

> There are some conclusions which we easily arrive at by using the most elementary logic, and which we dare not express. They seem to be in such flagrant contradiction to public opinion that we fear we should be stoned, morally speaking, and we prudently keep our light under a bushel. The problem of *liberty* is one of those *noli me tangere* ["do not touch me"] questions.
>
> If you submit it to a single individual in a theoretical discussion, in the absence of all elementary passion, he will have no difficulty in following your syllogisms; he will himself furnish you with arguments in favour of determinism. But address yourself to the masses, or to the individual when he is under the sway of emotion caused by a revolting crime, and you will call forth clamours of indignation – you will be put under the ban of public opinion.
>
> (*ibid.*)

The philosophical debate concerning "free will *vs*. determinism" in modern academic philosophy is incredibly complex. Dubois only engages with it at a very superficial level. However, one aspect of the debate can perhaps be made explicit by means of a very crude syllogism of the kind Dubois had in mind.

Most people assume that humans generally act with some sort of free will, albeit constrained to varying degrees by obstacles in their environment. So a person is typically regarded as being free from extrinsic restrictions or limitations and therefore completely *responsible* for his or her actions unless held at gunpoint, or brainwashed, etc. However, this popular way of talking about our actions risks confusing two different concepts of "freedom": that of freedom *from* the effects of preceding causal factors, and that of freedom *to* pursue future goals without obstruction. By contrast, the simple determinist position of Dubois can be outlined as follows.

1   All physical activity of the brain is wholly determined by antecedent causal factors.
2   All mental activity is wholly determined by physical activity in the brain.
3   Therefore, all mental activity is wholly determined by antecedent causal factors.

There are many variations of this argument, exhibiting different degrees of philosophical complexity and sophistication. However, this simple "premise-conclusion" format should at least be sufficient to expose the basic controversy. As Dubois observes, if we accept the physiological basis of the mind, "all thought being necessarily bound to the physical or the chemical phenomena of which the brain is the seat", we are ultimately forced to *abandon* the metaphysical theory of free will (Dubois & Gallatin, 1908, p. 9).

Doing so does not logically entail apathy and inertia, as many people falsely assume. Indeed, a man may be causally determined to respond to the perception of universal determinism with a sense of renewed commitment to his ideals, and to vigorous action.

> At the exact moment that a man puts forth any volition whatever his action is an effect. It could not either not be or be otherwise. Given the sensory motor state, or the state of the intellect of the subject, it is the product of his real mentality. . . . But it is nowhere written that the individual is going to persist henceforward in a downward course, that he is fatally committed to evil. But the fault having been committed, it should now be the time for some educative influence to be brought to bear, to bring together in his soul all the favourable motor tendencies and intellectual incentives, to arouse pity and goodness, or found on reason the sentiment of moral duty.
>
> (Dubois, 1904, pp. 55–56)

The defence of free will has been a central concern of medieval Christian ethics and traditionally depends upon making a sharp metaphysical division between the body and the mind, so that our will can be considered the unfettered activity of a soul which exists independently of the body, a "ghost in the machine", as Gilbert Ryle famously put it (Ryle, 1949).

However, if we accept the argument for determinism at face value it has radical implications for our attitudes toward ourselves and other people. It forces us to see other people as the product of genetics and environment and, therefore, acting in a manner for which they cannot be "blamed" in the ordinary sense of the word, that is, in an absolute, metaphysical sense. We are all, to a large extent, victims of circumstance, insofar as we do what we do with the brains and the upbringing that nature has given us. Dubois puts this quite eloquently:

> I know of no idea more fertile in happy suggestion than that which consists in taking people as they are, and admitting at the time when one observes them that they are never otherwise than what they can be.
>
> This idea alone leads us logically to true indulgence, to that which forgives, and, while shutting our eyes to the past, looks forward to the future. When one has succeeded in fixing this enlightening idea in one's mind, one is no more irritated by the whims of an hysterical patient than by the meanness of a selfish person.
>
> Without doubt one does not attain such healthy stoicism with very great ease, for it is not, we must understand, merely the toleration of the presence of evil, but a stoicism in the presence of the culprit. We react, first of all, under the influence of our sensibility; it is that which determines the first movement, it is that which makes our blood boil and calls forth a noble rage.
>
> But one ought to calm one's emotion and stop to reflect. This does not mean that we are to sink back into indifference, but, with a better knowledge of the mental mechanism of the will, we can get back to a state of calmness. We see the threads which pull the human puppets, and we can consider the only possible plan of useful action – that of cutting off the possibility of any renewal of wrong deeds, and of sheltering those who might suffer from them, and making the future more certain by the uplifting of the wrong-doer.
>
> (Dubois, 1904, p. 56)

In other words, contemplation of determinism, the idea that human actions are definitely *caused* by a complex network of multiple preceding factors, mitigates our anger toward other people and leads us close to a healthy sense of understanding and forgiveness. We are also more enlightened regarding our practical responses and more inclined to *reform* rather than *punish* wrongdoers. When Socrates argued in *The Republic* that the sage wishes to do good even to his enemies, he meant that we ought to educate and enlighten others, seeing that as their highest good. That *harmonious* attitude is the polar opposite of the one that seeks revenge through moralizing punishment. It leads instead to a sense of generosity and equanimity, and resolves anger, resentment, and contempt.

The paradox of free will vs. determinism

Like Dubois after them, the Stoics were determinists, who believed that all events in life, including our own actions, are predetermined to happen as they do. However, paradoxically, they were also passionately in favour of increased personal responsibility and belief in one's freedom to act and make decisions in accord with reason. Hence, Epictetus constantly reminds his students that no matter what happens to them, they still have the opportunity to make of life what they will.

> Sickness is an impediment to the body, but not to the faculty of choice, unless that faculty itself wishes it to be one. Lameness is an impediment to one's leg, but not to the faculty of choice. And say the same to yourself with regard to everything that befalls you; for you will find it to be an impediment to something else, but not to yourself.
>
> (*Encheiridion*, 9)

Epictetus himself was apparently lame, reputedly after being brutally crippled by his master when enslaved, so these remarks must have carried an extra poignancy, given his obvious physical disability.

To many people this seems confusing and contradictory. How can the Stoics emphasize both freedom *and* determinism? However, as is often the case in philosophy, it is not the answer that is confused, but the *question*. The Stoics evidently believe that the concepts of freedom and determinism are *compatible*.

> It is virtually certain that Epictetus' concept of a free will, far from requiring the will's freedom from fate (i.e., a completely open future or set of alternative possibilities or choices), presupposes people's willingness to comply with their predestined allotment. The issue that concerns him is neither the will's freedom from antecedent causation nor the attribution to persons of a completely open future and indeterminate power of choice. Rather, it is freedom from being constrained by (as distinct from going along with) external contingencies, and freedom from being constrained by the errors and passions consequential on believing that such contingencies *must* influence or inhibit one's volition.
>
> (Long, 2002, p. 221)

Confusion is caused because of a well-known and long-standing ambiguity in the popular notion of "free will". Metaphysical "freedom" refers to the freedom of the soul to act independently of antecedent causal factors, also known as metaphysical "libertarianism". However, by contrast, "freedom" in *common* parlance, in ordinary language usage, arguably refers to the ability of something to perform its prescribed function without external impediment or obstruction. A wheel turns *freely* unless, for instance, it is buckled or stopped by a rock. People act *freely* unless, for instance, other people restrain them physically or mentally. "For he is free for whom all things happen in accordance with his choice, and whom no one can restrain" (*Discourses*, 1.12.8).

Chrysippus, the great theorist of the Stoic school, explained their theory of free will and determinism by means of his famous "cylinder analogy". In this example, it is argued that if we roll a cylinder along the ground, the initial impetus to move is given by someone pushing it, but the direction in which the cylinder moves, in a straight line, is determined by its own shape. The push is an example of what Stoics call an "external cause" coming from without, whereas the shape of the cylinder is the "internal cause" of the direction it takes, its own constitution. External causes impinge upon the human mind through the senses, and through other effects upon the body. However, the constitution, or character, of our mind determines how we will respond, acting as an "internal cause" of our response.

The mind is, therefore, autonomous to the extent that it can determine the direction in which it acts on the basis of its own character. However, external events impinge upon it and trigger its responses. Our actions are like the movement of the cylinder, insofar as both are due to a combination of "internal" and "external" factors. The cylinder is free to move according to its own nature as long as no further external causes obstruct it.

> Whatever happens to you has been waiting to happen since the beginning of time. The twining strands of fate wove both of them together: your own existence and the things that happen to you.
>
> (*Meditations*, 10.5)

In this sense of the word "freedom", which, we should remind ourselves, happens to be the *normal* sense, there is no incompatibility whatsoever with the notion of determinism, because there is no reference made to the *preceding* causes that make the wheel turn, or the person act, in the first place. The cylinder rolls freely, its movement determined by antecedent events.

The notion of being free from preceding causes, by comparison, is a much more unusual and problematic concept. As Skinner argues at length in *Beyond Freedom and Dignity*, as our scientific understanding advances with regard to human behaviour, the notion that we were somehow exempt from universal determinism is very much eroded (1971, p. 21). He adds:

> Although people object when a scientific analysis traces their behaviour to external conditions and thus deprives them of credit and the chance to be admired, they seldom object when the same analysis absolves them of blame.
>
> (Skinner, 1971, p. 75)

But what of the *inner feeling* of free will? Whatever sensations or impressions we might feel of "effort", the *idea* that our actions are free is simply a sign that we are ignorant of their causes.

> We do not think enough about the yoke inside, the result of ideas so thoroughly adopted that they seem like our own. That is what Spinoza meant when he said, "Men think themselves free only because they get a clear view of their actions, they do not think of the motives that determined them".
>
> (Dubois, 1909, p. 53)

My freedom *toward* the future is a different matter and down to my specific circumstances in each situation, that is, whether I am obstructed by external events or not.

When people are told that things happen because they have been determined by the preceding chain of causes, they usually respond at first by complaining that there is no point trying to change anything in that case. The Stoics and other ancient philosophers knew this as the "lazy argument", and considered it an obvious fallacy. It's both an excuse for laziness and an example of lazy thinking. The theory of determinism does not hold, as this fallacy requires, that all events are completely determined only by *external* causes, that is, that people are completely passive in relation to the world. Rather, it holds that events are co-determined by the interaction of internal and external causes. My actions are part of the causal network and therefore have an effect upon the things that happen. Nevertheless, accepting those things that are genuinely beyond my control, with philosophical resignation, is a key rational therapeutic strategy and employed extensively by Stoics in the face of adversity.

Frustration tolerance and amor fati

Ellis repeatedly referred to the notion of "frustration tolerance" as a central component of REBT. People become disturbed, to a large extent, because they are unable to accept the frustration of their desires or actions, that is, they are bad losers and cannot cope with failure or even temporary setback or inconvenience. However, frustration is predominantly a self-imposed misery. If we relax the rigid demands that we impose upon ourselves, life, and other people, and learn to substitute flexible preferences, we develop "high frustration tolerance", an ability to accept the fact when things do not go as we desired. Hence, one of the key irrational ideas identified by Ellis as a root cause of emotional disturbance is "The idea that it is awful and catastrophic when things are not the way one would very much like them to be" (Ellis, 1962, p. 69). By contrast, Ellis' REBT approach recommends that as rational individuals we should do our best to change objectionable circumstances, but when we cannot we should "become philosophically resigned to our fate and accept things the way they are" (*ibid.*, p. 70).

The Stoic remedy for such frustration is virtually identical, though perhaps more radical. The sage desires only that he should do what he can to the best of his ability, no more and no less, and he accepts success or failure with equal serenity because he concerns himself only with the *quality* of his actions, and not their results. Seneca advises, "It is in no man's power to have whatever he wants; but he has it in his power not to wish for what he hasn't got, and cheerfully make the most of the things that do come his way" (*Letters*, 122).

One of the central recurring themes of Epictetus' philosophy is the advice that one should act as if one had chosen one's fate, or willed the present moment to happen as it does. "Don't ask things to happen as you wish, but wish them to happen as they do happen, and your life will go smoothly" (*Encheiridion*, 8).

Nietzsche, who was a professor not of philosophy, but of classical philology, steeped in Greek and Roman literature, referred to a similar notion using the Latin phrase *amor fati*, "love of [your] fate". It is unknown whether Nietzsche derived this phrase from an obscure source in classical literature or whether he simply coined it himself. It clearly expresses the sentiment found throughout Stoic literature, the notion of cultivating a willing acceptance of one's circumstances, although the phrase itself does not appear in any surviving Stoic writings. There is a similar expression, though, to be found among the Greek maxims of the Delphic Oracle reported by Stobaeus: *tuchen sterge*, "love fortune".

Stockdale's example in modern times provides a very remarkable instance of how this attitude can flourish even under the most extreme conditions. Stockdale, who was incarcerated in a Vietnamese prison and tortured severely, described his attitude as follows:

> Was I a victim? Not when I became fully engaged, got into the life of unity with comrades, helping others and being encouraged by them. So many times, I would find myself whispering to myself after an exhilarating wall tap message exchange: "I am right where I belong; I am right where I was meant to be".
>
> (Stockdale, 1995, p. 63)

Stockdale, following Epictetus' advice, embraced the reality of his confinement and rose to the challenges of the situation. He later thanked fate for giving him the opportunity to learn from the experience of imprisonment.

Ellis' criticism of Stoic fatalism

Ellis sometimes quoted the Stoic doctrine of acceptance very approvingly. For example, he advises those using REBT for self-help:

> If you face great frustrations and there seems no way to change them, then you had better gracefully *accept* them. Yes: not with bitterness and despair, but with dignity and grace. As Epictetus noted two thousand years ago: "Who, then, is unconquerable? He whom the inevitable cannot overcome".
>
> (Ellis & Harper, 1997, p. 145)

He adds:

> You can take a philosophy of acceptance to irrational extremes. But, within sensible limits, you can benefit from it.
>
> (*ibid.*)

However, in defending REBT against its critics, Ellis elsewhere wrote:

> It is sometimes objected that [REBT] is superficial in that it adjusts the patient all too well to his poor life situation and stoically induces him to tolerate what may well be intolerable conditions. This objection is a misinterpretation of the philosophy of Stoicism; and it assumes that rational emotive psychotherapy strictly follows Stoic teachings, which it does not.
>
> Epictetus, one of the main proponents of Stoicism, did not say or imply that one should calmly accept *all* worldly evils and should stoically adjust oneself to them. His view was that a person should first try to change the evils of the world; but when he could not successfully change them, *then* he should uncomplainingly accept them. This he wrote: "Is there smoke in my house? If it be moderate, I will stay; if very great, I will go out. For you must always remember, and hold to this, that the door is open".
>
> Some Stoics, such as Marcus Aurelius, took the doctrine of accepting the inevitable to extremes and were irrationally over-fatalistic. Thus, Marcus Aurelius advised: "Accept everything which happens, even if it seem disagreeable, because it leads to this, to the health of the universe and to the prosperity and felicity of Zeus. For he would not have brought on any man what he has brought, if it were not useful for the whole". To this kind of fatalistic philosophy, rational emotive therapists of course do *not* subscribe.
>
> (Ellis, 1962, pp. 361–362)

This interpretation of Stoicism should raise an eyebrow. First, we should ask ourselves how a philosophy so *obviously* over-fatalistic could have prospered for so many centuries without modification. Next, we should wonder whether Emperor Marcus Aurelius, for example, could have conceivably held the overly-fatalistic attitude Ellis attributes to him when he personally led the Roman legions, greatly depleted by a recent plague, to fight back the invading hordes of the Marcomanni and their allies. Was Seneca being *passive* in this way when he, reputedly, conspired to overthrow the corrupt and tyrannical Emperor Nero and lost his life in the process? Was Cato of Utica, the man who defied Julius Caesar, a *doormat*? In fact, many Stoics were famous political and military leaders, famed for their obstinacy and courage rather than for their passivity. The Stoics' greatest hero, Socrates, was himself a decorated (or nearly so) military hero and they also revered the legendary Hercules, who accomplished the 12 labours, despite being tormented by the goddess Hera. In short, the Stoics undoubtedly admired action, rather than passivity, in the face of adversity.

Ellis' portrayal of Stoic fatalism seems to echo a common misconception but one which clashes with the historical facts that we have about the lives of famous Stoics. How can we resolve this apparent contradiction? The Stoics recommend that we accept those things, as Ellis has already implied, which are outside our control. This advice constitutes a kind of truism, albeit a significant one: do not try to do the impossible. Of course, as the Serenity Prayer emphasizes, this requires a clear understanding of what is under our control and what is not. When Marcus Aurelius advised himself to accept everything that happens, he is taking it for granted that what has *already happened* is in the past and is, therefore, already unchangeable. It is only the immediate future that the Stoic can change, what is *about* to happen, not what has just *happened*. The ancient Stoics accepted reality, in other words, but nevertheless took vigorous action in the service of wisdom and justice.

Acceptance of the immediate past, or even the present moment, does not therefore preclude assertive action going forward. Acceptance does not mean defeat or surrender. A famous anecdote about Zeno, the founder of the Stoic school, helps to illustrate this point. He was once punishing a slave whom had been caught stealing when the culprit objected, "It was fated that I should steal", to which Zeno reputedly rejoined, "Yes, and that you should be beaten!" (*Lives*, 7.1).

Stoic determinism and empathy

Dubois recognized, like the Stoics, that the mere notion of determinism potentially moderated our emotional reactions and increased our empathy for others. According to Baudouin and Lestchinsky, Dubois said that:

> As soon as we realise that people are only what they think themselves to be, in virtue of the mentality they owe to their inherited disposition and to their education, we shall excuse them for their blunders and their faults.
>
> (Baudouin & Lestchinsky, 1924, p. 136)

Likewise, Marcus Aurelius reminds himself:

> Practice really hearing what people say. Do your best to get inside their minds.
>
> (*Meditations*, 6.53)

Elsewhere, he adds:

> When people injure you, ask yourself what good or harm they thought would come of it. If you understand that, you'll feel sympathy rather than outrage or anger. Your sense of good and evil may be the same as theirs, or near it, in which case you have to excuse them. Or your sense of good and evil may differ from theirs. In which case they're misguided and deserve your compassion. Is that so hard?
>
> (*Meditations*, 7.26)

In more recent decades, Ellis described one of the fundamental irrational ideas at the core of modern emotional disturbance as follows: "The idea that certain people are bad, wicked, or villainous and that they should be severely blamed and punished for their villainy" (Ellis, 1962, p. 65). Ellis himself traced this concept to the medieval Christian theology of sin and free will, the remnants of which still pervade our language and preconceptions about human nature, even though we live in a more secular and scientific era.

> The idea that people are bad or wicked springs from the ancient theological doctrine of free will, which assumes that every person has the freedom to act "rightly" or "wrongly", in relation to some absolute standard of truth and justice ordained by "god" or the "natural law"; and that if anyone uses his "free will" to behave "wrongly", he is a wicked "sinner". This doctrine has no scientific foundation, because its key terms . . . are purely definitional and can neither be proven or disproven in empirical, scientific terms.
>
> (*ibid.*, pp. 65–66)

By contrast, as Ellis observes, common sense suggests that people's seemingly offensive or immoral actions are often, at least partially, determined by ignorance, or other failings.

> When people perform acts which they (or others) consider "wrong" or "immoral", they appear to do so, in the final analysis, because they are too stupid, too ignorant, or too emotionally disturbed to refrain from doing so.
>
> (*ibid.*, p. 66)

Consequently, Ellis recommends that the rational individual should avoid irrational blame and adopt a more philosophical attitude toward the actions of others:

> He should not criticize or blame others for their misdeeds but should realize that they invariably commit such acts out of stupidity, ignorance, or emotional disturbance. He should try to accept people when they are stupid and to help them when they are ignorant or disturbed.
>
> (*ibid.*, p. 68)

Joseph Wolpe, the pioneer of modern behaviour therapy, likewise argued that the deterministic perspective of behavioural psychology inherently contributed to a sense of empathy.

> Objectivity, empathy, and sensitivity to suffering are intrinsic to the behavior therapist's approach to his patients. The objectivity follows from the knowledge that all behavior, including cognitive behavior, is subject to causal determination no less than is the behavior of falling bodies or magnetic fields. . . . To explain how the patient's neurosis arose out of a combination or chain of particular events helps [empathic] understanding.
>
> (Wolpe, 1990, p. 59)

Wolpe and his colleague, Lazarus, had earlier written of determinism as providing one of the "tactical principles" of behaviour therapy. "Since the patient has had no choice in becoming what he is, it is incongruous to blame him for having gone awry, or to disparage him for maintaining his unhappy state" (Wolpe & Lazarus, 1966, p. 16). By encouraging the client to recognize that "human behaviour is subject to causal determinism no less than that of billiard balls or ocean currents", they sought to counteract socially conditioned feelings of neurotic self-blame. On this point, Wolpe shared the simple determinist logic of the Stoic philosophy and Dubois' rational persuasion psychotherapy.

Contemplating psychological determinism is a key means of developing empathy. For this reason, like modern cognitive therapists, Epictetus said we should avoid labelling others as bad but rather view them as mistaken concerning the difference between good and bad (*Discourses*, 1.18.5). We should try to understand why they're acting as they do. Paradoxically, by judging others to be nothing but "idiots", we merely show our own ignorance of their motives and the paths that led them to their current way of thinking.

Moreover, the Stoic, if he is to be completely truthful and rational, must recognize that neither he nor other people are perfect, but, rather, all mortals are fallible. He cannot expect other people to act like the ideal sage. However, insofar as he empathizes with them, he must strike a careful balance, allowing himself to understand their distress, responding appropriately, but holding back internally from being drawn into the same errors of judgement. In a remarkable passage in the *Handbook*, Epictetus recognizes that sometimes the Stoic must *pretend* to share the distress of others in order to fit in and offer them support. "As far as words go, however, do not shrink from sympathizing with [a distraught person], and even, if the opportunity arises, from groaning with him; but be careful not to groan inwardly too" (*Encheiridion*, 16).

Likewise, those who place excessive value on superficial things such as wealth and reputation are treated like excitable children during the Roman festival of Saturnalia who come around clapping their hands with cries of joy. Epictetus says one should not try to disabuse them of their enthusiasm but humour them and clap along. "Thus when you are unable to change a person's views, recognise that he is a child, and clap your hands with him; or if you do not wish to do that, merely keep your silence" (*Discourses*, 1.29.31).

Epictetus could have used the analogy of the sympathy we feel for a child or an animal when they become unnecessarily distressed, "frightened of shadows", etc. In such cases we do not merely ridicule their lack of insight, but act sympathetically, offer reassurance, and accept their upset as genuine enough. Nevertheless, internally, we hold back from too much sympathy or over-identification because their anxieties are not based upon a perception of reality that we share. Indeed, we must concede that in a sense they are deluded or misguided. We would not merely *dismiss* a child's fears, though the perception on which they are based might be objectively false, because the emotional response they feel is real enough.

To feel affection for people even when they make mistakes is uniquely human. You can do it, if you simply recognise: that they're human too, that they act out of ignorance, against their will, and that you'll both be dead before long. And, above all, that they haven't really hurt you. They haven't diminished your ability to choose.

(*Meditations*, 7.22)

As a consequence, not only does the Stoic attempt to understand himself and other people as fallible, he even cultivates a kind of empathic understanding toward his enemies, as a remedy for the feelings of excessive or neurotic anger to which the human mind is prey when faced with opposition from others.

Empathy vs. blame

Philosophical empathy serves another crucial purpose: it acts as a potent inoculation against insult. Dubois clearly recognized this role of determinism in mitigating neurotic anger.

We give ourselves up to anger, that passion so contrary to the spirit of responsibility, even more disastrous to him who abandons himself to it than to him who is the object of it. Here again the idea of moral determinism is the one to set us right. Our fellowmen act only according to their actual mental representations; most frequently they think they are doing right, and are animated by good intentions. Even when they recognize an immoral character in their acts, when they revenge themselves, and intentionally wish to make trouble, it is because they consider they have reasons for so doing.

(Dubois, 1909, pp. 241–242)

Likewise, by attempting to understand his enemies, the Stoic either realizes that their criticisms of him are valid, in which case he is empowered to respond to them, or he sees through them as being the product of misconception or bias, in which case he invalidates them and ceases to be disturbed by them. The importance of this cognitive strategy in Stoicism is illustrated by the following quotes from *The Meditations*:

Enter their minds, and you'll find the judges you're so afraid of – and how judiciously they judge themselves.

(*Meditations*, 9.18)

When you face someone's insults, hatred, whatever . . . look at his soul. Get inside him. Look at what sort of person he is. You'll find you don't need to strain to impress him.

(*Meditations*, 9.27)

What their minds are like. What they work at. What evokes their love and admiration. Imagine their souls stripped bare. And their vanity. To suppose that their disdain could harm anyone – or their praise help them.

(*Meditations*, 9.34)

When asked whether he was offended by the rude comments of others, Socrates was said to reply confidently, "No, because that does not apply to me". Yet, he also welcomed being ridiculed by the comic playwrights, musing that if they had said anything worth hearing he would change his ways and if not he would simply ignore their comments as irrelevant (*Lives*, 2.5). When he was told that others spoke *badly* of him, he joked that was because they had never learned to speak *well* (*ibid.*). Indeed, according to legend, Socrates was frequently heckled and even beaten up by the crowd when speaking in the Athenian marketplace, but, says Diogenes Laertius, "he bore all this with great equanimity", adding:

> So that once, when he had been kicked and buffeted about, and had borne it all patiently, and some one expressed his surprise, he said, "Suppose an ass had kicked me, would you have had me bring an action against him?"
>
> (*ibid.*)

The moral of this story, and many other anecdotes about Socrates' disregard for the contempt of others, appears to be that there is no point taking offence at the insults of people who are ignorant of what they criticize. Epictetus similarly joked that when criticized by another, he can always complain that they obviously do not know what they are talking about or they would have mentioned all of his *other* vices as well.

Likewise, many jokes were made on the theme of Socrates' notoriously shrewish and quick-tempered wife, Xanthippe. Socrates himself dismissed her unruly behaviour in typically Stoic terms, as an opportunity to strengthen his moral fortitude by facing a challenge.

> And he used to say, that one ought to live with a restive woman, just as horsemen manage violent-tempered horses; "and as they", said he, "when they have once mastered them, are easily able to manage all others; so I, after managing Xanthippe, can easily live with any one else whatever".
>
> (*ibid.*)

One of the most important features of CBT is the disputation of irrational self-blame or blame of others. It is extremely common, for example, for a person disturbed by being involved in a car accident to engage in morbid recriminations, even if they had no *real* responsibility for the incident in question. It is equally common for people to blame others who upset or oppose them and label them "bitches" or "bastards", as if they were acting out of deliberate malice, with full awareness of doing so, and total control over their actions. Socrates, however, had famously argued that *no man does evil knowingly*, that is, that what we consider to be malice or vice in other people is really due to ignorance. Moreover, what is done unknowingly must also be done *unwillingly*.

> "Shouldn't this brigand and this adulterer be executed?"
> Don't ask this, but rather:

"Shouldn't that person be executed who has gone astray and erred over the most important things, blinded not in vision, which discriminates between black and white, but in the intelligence, which discriminates between good and bad?"

If you make your point like this, you will recognise how inhumane it is, just as if you were saying:

"This blind man or this deaf man should be executed".

For if loss of the most important things is the greatest harm, and what is most important in each person is correct volition, and someone is deprived of this, why are you still angry with him? My friend, if you must go against nature in your response to the plight of another person, pity him rather than hate him. Give up this retaliation and hostility.

(*Discourses*, 1.18.5–9)

Suppose, for a moment, that we could not decide whether it made more sense to blame our enemies for acting in a deliberately evil way, or to forgive them for acting in a misguided and confused way. The strategy of blaming the other person brings us *no* conceivable advantage and merely contributes to unhealthy emotions – it does us more harm than good to think about things that way. The strategy of viewing the other person's actions as confused and unenlightened, by contrast, is likely to moderate our emotional response and, if we are lucky, even to suggest possible ways of altering their actions by re-educating them. Hence, even if there were no way to decide which of these two interpretations were more accurate, the Socratic position, that no man does evil knowingly, would be preferable because it is generally the more healthy and pragmatic attitude.

However, the Stoics would argue that in addition to this practical advantage, the Socratic view has a right to claim greater philosophical consistency and to be not only more healthy but more accurate than the philosophy of blaming others. To understand this, we must remember the difference between Stoic and Christian ethics. The difference between good and bad, for the Stoic, is decided by reference to enlightened self-interest. Good actions are those that contribute to our long-term health and well-being and are consistent with the attainment of emotional freedom and intellectual enlightenment. No man would knowingly do evil, they argue, because to do so is against his own self-interest. Even if someone feels that they have deliberately set out to harm others for the sake of it, perhaps out of a sense of bitterness, they are presumably motivated to do so by the confused and irrational assumption that, in some way, it is better for them to follow their impulses rather than check them and rein them in. Epictetus, therefore, argues that it is no better to put to death "evil" men who are morally handicapped by ignorance than those who are physically handicapped by blindness or deafness.

If this ideal of empathy with one's enemies sounds idealistic or in any way unrealistic, consider the following remarkable example, once again from James

Stockdale. Describing the torture of "taking the ropes" he endured in the North Vietnamese Hao Lo prison:

> In a crucible like a torture prison, you reflect, you silently study what makes those about you tick. Once I had taken the measure of my torture guard, watched his eyes as he worked, watched him move, *felt* him move as he stood on my slumped-over back and cinched up the ropes pulling my shoulders together, I came to know that there was good in him. . . . Under orders, he put me through the ropes fifteen times over the years and rebroke my bad leg once, I feel sure inadvertently.
>
> (Stockdale, 1995, pp. 231–232)

Stockdale, influenced by the Stoic *Handbook* of Epictetus, empathized with his torturer, as a way of coping with the "buzz saw" of prison life, over a period of seven and a half years.

> In all those years, we probably had no more than twenty hours, one on one, together. But neither of us ever broke the code of an unvaryingly strict line of duty relationship. He never tricked me, always played it straight, and I begged no mercy. I admired that in him, and I could tell he did in me. And when people say, "He was a torturer, didn't you *hate* him?" I say, like Solzhenitsyn, to the astonishment of those about me, "No, he was a good soldier, never overstepped his line of duty".
>
> (*ibid.*, p. 232)

Further still, attempting to understand and empathize with one's opponents provides a much-needed check against vanity and may help us to identify and face up to our shortcomings. Reputedly, one of Antisthenes' maxims was, "One should pay attention to one's enemies, for they are the first to detect one's errors" (*Lives*, 6.1). The Stoics also consistently warned against the dangers of egotism, vanity, and the craving for fame and reputation. Epictetus makes this point very powerfully. A former slave himself, he fiercely rebuked his students, many of whom were wealthy aristocrats, for being the real "slaves!" In a famous Stoic paradox, Epictetus argued that only the man who has risen above the craving for wealth and reputation is truly a king, ruler of himself, and free from bondage.

> If someone handed your body over [as a slave] to anyone he met along the way, you would be angry. But are you not ashamed that you hand over your judgement to anyone who happens to come along, so that, if he abuses you, it is disturbed and confused?
>
> (*Encheiridion*, 28)

Empathy with others not only reduces anger but also punctures vanity, its cousin. The root cause of both is identical: a tendency to place too much value on the opinions and actions of others. When they praise us, we are flattered; when they criticize us, we are insulted. The Stoic attacks this emotional attachment to the views of others at root and attempts to see people as fallible and driven by their limitations in a way that mitigates both the egotistical pleasure and pain that comes from flattery and rebuke respectively. Equally, however, the Stoic is keen to stress that the views of others are their own business and outside our direct control. Once again, it is not things themselves, or other people, which disturb us, but our own judgements about them.

> So, whenever we are frustrated, or disturbed, or upset, let us never blame others, but only ourselves, that is, our own judgements. It is the action of a [philosophically] uneducated person to lay the blame for his own bad condition upon others; of one who has made a start on his education to lay the blame on himself; and of one who is fully educated, to blame neither others or himself.
>
> (*Encheiridion*, 5)

The actions or opinions of others mean nothing to us unless we attribute value to them; it is our own judgement that makes us offended by other people. Elsewhere, he restates the same point, adding that we should therefore try to spot our angry judgements early on, so that we can nip them in the bud and gain time to pause for thought, making it easier to control our feelings (*Encheiridion*, 20). However, as Epictetus seems to imply, blaming oneself is equally folly. Our present judgements are the source of our disturbance not our past actions. All blame errs by placing too much importance on the things that are judged blameworthy and not enough upon the internal act of judgement itself.

Chapter 13

The View from Above and Stoic metaphysics

Solon, seeing a very friend of his at Athens mourning piteously, brought him into a high tower and showed him underneath all the houses in that great city, saying to him "Think with yourself how many sundry mournings in times past have been in all these houses, how many at this present are, and in time to come shall be; and leave off to bewail the miseries of mortal folk, as if they were your own".

I would wish you, Lipsius, to do the like in this wide world. But because you cannot in deed and fact go to, do it a little while in conceit and imagination. Suppose, if it please, that you are with me on the top of that high hill Olympus; behold from there all towns, provinces, and kingdoms of the world, and think that you see even so many enclosures full of human calamities. These are but only theatres and places for the purpose prepared, in which Fortune plays her bloody tragedies. . . .

Which things think well upon, Lipsius, and by this communication or participation of miseries, lighten your own. And like they [Roman generals] which rode gloriously in triumph, had a servant behind their backs who in the midst of all their triumphant jollity cried out often times "you are a man" [and "remember you must die"], so let this be ever as a prompter by your side, that these things are human, or appertaining to men. For as labour being divided between many is easy, even so likewise is sorrow.

(Lipsius, 2006, pp. 127–128)

Many of the central metaphysical principles of ancient philosophy seem to converge within a single contemplative exercise or visualization technique. In its simplest form, this consists in the technique of picturing the world as if seen from very high above.

Mine are no weak or borrowed wings: they'll bear me, bard made bird, through the compliant air, earthbound no longer, leaving far behind the cities and the envy of mankind.

(Horace, *Odes*, 2.20)

This technique, in other words, is a kind of dissociation through mental imagery. One takes a step back surveying life as a whole from a bird's eye view. Indeed, we have several familiar clichés in our language that relate to this notion, another indication of its perennial appeal. We take the "long view", the "bird's eye view", look at "the bigger picture", "take a step back and look at ourselves", talk about how events fit into "the grand scheme of things", etc.

Contemplating the View from Above

The practise of meditating upon an expansive vision of the world appears in Stoicism but was certainly common to many different schools of ancient philosophy. Hadot refers to it as the "View from Above". This concept recurs throughout classical philosophy and poetry.

> Such a procedure is the very essence of philosophy. We find it repeated – in identical from, beneath superficial differences of vocabulary – in all the philosophical schools of antiquity. Plato, for instance, defines the philosophical nature by its ability to contemplate the totality of time and being, and consequently of human affairs, in contempt.
>
> (Hadot, 1995, p. 184)

As is often the case in classical literature, the term "contempt" would be better translated "indifference", or perhaps "detachment". As Stockwell writes, "So make sure in your heart of hearts, in your inner self, that you treat your station in life with *indifference*, not with contempt, only with *indifference*" (Stockdale, 1995, p. 191). Hence, the Stoics in general aimed to cultivate a kind of rational *love* toward the totality of existence, to the world, and the whole cosmos.

When rephrased in more contemporary language, I have consistently found this to be one of the classical philosophical exercises that hold most widespread appeal among modern therapy students. However, surprisingly, it has relatively few equivalents in modern therapeutic practise. It is tempting to call the View from Above an "archetypal" technique of psychotherapy insofar as it can be found, in different forms, as far back as history records, in many different nations across the earth, in the philosophies, religions, and schools of thought of many different people and many different ages. Perhaps it is somehow innate in the human mind to make this psychological manoeuvre in order to deal with certain concerns and stresses in life.

Self-interest vs. cosmic consciousness

In *Philosophy as a Way of Life* (1995), Hadot responds to an analysis of Stoicism published by the French philosopher Michel Foucault in his *The Care of the Self* (1986) and elsewhere. Foucault had assimilated some ideas from Hadot's earlier writings into his thesis that the Stoics present a model of "care of the self" through what Foucault variously described as "practices of the self", "arts of existence", and "techniques of the self". Foucault's writings are of considerable interest in relation to modern psychotherapy. However, Hadot disagreed with his interpretation of Stoicism, especially with regard to the sense of selfhood in Stoic philosophy.

> The psychic content of these exercises seems to me to be something else entirely. In my view, the feeling of belonging to a whole is an essential element: belonging, that is, both to the whole constituted by the human community, and to that constituted by the cosmic whole. Seneca sums it up in four words: *Toti se inserens mundo*, "Plunging oneself into the totality of the world".
>
> (Hadot, 1995, p. 208)

Indeed, at the heart of Stoic ethics and psychotherapy there lies an obscure doctrine about the nature of personal identity and the relationship between the mind and the world. It would take us beyond the scope of this text to attempt to reconstruct, elaborate, and defend this aspect of Stoicism in detail. However, in brief, the Stoics repeatedly allude to the importance of seeing the totality of all things in unity, the whole of space and time as *one* multifaceted entity. Indeed, doing so is part of their broadly *pantheistic* orientation, the notion that God is synonymous with the totality of existence. In particular, they emphasize the psychological importance of seeing *oneself* and other human beings, metaphorically, as *parts* (different "limbs") of one great organism (*Meditations*, 2.1).

We must therefore keep in mind the idea of the world as one, all-encompassing, living being (*Meditations*, 4.40). The Stoic and his environment, the brotherhood of mankind and the universe as a whole, form a single organic system, therefore, and not a mere collection of *atomized* and fragmentary individuals. For the Stoic to care for himself is to care for *part* of the universe in its relationship with the *whole*. Stoic ethics is indeed based upon self-interest. However, any change in our view of the self requires changing our assumptions about what self-interest actually means. A metaphysical theory about personal identity therefore determines Stoic ethics. I am essentially part of a greater whole. My interests are therefore bound up with the question of what it means for me to function well and *harmoniously* in relation with the whole.

The exercise itself can take several different forms. Perhaps the first distinction that should be made is between the notion of contemplating the earth seen from high above, and the notion of attempting to contemplate the whole cosmos in one vast perspective. For simplicity, we can refer to these as the "View from Above" and the "cosmic perspective", respectively, as Sellars refers to the latter as the "point of view of the cosmos" (Sellars, 2003, p. 147). Indeed, it is tempting to draw the following analogy. The View from Above is the "Olympian" view and comes from the primitive notion of Zeus and the other gods looking down upon mortal life from atop Mount Olympus. The cosmic perspective perhaps comes from a more sophisticated and philosophical theology, in which God is everywhere and sees everything in one grand unified vision, encompassing past, present, and future in a single timeless and omniscient perception.

However, although such visions have obvious theological connotations, Bertrand Russell, perhaps influenced by his own study of Spinoza, described a similar contemplative practise in *The Conquest of Happiness* from a thoroughly *atheistic* point of view (Russell, 1930). Ironically, even Russell's atheistic vision of the universe takes on a slightly mystical tone.

> If you have attained to this outlook, a certain deep happiness will never leave you, whatever your personal fate may be. Life will be a communion with the great of all ages, and a personal death no more than a negligible incident.
>
> (Russell, 1930, p. 173)

Some ancient philosophers were probably also able to engage in cosmological meditation practises of this kind while remaining relatively *agnostic* with regard to the existence of God, and yet to have found a kind of spiritual fulfilment from the exercise.

Philosophical cosmology

In the meditation that Hadot calls "cosmic consciousness", we can perhaps see the ancient practise of cosmology taking on a new dimension, as a contemplative exercise in its own right.

> By "cosmic consciousness", we mean the consciousness that we are a part of the cosmos, and the consequent dilation of our self throughout the infinity of universal nature. In the words of Epicurus' disciple Metrodorus: "Remember that, although you are mortal and have only a limited life-span, yet you have risen, through the contemplation of nature, to the infinity of space and time, and you have seen all the past and all the future".
>
> (Hadot, 1995, p. 266)

Those philosophers who drew diagrams of the universe and tried to imagine it as a whole must have shared a similar subjective experience, a psychological effect of deeply contemplating the very idea of cosmology. Plato's *Timaeus*, for example, rather than simply being an outdated theory of the universe, can perhaps be seen as an attempt to *actively* contemplate cosmology at length through the use of complex diagrams and reflective discussion, a meditation upon the cosmic perspective. For ancient thinkers listening to Plato's dialogue being read aloud, perhaps it felt as though they were being taken on an imaginative journey to the outer reaches of time and space. Hadot says that putting philosophical theory into practise begins with the exercise that consists in "recognizing oneself as a part of the

Whole, elevating oneself to cosmic consciousness, or immersing oneself within the totality of the cosmos" (Hadot, 2002, p. 136). He says that while "meditating on Stoic physics", we are to try to imagine seeing things from the perspective of Zeus, or universal Reason, by first picturing the whole world as though seen from above.

The ancient Pythagoreans appear to have explicitly treated cosmology as a form of meditation before the time of Socrates. The Stoics apparently inherited this and other contemplative practises from them. For example, Marcus Aurelius writes:

> The Pythagoreans tell us to look at the stars at daybreak. To remind ourselves how they complete the tasks assigned them – always the same tasks, the same way. And their order, purity, nakedness. Stars wear no concealment.
>
> (*Meditations*, 11.27)

Although the human body is minute by comparison with the rest of the universe, the same scale does not apply to the mind. Paradoxically, it is the very ability of the mind to conceive of *vastness* that allows us to perceive the minuteness and transience of our own physical existence.

> Do you not know how very small a part you are compared to the whole? That is, as to the body; for as to reason, you are neither worse, nor less, than the gods. For the greatness of reason is not measured by length or height, but by its judgements.
>
> (*Discourses*, 1.12.26)

Some of the most compelling references to the View from Above occur throughout *The Meditations* of Marcus Aurelius. At one point, he explicitly attributes the technique to Plato's dialogues, written over 500 years earlier.

> Plato has a fine saying, that he who would discourse of man should survey, as from some high watchtower, the things of earth; its assemblies for peace or war, its husbandry, matings, and partings, births and deaths, noisy law-courts, lonely wastes, foreign peoples of every kind, feasting, mourning, bargaining – observing all the motley mixture, and the harmonious order that is wrought out of contrariety.
>
> (*Meditations* 7.48)

This practise seems naturally to evoke feelings of the transience and triviality of things which might otherwise have caused undue concern.

> To see them from above: the thousands of animal herds, the rituals, the voyages on calm or stormy seas, the different ways we come into the world, share it with one another, and leave it. Consider the lives led once by others,

long ago, the lives led by others after you, the lives led even now, in foreign lands. How many people don't even know your name. How many will soon have forgotten it. How many offer you praise now – and tomorrow, perhaps, contempt.

(Meditations, 9.30)

More fundamentally, the View from Above seems to be associated with a technique that involves thinking of events within the context of the totality of time and space. In a sense, this cosmic perspective is simply a case of putting things in their true context – the *totality* is reality.

Continual awareness of all time and space, of the size and life span of things around us. A grape seed in infinite space. A half twist of a corkscrew against eternity.

(Meditations, 10.17)

The most obvious benefit of this technique is the fact that it seems to encourage that sense of philosophical tranquillity called *apatheia* or *ataraxia*, one of the defining characteristics of the enlightened sage. Marcus Aurelius describes this state of serenity in quite beautiful terms:

Let it be clear to you that the peace of green fields can always be yours, in this, that, or any other spot; and that nothing is any different here from what it would be either up in the hills, or down by the sea, or wherever else you will. You will find the same thought in Plato, where he speaks of living within the city walls "as though milking his flocks in a mountain sheepfold".

(Meditations, 10.23)

Cognitive therapists frequently emphasize the notion of "selective abstraction" to their clients, the thinking error or cognitive distortion that occurs when we take things out of context. Beck calls this "tunnel vision", though we might also call it a "lie of omission" made to oneself. Normally in CBT, addressing this cognitive distortion entails helping the client to acknowledge overlooked details of a specific situation. One method for doing this involves broadening the client's perspective to encompass a longer period of time.

Judith Beck, for instance, described a series of mental imagery techniques for use in cognitive therapy, including a temporal "distancing" method that asks the client to picture events changing over time:

Another distancing technique helps a patient deal with the imagined aftermath of a catastrophe. Marie . . . fears that her children would be devastated forever if she dies. Her therapist has her imagine their realistic level of distress at different points in time, instead of just immediately after the accident.

(Beck, 1995, p. 246)

Lazarus had previously described a very similar method called "time projection", through which the client may consider an upsetting event from progressively distant perspectives in time (Lazarus, 1971). Beck and his colleagues also adopted this technique in cognitive therapy, which they saw as a means for clients to obtain "detachment from", and perspective on, feared events (Beck, Emery, & Greenberg, 2005, p. 217).

The same psychological effect can be achieved by contemplating the present moment as part of a greater expanse of time, "enlarging perspective" as Beck and colleagues put it:

> The anxious patient usually takes the "worm's eye view" of his situation, and one of the functions of therapy is to provide him with a broader perspective: that is, the "long" or bird's-eye" view of the situation.
>
> (Beck, Emery, & Greenberg, 2005, p. 206)

The Stoics can be seen as taking the same principle to the extreme by continually reminding themselves to place things within the *ultimate* context, the whole of space and time. Of course, nobody could possibly visualize all of those things at once. Nevertheless, the abstract *concept* is available to us at all times.

The contemplation of determinism and transience

One implication of contemplating the cosmic perspective is that it highlights the causal network of determinism. We see ourselves as part of a vast sequence of events.

> If you consider yourself as a detached being, it is [seemingly] natural for you to live to old age and be rich and healthy; but if you consider yourself as a [mortal] man, and as part of the whole, it will be fitting, on account of that whole, that you should at one time be sick, at another take a voyage and be exposed to danger, sometimes be in want, and possibly – it may happen – die before your time.
>
> (*Discourses*, 2.5.25)

Likewise:

> For everything that happens in the universe one can readily find reason to praise providence, if one has within oneself these two qualities, the ability to see each particular event in the context of the whole, and a sense of gratitude.
>
> (*Discourses*, 1.6.1)

By contemplating the bare unembellished facts, within the total context of time and space, the Stoic attempts to think of life in the most objective manner possible.

Keep reminding yourself of the way things are connected, of their related-
ness. All things are implicated in one another and in sympathy with each
other. This event is the consequence of some other one. Things push and pull
on each other, and breathe together, and are one.

(*Meditations*, 6.38)

An inevitable consequence of the attempt to think all of space and time is the
sense not only of physical insignificance in space, but also the transience of
things in relation to the vast river of cosmic time. Hadot says that to achieve
cosmic consciousness we must practise "the exercise that consists in seeing all
human things from above" (Hadot, 2002, p. 136). From that perspective, he
says, we are to also view all of existence as being in a "constant state of metamorphosis". He notes that the contemplation of universal metamorphosis and
the transience of all material things must inevitably also lead us to the meditation on death. As Epictetus puts it, "I am not eternal, but a man; a part of the
whole, as an hour is of the day. Like an hour I must come and, like an hour, pass
away" (*Discourses*, 2.5.13).

Hence, in one of the most startling and controversial passages in Stoic literature, Epictetus recommends that we practise seeing even the lives of our friends
and loved ones as transient. He describes this method as "the highest and principal
form" of Stoic training, and the one which marks initiation into the philosophical
life. Things that are normally seen as desirable are to be viewed as transient, like
an earthenware cup, a disposable object.

So in this, too, when you kiss your child, or your brother, or your friend,
never entirely give way to your imagination, nor allow your elation to
progress as far as it will; but curb it in, restrain it, like those who stand
behind generals when they ride in triumph and remind them that they are
mortal. In a similar way, you too should remind yourself that what you
love is mortal, that what you love is not your own. It is granted to you
for the present while, and not irrevocably, nor for ever, but like a fig or
a bunch of grapes in the appointed season; and if you long for it in the
winter, you are a fool.

So, if you long for your son or your friend when he is not granted to you,
know that you are longing for a fig in winter. For as winter is to a fig, so is
every state of affairs that arises from the order of things in relation to what
is destroyed in accordance with that state of affairs. Henceforth, when you
take delight in anything, bring to mind the contrary impression. What harm is
there while you are kissing your child to say softly, "Tomorrow you will die";
and likewise to your friend, "Tomorrow either you or I will go away, and we
shall see each other no more"?

(*Discourses*, 3.24.84–8)

The sage moderates emotional attachment by, philosophically, reminding himself that he is mortal and must die, that his loved ones are mortal, and that wealth and reputation are fickle and transient things, in the hands of fortune and beyond his ultimate control. As Dubois writes, "let us beware of placing all our happiness on cards liable to be shuffled at any moment by others' hands or blown away by the least wind" (1909, p. 26).

Chapter 14

Stoicism and third-wave CBT

Since the first edition of this book was published in 2010, the third wave of CBT has become increasingly influential. The first wave really began in the 1950s and consisted in the early forms of behaviour therapy promoted by Wolpe, Lazarus, Eysenck, and others. Following the cognitive revolution in psychotherapy, this was gradually superseded by the second wave, consisting in various forms of *cognitive*-behavioural therapy. These became increasingly prominent from the late 1970s onward, although Albert Ellis had already pioneered a cognitive approach to psychotherapy, which became known as REBT, as far back as the mid-1950s.

From around the 1990s onward, though, a new trend emerged in CBT, which placed more emphasis on modifying our relationship *toward* our cognitions rather than the disputation of their content. This wasn't a single therapy but a movement comprised of several quite different therapeutic approaches, developed by different teams of researchers, which nevertheless shared certain themes in common. They became known collectively as the "third wave" of CBT and are sometimes described as mindfulness and acceptance-based approaches. Some of the best known examples include Mindfulness-Based Cognitive Therapy (MBCT), Acceptance and Commitment Therapy (ACT), Metacognitive Therapy (MCT), Dialectical Behaviour Therapy (DBT), and so on.

So far I've been unable to identify any references to Stoicism in the literature of third-wave CBT, with the exception of my own book *Build Your Resilience* (2012) which combines elements of Stoicism with ACT and other third-wave approaches. This is surprising because some of the main themes found in third-wave CBT clearly resemble aspects of Stoic philosophical therapy. Third-wave researchers and clinicians have mainly looked to Eastern religions, particularly Buddhism, for inspiration rather than to Stoicism or Western philosophy, despite the influence of Stoicism on the development of *second*-wave CBT. Some forms of third-wave CBT drew inspiration from Jon Kabat-Zinn's influential book *Full Catastrophe Living* (1990), which adapted Buddhist mindfulness as a form of stress management training. Kabat-Zinn defined the concept of mindfulness there as "Paying attention in a particular way: on purpose, in the present moment, non-judgmentally" (1990, p. 4). As we'll see, this closely matches the Stoic conception of *prosoche*, which consists in paying attention on purpose, in the present moment, with indifference, i.e., while suspending value judgements – and so we may indeed speak of *prosoche* as "Stoic mindfulness".

Stoic mindfulness, however, doesn't involve attention to physical sensations such as are found in the body scan exercise or mindfulness of breathing. For Stoics, *prosoche* or mindfulness is centred on the moment-to-moment use we make of our *prohairesis* or faculty of making value judgements and choices, which is part of the *hegemonikon* or "ruling faculty". In particular, it entails continual attention to the distinction between our value judgements and external objects to which they refer. For example, Epictetus dedicated a whole discourse to *prosoche* or attention to our ruling faculty, in which he warns students that if they allow their attention to lapse for a moment it can be difficult to recover, and if we do this regularly a habit easily forms of mindless *inattention* to the most important things in life. Even if they play games or sing, he says, they should continue to do so with attention, or mindfulness. "If it is good to use attention tomorrow, how much better is it to do so today?" (*Discourses*, 4.41). One of the main things to which Stoics pay attention happens to be the distinction expressed in the famous saying "It's not things that upset us but our judgements about them" (*Encheiridion*, 5). Stoic mindfulness therefore happens to be based upon the premise Stoicism shares with CBT, the cognitive theory of emotion, and therefore the concept of "cognitive distancing".

As it happens, one of the initial reasons for the growth of third-wave CBT as a distinct movement from traditional CBT was that researchers began to converge on the finding that in most cases cognitive distancing could potentially replace disputation as a therapeutic procedure. Ellis, Beck, and their contemporaries had largely assumed that the content of dysfunctional beliefs needed to be modified, through verbal disputation (Socratic questioning) or empirical testing (behavioural experiments), in order for clients' symptoms to improve. Someone with social anxiety disorder, for instance, might have the belief "People think I look like an idiot". Second-wave therapists would encourage clients to question the evidence for this assumption and to carry out behavioural experiments to test it out in practise, perhaps by obtaining feedback from audience members on the client's appearance during a talk. However, third-wave practitioners increasingly found that it was sufficient for clients to change their psychological *relationship toward* beliefs of this kind without necessarily having to go to the trouble of questioning or disproving their content, something that can take time and in some cases can lead clients to get "lost in the weeds" of their own thinking.

Third-wave practitioners discovered that it was often sufficient for clients to learn an attitude of greater detachment from dysfunctional thoughts and beliefs, something that is generally much quicker and easier to teach. Whereas Beck referred to this attitude of detachment as "cognitive distancing", later behaviour therapists introduced the term "verbal defusion" to denote a broadly similar process construed in terms of behavioural psychology. Although Stoicism has much in common with second-wave CBT, it also has similarities with the third-wave approaches. In particular, Stoic philosophers appear to have focused more on transforming their attitude toward certain pathological beliefs, in quite general terms, than upon questioning the individual content of such beliefs.

The third-wave consists of a variety of quite distinct approaches, drawing on different theoretical frameworks, including both cognitive and behavioural psychology. However, for the purposes of our comparison, Acceptance and Commitment Therapy (ACT) arguably provides the best model. Whereas some third-wave CBT approaches have taught Buddhist-style meditation practises, this is not essential, and is indeed uncommon, for ACT training (Hayes, Strosahl, & Wilson, 2016, p. 204). Instead, ACT teaches psychological skills, including mindfulness, through a diverse range of experiential techniques and metaphors, some of which easily lend themselves to comparison with Stoicism. The emphasis on "reason" in Stoicism does potentially conflict with ACT's more experiential orientation and wariness of verbal rule-governed behaviour. However, our discussion in this chapter will focus on the points of convergence between the two approaches.

ACT divides the mechanisms of therapeutic change into six distinct categories, which are broad enough to encompass many aspects of other third-wave approaches (Hayes, Strosahl, & Wilson, 2016). This model, known as the "hexaflex", includes the processes called "acceptance", "verbal defusion", "present moment awareness", "values clarification", "committed action", and "dimensions of self". We'll now examine each in turn, in order to draw several important analogies with Stoicism.

Acceptance

The concept of Stoic acceptance is a good place to begin when drawing analogies with third-wave therapies because the authors of the main clinical textbook on ACT actually compare this aspect of their own approach with *The Serenity Prayer*:

> God, grant me the serenity to accept the things I cannot change,
> Courage to change the things I can,
> And wisdom to know the difference.

As we've already seen, *The Serenity Prayer* encapsulates the central psychological doctrine of Stoicism, often known today as the "dichotomy of control". This distinction is also recognized as crucial in ACT.

> This prayer says it takes a certain kind of "wisdom" to live life well. We must learn what can be controlled and what can't and then redirect our energy accordingly.
>
> (Hayes, Strosahl, & Wilson, 2016, p. 270)

It takes both wisdom and courage to live a vital life, as they put it, "and *our culture offers little guidance* on how to do this" (*ibid.*, italics added). However, as we've seen, Western culture *does* offer us guidance on how to do this, although it's largely been forgotten or has become fragmented – it was once provided by the Stoics and other ancient schools of philosophy.

In ACT, "acceptance" is defined as a form of voluntary non-judgemental exposure to unpleasant experiences.

> Acceptance, as we mean it, is *the voluntary adoption of an intentionally open, receptive, flexible, and nonjudgmental posture with respect to moment-to-moment experience.* Acceptance is supported by a "willingness" to make contact with distressing private experiences or situations, events, or interactions that will likely trigger them.
>
> (Hayes, Strosahl, & Wilson, 2016, p. 272)

This resembles the ancient practise of "voluntary hardship" (or discomfort). The Cynics had many ways to express the value of actively embracing pain and discomfort, which sound remarkably similar to ACT metaphors. For example, they would say that someone who turns and flees in panic trying to escape from wild dogs is more likely to be pursued by them and attacked than someone who stands and faces them calmly and confidently. Likewise, someone who grabs a snake confidently behind the head is less likely to be bitten than someone who picks it up gingerly by its tail. In other words, the Cynics knew that by facing our pain, and accepting it, we often suffer less than when we try to struggle and avoid experiencing it. The Stoics inherited this willingness to voluntary embrace uncomfortable feelings from their predecessors, the Cynics.

However, Stoic acceptance is also inherently related to their doctrine of philosophical "indifference". For Stoics, unpleasant experiences are neither intrinsically good nor bad. To put it bluntly, because they're not inherently bad, harmful, or evil, they're generally to be regarded with studied indifference (*apatheia*) rather than avoided or suppressed, especially insofar as living in accord with wisdom and virtue actually requires us to experience them. For example, a Stoic would potentially accept the pain and discomfort of rigorous physical exercise, as something neutral rather than bad, insofar as it's natural and inevitable if they want to exercise the inner virtue of self-discipline and pursue the external goal of becoming fitter.

> So let us accept what fate prescribes as we accept what Asclepius [the god of medicine] prescribes for us. For there is surely much in these prescriptions that is none too agreeable, but we welcome them in the hope of regaining our health.
>
> (*Meditations*, 5.7)

In other words, it's healthier to reconcile ourselves to painful experiences and swallow the bitter pill than to struggle against aspects of life beyond our direct control.

When attempting to articulate this concept of acceptance, the ACT researchers found themselves struggling with the same objections faced thousands of years earlier by the Stoics.

> Acceptance also does not mean wanting or liking something, wishing it were here, or judging it to be fair, right, or proper. It does not mean leaving changeable situations unchanged – it means to embrace experiences as they are, by choice, and in the moment.
>
> (Hayes, Strosahl, & Wilson, 2016, p. 272)

Likewise, Stoic acceptance doesn't mean masochism, or actively enjoying unpleasant experiences. For Stoics, pain is "indifferent"; it is not bad but *neither* is it inherently good. (The same goes for any unpleasant feeling, such as fatigue or discomfort.) Stoic acceptance also doesn't mean behavioural inertia or passivity. Stoics reconcile the acceptance of their experiences (the discipline of desire and aversion) with commitment to change in the service of appropriate external goals (the discipline of action). As ACT explains, acceptance is actually required for change because changing things we control inevitably leads to other events that can't be controlled. We control our own voluntary actions, by definition, but then we have to be willing to accept the feelings and other consequences that follow from those actions. Both ACT and Stoicism therefore stress that acceptance, in this sense, does not mean passivity or "giving in" to things such as domestic abuse, for example. It means accepting the reality of our situation and the feelings we have to go through in order to improve our lives. As Epictetus puts it, when there is smoke in my chamber, if it is bearable I will stay but if it becomes excessive then I will leave (*Discourses*, 1.25).

In ACT, the value of acceptance is also explained by talking about "clean" vs. "dirty" pain. Clean pain consists in the unpleasant feelings that aren't directly under our control. We either accept those feelings or struggle against them. Dirty pain comes when we fight against our feelings and try to control or avoid them, something ACT researchers call "experiential avoidance". Dirty pain is *unnecessary* suffering. One ACT exercise consists in drawing a large circle on a piece of paper. Clients are asked to divide it into a pie chart showing how much suffering comes from clean vs. dirty pain (Hayes, Strosahl, & Wilson, 2016, p. 281). Of course, this is bound to remind us of the anecdote presented earlier in which psychotherapist Paul Dubois had his patient draw a circle to represent the Stoic philosophy of acceptance, showing the initial suffering enclosed by additional circles symbolizing preoccupation, worry, and other layers of unnecessary additional suffering. Dubois said that Stoic acceptance consists in letting go of those extra layers that magnify the initial suffering. The paradox of acceptance is that when we accept painful or unpleasant feelings they often diminish in intensity as a result, and sometimes the feelings may also reduce in terms of frequency and duration. However, ACT practitioners are keen to emphasize that that's not a rationale conducive to acceptance. Acceptance shouldn't be viewed as a trick "to accept something out of existence", as they put it (Hayes, Strosahl, & Wilson, 2016, p. 284). Approaching it with that intention would just disguise an underlying *refusal* to accept, which is just another form of experiential avoidance. The main benefit of acceptance is that by letting go of our struggle we alleviate much of our second-level suffering, the dirty pain, and that allows us to respond more flexibly to the situations we face. Although the initial feelings are often alleviated as well, that should be viewed more like an added bonus rather than the goal of acceptance.

One of the most popular ACT strategies for facilitating acceptance is also strikingly similar to an approach found in ancient Stoicism. The ACT "Tin Can Monster" exercise provides a good example. Clients are asked to think of their problem as if it were a 30-foot monster made of tin cans and string. It might appear overwhelming at first but if we take it apart and confront one piece at a time then it becomes easier to practise acceptance. The ACT practitioner may ask a client to "divide and conquer" unpleasant feelings by focusing on one element at a time and letting go of the struggle, i.e., accepting rather than trying to control or avoid that experience.

As noted earlier, the psychotherapist Baudouin described a Stoic method he named "depreciation by analysis", which involves dividing events into their component parts in order to be able to accept them with indifference. It should be clear by now that this isn't a begrudging acceptance, or reluctant tolerance, like the modern word (lower case) "Stoicism" might suggest. Rather ancient Stoicism taught a more psychologically nuanced form of acceptance, based upon a complete philosophy of life and set of values, which regard such experiences as "indifferent" in the sense of being undeserving of struggle. What people mean by "Stoic" would often be more like the superficial pretense of being "Stoic" – trying to act *as if* you accept unpleasant feelings rather than actually accepting them at a deeper philosophical level.

Verbal defusion/cognitive distancing

Beck realized that in order for clients to critically evaluate their own thoughts or beliefs (cognitive disputation) they would first have to be able to distinguish between them and reality, and treat them as hypotheses, which could potentially be either true or false (cognitive distancing). That's the difference between saying to yourself "This situation *is* a catastrophe" and saying "I'm *viewing* this situation as if it were a catastrophe". Sometimes our beliefs are so tightly fused with reality that we lose sight of the distinction between thoughts and facts, and therefore can't imagine viewing things any other way. It's impossible to dispute our own cognitions, in other words, unless we first gain enough distance or separation between them and external reality.

Beck suggested a variety of techniques to help clients gain cognitive distance early in the therapy process, viewing it as a prerequisite for cognitive therapy proper. However, researchers began to wonder what would happen if clients simply engaged more rigorously in this process without necessarily proceeding to dispute the content of their cognitions. Enthusiasm for cognitive distancing techniques was partly inspired by the observation that similar processes appear to be at play in Buddhist mindfulness meditation, where thoughts are viewed with a similar form of detachment but practitioners typically *refrain* from struggling against or disputing them. Hence, the approach that was later developed by ACT researchers into "verbal defusion" was initially referred to as "comprehensive distancing", i.e., a more thorough version of the technique employed by Beck and his associates.

In ACT, "fusion" is defined as "the pouring together of verbal/cognitive processes and direct experience such that the individual cannot discriminate between the two" (Hayes, Strosahl, & Wilson, 2016, p. 243). We could also say that "fusion" occurs when there's no "distance" between our cognitions and the experiences to which they relate. That is, our words and concepts become so blended with our experiences that we become temporarily unable to distinguish one from the other. This might be useful when we're immersed in reading a novel and want to lose ourselves in the story and experience it as if it were really happening. However, suppose the story we tell ourselves consists of pathological ruminations about our own worthlessness as a human being or anxiety-provoking worries about hypothetical future catastrophes. Some stories and beliefs, the unhealthy ones, are better kept at arms length and viewed with a sort of detachment or studied indifference.

Because Stoic therapy is *philosophical* it tends to focus on what Stoics consider to be the most fundamental and important beliefs in life. Those are our beliefs concerning the nature of the supreme good, the goal of life – we could even say the "meaning of life". The main concern that runs throughout Stoic writings is specifically to challenge the assumption – considered false by them – that our supreme good consists in experiencing pleasure or obtaining other externals. Sometimes the Stoics do this by philosophically disputing the belief that something external is more important than wisdom and virtue. However, more often they simply remind themselves that values do not exist in nature and that when we judge something intrinsically good or bad we're projecting our values on to it, i.e., fusing our own value judgements (cognitions) with our perception of external events. Epictetus reminds his students of this in the famous passage frequently quoted by Ellis and later second-wave CBT practitioners: "It's not things that upset us but our judgements about them" (*Encheiridion*, 5). Epictetus here encourages his students to gain cognitive distance by separating or *defusing* their (value) judgements from the external events to which they refer. Indeed, we're told that fusion "creates the illusion that experiences are what they say they are" (Hayes, Strosahl, & Wilson, 2016, p. 270). Epictetus, by contrast, tells his students that when they're confronted by a troubling impression they should train themselves to say to it: "You are just an impression and not at all what you claim to be" (*Encheiridion*, 1).

The ACT researchers note that "evaluations" (value judgements) are a particularly insidious form of fusion and that it's critical for their approach to help clients distinguish these from objective descriptions (Hayes, Strosahl, & Wilson, 2016, p. 263). They describe it as "one of the worst tricks language plays on us". Clients typically respond to their own value judgements as if they were literal descriptions of fact.

> Our language makes almost no distinction between the primary properties of events themselves and the secondary properties that are injected by the responder. This creates a significant problem. Not only is the client fusing with verbal products, but also the fusion itself confuses primary properties and injected properties.
>
> (Hayes, Strosahl, & Wilson, 2016, p. 264)

To borrow their example, saying "This is a good cup" or "This is a beautiful cup" sounds just like saying "This is a ceramic cup". However, the value judgements don't describe physical properties of the cup, like being ceramic. Rather they express our relationship toward it and the value we choose to assign to it. The language used conceals this evaluative activity, though, and makes it appear as though we're just *passively* perceiving the goodness or beauty of the cup and reporting that as if stating an observable fact. Epictetus likewise tells his students that in every case where they're troubled by love or desire for something they should pause to describe it to themselves objectively, stripped down to its physical properties. The example Epictetus gives, which was cited by Ellis in his writings on REBT, happens also to be a ceramic cup (*Encheiridion*, 3).

Present moment awareness

Awareness of the present moment is linked, in a fundamental sense, to all of the other ACT processes. Acceptance and defusion are only possible in the here and now, and we can only take committed action directly in accord with our values in the here and now. Although ACT researchers originally avoided the term, they concede that the methods they teach for returning attention to the now "can rightly be called *mindfulness* strategies" (Hayes, Strosahl, & Wilson, 2016, 202).

In a sense, we can only live in the present, and so returning our focus to it is a return to philosophical truth. Indeed, ACT practitioners "assume that the past is gone forever and the future is not here yet" (Hayes, Strosahl, & Wilson, 2016, p. 201). This could almost have been a quote from the Stoics. The same concept is emphasized frequently throughout *The Meditations* of Marcus Aurelius. For example:

> For the present is equal for all, and what is passing must be equal also, so what can be lost is shown to be nothing more than a moment; and no one could lose either the past or the future, for how could he be deprived of what he does not possess?
>
> (*Meditations*, 2.14)

Stoicism therefore teaches us to centre our attention in the present moment and place most importance upon our own voluntary actions here and now. Marcus says that even in relation to its own activities, the mind "is concerned only with the present; for its future and past activities are themselves indifferent at that moment" (*Meditations*, 6.32). He therefore advises himself that the sense of fulfilment he hopes to attain by roundabout means in life could be secured here and now if only he would "leave all the past behind" and "entrust the future to providence", concerning himself with the present alone and aligning his actions with virtue (*Meditations*, 12.1).

Letting go of the past and future in this sense has proven therapeutic value. Clients ruminate about the past and worry about the future because, in most cases, they believe that in some sense it will be helpful for them to do so. However, the opposite is true. Higher levels of rumination and worry are actually predictive of *poorer* psychological adjustment. It feels like dwelling on distant events should help us but beyond a certain level it often just makes things worse.

There are many other reasons why clients potentially benefit from paying more attention to the present moment.

> Therapists might also begin with the oft-quoted advice to "Stop and smell the roses", which is both widely known and widely ignored.
>
> (Hayes, Strosahl, & Wilson, 2016, p. 205)

This is ancient advice, as we've seen, familiar from Robert Herrick's line "Gather ye rosebuds while ye may", which is derived in turn from the Latin poem *De rosis nascentibus*. Many people are familiar with the Latin phrase *carpe diem* ("seize the day"), from the poet Horace, who had studied both Stoicism and Epicureanism.

There are many techniques used in third-wave CBT to help clients gain more attunement to the present. For instance, ACT sometimes recommends *slowing down* as a way of returning to the now.

> Changing pace, particularly slowing down, can break up old patterns and allow their functions to be seen. . . . Fused and avoidant behavior can seem like running, in a figurative sense.
>
> (Hayes, Strosahl, & Wilson, 2016, p. 209)

The Stoic Chrysippus used the same metaphor: describing the unhealthy passions as like someone running too quickly to stop or change direction. When we slow things down, our patterns of emotional thinking and behaviour often come apart and become more amenable to voluntary control. Epictetus therefore advised his students to pause and wait when they noticed an unhealthy passion arising in order to avoid rushing to judgement and being swept along with their feelings.

However, many ACT exercises train clients "to contact psychological content and simply to describe it without adding or subtracting anything" (Hayes, Strosahl, & Wilson, 2016, p. 216). Currently experienced thoughts and emotions, etc.

are simply noticed and named, or briefly described, without adding any value judgements. This also restores attention to the present moment. This obviously resembles the Stoic technique of *phantasia kataleptike* or "Objective Representation", which consists in describing objects as clearly as possible, in a detached and matter-of-fact way, without strong value judgements. This exercise both defuses our value judgements from external events and returns our awareness to the solid ground of our sensory experience in the here and now.

Connecting with values

ACT is essentially a behaviour therapy, based on a modern form of behavioural psychology. It addresses thoughts and feelings through processes like verbal defusion and acceptance. However, its main priority is really behaviour change. The purpose of behaviour change is more values-oriented in ACT, though. Whereas older forms of behaviour therapy might, for example, prescribe certain behaviours in order to help alleviate anxiety, ACT encourages the client to behave in new ways that accord with their authentic values in life. To do this the client has to both have a clear understanding of their values and commit to acting in ways aligned with them. Strategies such as defusion and acceptance can then help them to get past psychological barriers to valued action, such as anxiety or poor self-esteem. Values are generally a more reliable guide to action than feelings, which can be unpredictable and may often lead us into avoidance. Following our values tends to lead to a more *consistent* and fulfilling pattern of life.

To understand the role of valued action in ACT it's essential to grasp the technical sense in which the word "value" is being used. ACT practitioners teach their clients to make a sharp distinction between values and goals. Values are qualities of our actions, such as being generous or creative, which we can instantiate in an ongoing way but never completely. Goals, by contrast, are consequences, which may or may not be achieved at a specific date and time. ACT suggests that problems are caused when we become overly goal-oriented at the expense of our authentic values. This is partly because goals are posited in the future so that we don't experience satisfaction from achieving them immediately and when we do it's often inherently fleeting. By contrast, as soon as I make a first step or even have the intention to act in accord with a value, such as friendship, I potentially experience a sense of accomplishment in the present moment, which can continue indefinitely as long as I maintain my commitment.

> In ACT, values are freely chosen, verbally constructed consequences of ongoing, dynamic, evolving patterns of activity, which establish predominant reinforcers for that activity that are intrinsic in engagement in the valued behavioral pattern itself.
>
> (Hayes, Strosahl, & Wilson, 2016, p. 297)

The key phrase is "intrinsic in engagement", i.e., when we value a way of acting in this sense we experience it as its own reward. Most external goals, by contrast, are only valued as means of achieving something else. Health, wealth, and reputation are valued by many people, because they assume they'll lead to happiness or fulfilment of some kind – something which may or may not be true in practise. Clients often forget, however, that such goals are merely of value as means to an end and confuse them with ends in themselves.

> Some "values" are really means to an end, in which case they are not values at all. One way to think of values is as means values versus ends values.
>
> (Hayes, Strosahl, & Wilson, 2016, p. 323)

For example, many people fall into the trap of pursuing wealth as if it were an end in itself when in fact, on reflection, they may find that they only really came to value wealth as a means to securing other things in life such as the ability to care for their loved ones.

For Socrates and those schools of philosophy influenced by him, *virtue is its own reward*. ACT's technical definition of "value" is therefore obviously very similar to the concept of "virtue" in the ancient Socratic tradition, particularly in Stoicism. It's true that ACT values are meant to be "freely chosen" but the virtues in Stoicism are also freely chosen, in a different sense. The Stoics assume that any rational being who reflects on their values philosophically should arrive at the same basic conclusions about the nature of virtue, or what's intrinsically valuable in human life. Primarily, they should conclude that moral wisdom is intrinsically valuable. That's partly because this particular form of practical wisdom, by definition, allows us to assign value appropriately to everything else in life so neglecting it would potentially be self-defeating. However, individuals also tend to agree on other broad values such as courage, self-discipline, fairness, and kindness. This is supported by modern empirical research on values, which tends to show a surprising consistency in the abstract values held by individuals across different cultures, although there are marked differences in the way they're applied to specific situations.

ACT employs a variety of strategies to help clients clarify their own values. These can typically be expressed as questions, one of the most common being "What do you want your life to stand for?" (Hayes, Strosahl, & Wilson, 2016, p. 304). Mental imagery exercises such as picturing their own funeral and what they'd like people to say about them in eulogies can help clients answer the related question: "What would you like to be remembered for by your friends?" This perspective, which asks us to directly consider what makes our lives worthwhile, is common in Stoicism. The Stoics also ask us to reflect upon the qualities we most admire in *other* people and to consider how our lives would be changed if we exemplified those virtues more ourselves. For instance, in the first chapter of *The Meditations* of Marcus Aurelius he reviews in detail the qualities he most admires in his friends and teachers. Marcus makes it clear that he's doing this, in part, because he wants to learn to emulate them and embody similar values in his own life.

ACT also encourages clients to think about values in relation to different domains of life, e.g., what traits they'd like to exhibit as a spouse, or parent, or employee, etc. Epictetus and other Stoics likewise referred to our fulfilment of different roles in life as a way of clarifying the virtues.

> Remember that you are an actor in a drama, which is as the playwright wishes; if the playwright wishes it short, it will be short; if long, then long. . . . For this is what is yours: to finely play the role that is given; but to select [that role] itself is another's.
>
> (*Encheiridion* 17)

If you're a parent, consider what it means to you to be a good parent; if you're a soldier, what it means to be a good soldier; if an athlete, what it means to excel in that role, and so on.

Values clarification work usually exposes a wide discrepancy between the client's values and their existing patterns of behaviour. That inevitably leads into the next process, which involves making and maintaining a commitment to act in accord with one's authentic values in daily life. As Marcus Aurelius famously wrote: "Waste no more time arguing about what a good man is and just be one" (*Meditations*, 10.16).

Committed action

Having clarified their true values, the next step for most clients is to make the commitment to living more in accord with them, although there's often a reciprocal relationship between these two processes. By clarifying our values we're more able to live in agreement with them but by trying to live in accord with them, we can also become clearer about their meaning. The ACT concept of "commitment" emphasizes the intention to act in a certain way, while recognizing that our intent is sometimes thwarted or falters over time. Success in exemplifying a value might be judged over a period of time, in one respect, but our *commitment* to doing so occurs instantly, in the present moment, as soon as we take the very first step in the right direction.

> Thus, in ACT, committed action is a values-based action that occurs at a particular moment in time and that is deliberately linked to creating a pattern of action that serves the value.
>
> (Hayes, Strosahl, & Wilson, 2016, p. 328)

This could be observable behaviour or entirely private, mental activity. What matters is that actions, of whatever kind, are being taken in the service of some authentic personal value.

As noted earlier, the majority of clients tend to orient their actions more around external goals, or outcomes, than intrinsic values. ACT suggests that this implies a sense of deprivation because having future goals entails the assumption that the present is incomplete and satisfaction is at some distance from now in time. Too much of this way of thinking can negatively affect our mood, causing anxiety about the possibility of failing to achieve goals in the future or depression based on the sense of loss that comes from having already failed to achieve them. By contrast, when we orient our actions around intrinsic values – such as being a loving parent – we're prizing something that's already capable of being experienced right here in the present moment and which is entirely up to us as long as we're genuinely willing to commit ourselves to it.

ACT recognizes that external goals are necessary, although they're generally healthier when subordinated to our values rather than being viewed as ends in themselves. For instance, I might seek to acquire a certain amount of wealth insofar as it helps me to behave as a loving parent by providing for my children. Nevertheless, being prevented from achieving the goal of acquiring money – something not entirely under my control – wouldn't actually stop me from being a loving parent, I'd just need to express that value in another way. Stoics, likewise, as we've seen, pursue external goals with the "reserve clause", an implicit caveat that says, "I will do such-and-such, fate permitting". That mindset helps them to maintain their commitment to the intention, while adapting flexibly to external setbacks.

Dimensions of self

ACT is particularly influenced by various spiritual and philosophical traditions in proposing that our ability to take different perspectives on our experience has the capacity to help free us from entanglement with toxic beliefs, rules, and patterns of behaviour (Hayes, Strosahl, & Wilson, 2016, p. 220). The pure awareness of ourselves as observers of our own experience provides a way of rising above identification with our everyday ego and self-image.

> That sanctuary is the simple experience of being aware that we are the ones who contain and look at our private experience.
>
> (*ibid.*)

One of the exercises ACT uses to teach this perspective to clients is called the "Expanding Balloon" metaphor:

> Think of yourself as an expanding balloon. At the edge of the balloon is a zone of growth where the same question keeps being asked: "Are you big enough to have this?" No matter how big you get, you can always get bigger.
>
> (Hayes, Strosahl, & Wilson, 2016, p. 289).

The client is thereby helped to experience a "larger notion of self", which tends to make unpleasant experiences feel less overwhelming. However, whereas this is an exercise in behaviour therapy, certain ancient traditions teach it as a philosophical truth. The Stoics, for instance, emphasize that the individual must learn to expand his self by viewing it as part of a greater whole, which consists of cosmic Nature in its entirety. Wisdom entails viewing events, insofar as possible, as belonging within the context of the whole of time and space. Taking events in isolation from the whole is a lie of omission.

> ACT therapists take the view that vitality, purpose, and meaning occur when the person voluntarily and repeatedly engages in a kind of conceptual suicide, in which the boundaries of the conceptualized self are softened and there is a more open approach to experiences that are but echoes of one's history. The ACT phrase for this is "kill yourself every day".
>
> (Hayes, Strosahl, & Wilson, 2016, p. 221)

This could also have been a quote from the Stoics, who believed that in a sense we are all already dying every day. Recognizing the transience of life helps us to remain grounded in the present. For example:

> Consider individuals, survey men in general; there is none whose life does not look forward to the morrow. "What harm is there in this", you ask? Infinite harm; for such persons do not live, but are preparing to live. They postpone everything. Even if we paid strict attention, life would soon get ahead of us; but as we are now, life finds us lingering and passes us by as if it belonged to another, and though it ends on the final day, it perishes every day.
>
> (Seneca, *Letters*, 45)

Marcus Aurelius likewise tells himself to remember that nothing in the composition of his body or soul dates to the beginning of his life. We are constantly dying and transforming into something new and this body is not the one to which his mother gave birth (*Meditations*, 10.7).

Although ACT often encourages clients to experience things from the "I-here-now" point of view, many exercises involve cultivating flexibility by exploring other perspectives.

> For example, clients may be asked to go to a "wiser" future and look back at themselves now, perhaps even writing a letter to oneself about how to engage with the current situation in a healthy way. The client might be asked to put him- or herself into an empty chair and talk to him- or herself from the perspective of another. Upon hearing a new bit of clinical material, the client might be asked what he or she supposes you, the therapist, might be thinking.
>
> (Hayes, Strosahl, & Wilson, 2016, p. 224)

As we've seen, Stoicism encourages perspective shifting by posing the question of what the ideal sage would say or do in response to the situations faced by the student, or simply asking, "What would Socrates or Zeno do?" Marcus Aurelius makes it clear that Stoics practised imaginatively entering into the minds of others and exploring their perspectives on events.

However, the Stoics also got in touch with a "larger sense of self", as ACT puts it, by attempting to imagine their minds expanding to encompass the View from Above, or even the whole of time and space as if seen from the perspective of Zeus or universal Nature. The literature of Stoicism is replete with references to shifting perspective, usually by broadening awareness of time and/or space, or by trying to adopt the perspective of an ideal sage, or the whole of Nature. The ACT researchers refer to these sorts of strategies as "perspective-taking skills of looking across time, place, and person " (Hayes, Strosahl, & Wilson, 2016, p. 230).

The self in ACT is typically construed as the *context* of our experience, pure consciousness, as opposed to being identified with the individual contents of our conscious experience. For Stoics, the self is part of a greater whole and we are led into error by viewing ourselves in isolation, alienated from the rest of mankind or cosmic Nature. The sense of self is therefore expanded by Stoics in this way, by relocating our lives within the wider context of space and time in their totality.

Viewing the self in broader and more flexible terms is linked to the development of compassion for others by the ACT researchers.

> Just as often, self-work naturally stimulates values and action work. It is no accident that many spiritual and religious traditions hold that a stance of awareness naturally leads to a state of compassion for self and others and a profound appreciation of the interconnectedness of all things. This observation may be true because attachment to the conceptualized self draws the person out of contact with the surrounding world. Humans are naturally social creatures, but the direction that a person's social vision takes is heavily influenced by social conditioning and cultural practices.
>
> (Hayes, Strosahl, & Wilson, 2016, p. 238).

This also sounds very reminiscent of the Stoics whose philosophy was based on the assumption that humans are by nature both essentially reasoning (conscious and language-using) and *social*. Marcus Aurelius, in particular, stresses the view throughout *The Meditations* that connecting our actions and sense of self with cosmic Nature entails developing a greater sense of kinship toward other people.

The ACT experts have noted the "poor fit between the language of mindfulness and the experiences and biases of many clients", who may be "skeptical or even hostile to anything that smacks of Eastern spirituality or New Age ideas" (Hayes, Strosahl, & Wilson, 2016, p. 218). They consider it safer in many cases to replace "mindfulness" with more neutral terms such as "attention training" so that clients do not "think they are being encouraged to be Buddhists" (*ibid.*).

Sometimes links must be made instead with other spiritual or philosophical traditions, such as Christianity. However, they could also potentially address this problem by framing ACT concepts and techniques in relation to the literature of *Western* rather than Eastern philosophy, as I hope the discussions throughout this book have amply shown.

Conclusion

Fate guides the willing

Lead me, Zeus, and thou, O Destiny, Lead me wherever your laws assign me.
I follow fearless, for even if I should become reluctant, Wretched though I may be, I shall follow still. . . .
Fate guides the willing, but drags the unwilling with it.
— (The Hymn to Zeus, Cleanthes of Assos, quoted in *Encheiridion*, 53, modified)

I hope to have shown that the origins of psychotherapy and self-help, especially of a cognitive orientation, can quite reasonably be traced to classical philosophical schools such as Stoicism. I think the reader will also perceive that the philosophical tradition contains a number of concepts, strategies, and techniques that might expand the clinical armamentarium of modern psychotherapy, providing new means of facilitating cognitive, behavioural, and emotional improvement in today's clients.

As discussed in the introduction to this book, the Socratic tradition may also offer a broader and, unsurprisingly, more *philosophical* perspective on therapeutic practise, unconstrained by modern presuppositions about the nature of psychotherapy as a profession. Considering the bigger picture, the place of modern cognitive therapy within a philosophical tradition stretching back roughly 2,500 years allows us to see modern therapeutic concepts, strategies, and techniques as part of a philosophical "art of living", rather than merely the tools of a trade. Looking at the bigger picture in this way is itself a strategy familiar from Stoic texts, and it can quite reasonably be applied not merely to a person's life but also to the subject of modern psychotherapy itself. It prompts the question: "What is a therapist?", meaning, "What role should a therapist adopt toward life in general?" I believe that the Stoic literature provides a wonderful example of a whole system of philosophy whose attempts to express such large questions might provide a foundation for future enquiry in this area.

The enormous literary and philosophical value of classical texts, such as the works of Seneca, Epictetus, and Marcus Aurelius, add another dimension to the study of psychotherapy for those drawn to the beauty of thought and expression in ancient literature. These works have survived many centuries, and certain individuals in one generation after another have been drawn to them for both consolation and inspiration. The life stories of these philosophers, too, are often remarkable. Seneca? Epictetus? Marcus Aurelius? Our knowledge of their character and circumstances, and the times in which they lived, undoubtedly adds something to our appreciation of their wisdom when it comes to coping with adversity in all its hues. These Stoics were philosophical *heroes*, veritable warriors of the *psyche*, who knew bereavement, torture, exile, infirmity, warfare, political intrigue, and betrayal. Vice admiral James Stockdale, the Vietnam veteran, is perhaps our closest modern equivalent. He described the ancient world of Epictetus as a dangerous "buzzsaw" of adversity and misfortune, and he found himself against a similar metaphorical buzzsaw in the dungeons of the Hanoi Hilton prison, where he almost gave his life to avoid betraying the incarcerated soldiers under his command.

I hope to have been able to provide a little more scaffolding within which others may erect a more comprehensive and refined account of modern psychotherapy within the Socratic tradition, inspired by Stoicism and other ancient therapeutic approaches. My grasp of ancient languages is limited but where necessary I have modified the existing translations, or produced hybrids of them, which seemed to me to better convey their meaning to modern readers, especially psychotherapists. Where possible, I have tried to check my translations with others more adept in these matters. Undoubtedly, one of the greatest obstacles to the reception of ancient texts among modern professionals engaged in similar work is the language used in common translations, which are often quite dated and anachronistic. I would like to think that one day translations could be made of key texts, such as the *Encheiridion*, using the same terminology of modern psychotherapy, where appropriate. Perhaps most crucially, I would suggest that the term "emotional disturbance" better and more accurately conveys the meaning to modern practitioners of psychotherapy than the conventional translation as "passion". The false notion of the Stoic as a "cold fish", someone "intellectualizing" or "rationalizing" things defensively, at the expense of feeling, has done more to deter modern readers than any other misconception, and even resulted in Ellis expressing somewhat unfounded, mixed feelings toward the Stoics. This could be redressed, perhaps, by emphasizing the opposite view and formulating an explicit account of Stoicism, as previously discussed, which centres upon its theory of the ideal sage as being animated by a philosophical *love* of virtue – free from passion, in the sense of emotional disturbance, but nevertheless full of love, as Marcus Aurelius put it. The analogy with Spinoza's "intellectual love of God" or Nature, might perhaps act as a guide in this respect. Spinoza himself presents a system of philosophical therapeutics so similar to Stoicism that it is tempting to see him as their early modern heir in this respect.

To further assist the reader, I have provided the script of an exercise called the "View from Above" which can easily be read to groups of students, and which I hope provides some taste of the kind of mental exercise of which Socrates or

Epictetus might have approved. I have used this script with several thousand people over the years, on courses and workshops, and have consistently found that they enjoyed the experience and found it gave them a more serene perspective on troubling life events. Some people find these exercises so appealing that they repeat them on a daily basis. Indeed, I have also attempted to provide a schematic reconstruction of the daily regime or routine of a Stoic philosopher, to try to help modern readers better envisage their use of the various exercises discussed. This cannot be a perfect reconstruction, but support for it can be found in the preceding chapters, and I hope that it will make the overall "art of living" clearer, as well as highlighting the kind of self-discipline apparently required to follow the Stoic path.

In relation to modern "evidence-based" practise in psychotherapy, we are clearly discussing a subject that has no real basis in the research literature. As far as I am aware, nobody has conducted research suitable to establish the therapeutic efficacy of Stoicism. We can obviously draw some indirect support for certain Stoic ideas from the literature supporting related techniques in the field of modern CBT. However, this can only be speculation, and principles and techniques derived from Stoicism need to be tested directly before we can be confident that they are effective for a modern client, and certainly before we can assume that they are equal or superior to modern methods of psychotherapy and self-help. However, strange as it may sound, I do believe that certain aspects of Stoic psychotherapy are testable by empirical means and, for example, one day it may be possible to confirm the extent to which regular use of meditation techniques such as the View from Above, conceptualized in Stoic terms, might reduce anxiety or contribute to well-being in some other, measurable, regard.

The holy grail of mental health is prevention – everyone knows that *prevention is better than cure*. My belief is that whereas CBT is mainly a short-term remedial approach Stoicism especially holds promise as a long-term preventative, or resilience-building, approach, based on similar concepts and practises.

In conclusion, I hope that this work can be extended to form the basis of a more coherent appraisal and assimilation of classical philosophy within the field of modern psychotherapy. I have found the literature of classical philosophy to be of tremendous personal value and have also drawn inspiration from it in teaching, supervision, and clinical psychotherapy. I am certain that others will benefit from it in similar ways, and if this book inspires them to read Seneca, Epictetus, Marcus Aurelius, or other ancient philosophers, then I will be satisfied that it has achieved something indisputably worthwhile from a philosophical perspective and hopeful that therapeutic benefit or well-being may be achieved by those bold enough to experiment systematically with the Stoic methods, as many others seem to have found over the centuries.

References

Anon (1988). The golden verses of Pythagoras. In: K. S. Guthrie (Ed.), *The Pythagorean Sourcebook and Library*. Grand Rapids, MI: Phanes.

Araoz, D. (1981). Negative self-hypnosis. *Journal of Contemporary Psychotherapy, 12*(1): 45–52.

Aurelius, Marcus (2003). *Meditations: Living, Dying and the Good Life* (G. Hays, Trans.). London: Phoenix.

Azrin, N. H., & Nunn, R. G. (1977). *Habit Control in a Day*. New York: Simon & Schuster.

Baudouin, C. (1920). *Suggestion and Autosuggestion* (E. Paul & C. Paul, Trans.). London: George Allen & Unwin.

Baudouin, C., & Lestchinsky, A. (1924). *The Inner Discipline*. London: George Allen & Unwin.

Beck, A. T. (1976). *Cognitive Therapy and the Emotional Disorders*. New York: International Universities Press.

Beck, A. T., & Alford, B. A. (2009). *Depression: Causes and Treatment* (2nd ed.). Philadelphia, PA: University of Philadelphia Press.

Beck, A. T., Emery, G., & Greenberg, R. (2005). *Anxiety Disorders and Phobias: A Cognitive Perspective* (20th Anniversary ed.). Cambridge, MA: Basic Books.

Beck, A. T., Rush, A. J., Shaw, B. F., & Emery, G. (1979). *Cognitive Therapy of Depression*. New York: Guilford Press.

Beck, J. S. (1995). *Cognitive Therapy: Basics & Beyond*. New York: Guilford Press.

Becker, L. C. (2004). Stoic emotion. In: S. Strange & J. Zupko (Eds.), *Stoicism: Traditions and Transformations*. Cambridge: Cambridge University Press.

Bernheim, H. (1887). *Suggestive Therapeutics: A Treatise on the Nature and Uses of Hypnotism (De la Suggestion et de son Application à la Thérapeutique)* (2nd ed., C. A. Herter, Trans., 1889). New York: G.P. Putnam's Sons.

Braid, J. (2009). *The Discovery of Hypnosis: The Complete Writings of James Braid, the Father of Hypnotherapy* (D. Robertson, Ed.). Studley: The National Council for Hypnotherapy (NCH).

Brookshire, S. A. (2007). Utilizing Stoic philosophy to improve cognitive behavioral therapy. *NC Perspectives, 1*(1): 30–36.

Brown, D. (2016). *Happy: Why More or Less Everything Is Absolutely Fine*. London: Corgi Books.

Burkeman, O. (2013). *The Antidote: Happiness for People Who Can't Stand Positive Thinking*. Edinburgh: Canongate.

Carroll, R. P., & Prickett, S. (Eds.). (1998). *The Bible: Authorized King James' Version. New Testament.* Oxford: Oxford University Press.

Chakrapani, C. (2016). *Unshakable Freedom: Ancient Stoic Secrets Applied to Modern Life.* Toronto: The Stoic Gym.

Cicero (2009). *Treatises on Friendship and Old Age* (E. S. Shuckburgh, Trans.). Dodo Press.

Coué, É. (1923). *My Method.* New York: New York World.

Covey, S. R. (1989). *The Seven Habits of Highly Successful People.* New York: Free Press.

Curwen, B., Palmer, S., & Ruddell, P. (2000). *Brief Cognitive Behaviour Therapy.* London: Sage.

DeBrabander, F. (2004). Psychotherapy and moral perfection: Spinoza and the Stoics on the prospect of happiness. In: S. K. Strange & J. Zupko (Eds.), *Stoicism: Traditions & Transformations* (pp. 198–213). Cambridge: Cambridge University Press.

Descartes, R. (1998). *Discourse on Method and Meditations on First Philosophy* (4th ed., D. A. Cress, Trans.). Indianapolis, IN: Hackett.

Dobson, K. S., & Dozois, D. J. (2001). Historical and philosophical bases of the cognitive-behavioral tradition. In: K. S. Dobson (Ed.), *Handbook of Cognitive-Behavioral Therapies* (2nd ed., pp. 3–39). New York: Guilford Press.

Dryden, W., & Ellis, A. (2001). Rational emotive behaviour therapy. In: K. Dobson (Ed.), *Handbook of Cognitive-Behavioral Therapies* (pp. 295–348). New York: Guilford Press.

Dubois, P. (1904). *The Psychic Treatment of Nervous Disorders: The Psychoneuroses & Their Moral Treatment.* New York: Funk and Wagnall.

Dubois, P. (1909). *Self-Control and How to Secure It* (H. H. Boyd, Trans.). New York: Funk and Wagnalls.

Dubois, P., & Gallatin, L. (1908). *The Influence of the Mind on the Body.* New York: Funk and Wagnalls.

Ellenberger, H. F. (1970). *The Discovery of the Unconscious: The History and Evolution of Dynamic Psychiatry.* New York: Basic Books.

Ellis, A. (1962). *Reason and Emotion in Psychotherapy: A Comprehensive Method of Treating Human Disturbance.* Secaucus, NJ: Citadel.

Ellis, A. (2004). *The Road to Tolerance: The Philosophy of Rational Emotive Behavior Therapy.* New York: Prometheus Books.

Ellis, A., & Harper, R. A. (1997). *A Guide to Rational Living* (3rd Revised ed.). Chatsworth, CA: Wilshire.

Ellis, A., & MacLaren, C. (2005). *Rational Emotive Behavior Therapy: A Therapist's Guide* (2nd ed.). Atascadero, CA: Impact.

Epictetus (1995). *The Discourses, the Handbook, Fragments* (R. Hard, Trans.). London: Everyman.

Eysenck, H. J. (1977). *You and Neurosis.* London: Temple Smith.

Eysenck, H. J. (1990). *Rebel with a Cause: The Autobiography of Hans J. Eysenck.* London: W. H. Allen.

Farnsworth, W. (2018). *The Practicing Stoic: A Philosophical User's Manual.* Jaffrey, NH: David R. Godine.

Ferriss, T. (2017). *The Tao of Seneca*, vols. 1–3. https://tim.blog/2017/07/06/tao-of-seneca/.

Foucault, M. (1986). *The History of Sexuality Volume 3: The Care of the Self* (R. Hurley, Trans.). London: Penguin.

Foucault, M. (1988). Technologies of the self. In: L. H. Martin, H. Gutman, & P. H. Martin (Eds.), *Technologies of the Self: A Seminar with Michel Foucault* (pp. 16–49). Amherst, MA: University of Massachusetts Press.

Frankl, V. E. (1959). *Man's Search for Meaning*. Boston, MA: Beacon.

Gibbon, E. (1909). *The Decline and Fall of the Roman Empire* (Vol. I). London: Methuen.

Guthrie, K. S. (1988). *The Pythagorean Sourcebook and Library*. Grand Rapids, MI: Phanes.

Hadot, P. (1995). *Philosophy as a Way of Life* (A. I. Davidson, Ed., M. Chase, Trans.). Malden, MA: Blackwell.

Hadot, P. (1998). *The Inner Citadel: The Meditations of Marcus Aurelius* (M. Chase, Trans.). Cambridge, MA: Harvard University Press.

Hadot, P. (2002). *What Is Ancient Philosophy?* (M. Chase, Trans.). Cambridge, MA: Harvard University Press.

Hayes, S. C., Strosahl, K. D., & Wilson, K. G. (2016). *Acceptance and Commitment Therapy: The Process and Practice of Mindful Change* (2nd ed.). New York: Guilford Press.

Herbert, J. D. (2004). Connections between ancient philosophies and modern psychotherapies: Correlation doesn't necessarily prove causation. *The Behavior Therapist, 27*(3): 53–54.

Holiday, R. (2014). *The Obstacle Is the Way: Turning Adversity into Advantage*. New York: Penguin.

Holiday, R., & Hanselman, S. (2016). *The Daily Stoic: 366 Meditations on Wisdom, Perseverance, and the Art of Living: Featuring New Translations of Seneca, Epictetus, and Marcus Aurelius*. New York: Penguin.

Horace (1964). *The Odes of Horace* (J. Michie, Trans.). Harmondsworth: Penguin.

Iamblichus (1988). The life of Pythagoras. In: K. S. Guthrie (Ed.), *The Pythagorean Sourcebook and Library* (pp. 57–122). Grand Rapids, MI: Phanes.

Inwood, B. (2018). *Stoicism: A Very Short Introduction*. Oxford: Oxford University Press.

Irvine, W. (2009). *A Guide to the Good Life: The Ancient Art of Stoic Joy*. Oxford: Oxford University Press.

Kabat-Zinn, J. (1990). *Full Catastrophe Living*. New York: Bantam.

Kant, I. (1996). On the power of the human mind to master its morbid feelings merely by a firm resolution. In: I. Kant (Ed.), M. J. Gregor & R. Anchor (Trans.), *The Cambridge Edition of the Works of Immanuel Kant: Religion and Rational Theology* (pp. 314–326). Cambridge: Cambridge University Press.

Kipling, R. (1994). *The Collected Poems of Rudyard Kipling*. Ware: Wordsworth.

Korzybski, A. (1958). *Science and Sanity*. Lakeville, CO: International Non-Aristotelian Publishing.

Laertius, D. (1853). *The Lives and Opinions of Eminent Philosophers* (C. Yonge, Trans.). London: Henry G. Bohn.

Lazarus, A. A. (1971). *Behavior Therapy & Beyond*. Englewood Cliffs, NJ: Jason Aronson.

Lazarus, A. A. (1981). *The Practice of Multimodal Therapy*. Chicago, IL: Johns Hopkins University Press.

Lipsius, J. (2006). *On Constancy* (J. Sellars, Ed., S. J. Stradling, Trans.). Exeter: Bristol Phoenix Press.

Long, A. (2002). *Epictetus: A Stoic and Socratic Guide to Life*. Oxford: Oxford University Press.

Lucretius (1951). *The Nature of the Universe* (R. Latham, Trans.). Harmondsworth: Penguin.

Marinoff, L. (2002). *Philosophical Practice*. San Diego, CA: Academic Press.

McGlinchey, J. B. (2004). On Hellenistic philosophy and its relevance to contemporary CBT: A response to Reiss (2003). *The Behavior Therapist*, *27*(3): 51–52.

Meichenbaum, D. (1977). *Cognitive-Behavior Modification: An Integrative Approach*. New York: Plenum Press.

Montgomery, R. W. (1993). The ancient origins of cognitive therapy: The reemergence of Stoicism. *Journal of Cognitive Psychotherapy*, *7*(1): 5–19.

Nietzsche, F. (1996). *Human All too Human* (R. Hollingdale, Trans.). Cambridge: Cambridge University Press.

Peck, M. S. (1978). *The Road Less Traveled*. New York: Simon & Schuster.

Pietsch, W. V. (1990). *The Serenity Prayer Book*. New York: HarperCollins.

Pigliucci, M. (2018). *How to Be a Stoic: Using Ancient Philosophy to Live a Modern Life*. New York: Basic Books.

Plato (1997). *Complete Works* (J. M. Cooper, Ed.). Indianapolis, IN: Hackett.

Plutarch (1992). *Essays* (R. Waterfield, Trans.). London: Penguin.

Porphyry (1988). The life of Pythagoras. In: K. S. Guthrie (Ed.), *The Pythagorean Sourcebook and Library* (pp. 123–135). Grand Rapids, MI: Phanes.

Raimy, V. (1975). *Misunderstandings of the Self: Cognitive Psychotherapy and the Misconception Hypothesis*. San Francisco, CA: Jossey-Bass.

Reiss, S. (2003). Epicurus: The first rational emotive therapist. *The Behavior Therapist*, *26*(8): 405–406.

Robertson, D. (2005). Stoicism: A lurking presence. *Counselling & Psychotherapy Journal*, *16*(6): 35–40.

Robertson, D. (2009). James Braid's life and work. In: D. Robertson (Ed.), *The Discovery of Hypnosis: The Complete Writings of James Braid* (pp. 6–16). Studley: NCH.

Robertson, D. (2012). *Build Your Resilience*. London: Hodder.

Robertson, D. (2018). *Stoicism and the Art of Happiness* (2nd ed.). London: Hodder.

Robertson, D. (2019). *How to Think Like a Roman Emperor: The Stoic Philosophy of Marcus Aurelius*. New York: St Martin's.

Russell, B. (1930). *The Conquest of Happiness*. London: Routledge.

Ryle, G. (1949). *The Concept of Mind*. Middlesex: Penguin.

Segal, Z., Teasdale, J., & Williams, M. (2002). *Mindfulness-Based Cognitive Therapy for Depression*. New York: Guilford Press.

Sellars, J. (2003). *The Art of Living: The Stoics on the Nature and Function of Philosophy*. Burlington, VT: Ashgate.

Seneca (1917–1925). *Moral Epistles: The Loeb Classical Library* (Vol. 1, R. M. Gummere, Trans.). Cambridge, MA: Harvard University Press.

Seneca (2004). *Letters from a Stoic* (R. Campbell, Trans.). Harmondsworth: Penguin.

Skinner, B. (1971). *Beyond Freedom and Dignity*. Cambridge, MA: Hackett.

Sorabji, R. (2004). Stoic first movements in Christianity. In: S. K. Strange & J. Zupko (Eds.), *Stoicism: Traditions & Transformations* (pp. 95–107). Cambridge: Cambridge University Press.

Spinoza, B. de (1955). *Works of Spinoza: Vol. II* (R. Elwes, Trans.). New York: Dover.

Still, A., & Dryden, W. (1999). The place of rationality in Stoicism and REBT. *Journal of Rational Emotive & Cognitive-Behavior Therapy*, *17*(3): 143–164.

Stockdale, J. (1995). *Thoughts of a Philosophical Fighter Pilot*. Stanford, CA: Hoover Institute Press.

Taleb, N. (2012). *Antifragile: How to Live in a World we Don't Understand*. London: Allen Lane.

Wolpe, J. (1990). *The Practice of Behavior Therapy* (4th ed.). New York: Pergamon.

Wolpe, J., & Lazarus, A. A. (1966). *Behavior Therapy Techniques: A Guide to the Treatment of Neuroses*. Long Island City, NY: Pergamon.

Xenophon (1970). *Memoirs of Socrates and the Symposium* (H. Tredennick, Trans.). Harmondsworth: Penguin.

An example of Stoic therapeutic regime

It is difficult, probably impossible, to do justice to the variety of therapeutic concepts, strategies, and techniques recommended by Stoic philosophers in an outline such as this. Nevertheless, I hope that by attempting to do so in relatively plain English, I will help to clarify their "art of living" somewhat, in a manner that may be of service to modern psychotherapists who wish to make use of classical philosophy in modern life. It probably requires the self-discipline for which Stoics were renowned to follow a regime like this in full, and I imagine that the intention was to begin by attempting one step at a time. I certainly do not propose this as an evidence-based treatment or self-help protocol but, rather, as an attempt to reconstruct the Stoic regime for discussion.

Mornings

1   Take time to calm your mind and gather your thoughts before preparing for the day ahead. Observe (or just imagine) the rising sun and the stars at daybreak, and think of the whole cosmos and your place within it (the View from Above).
2   Mentally rehearse the main events of the day ahead and picture the consequences of being guided by passion (strong, irrational desires or emotions) then contrast this with the consequences of responding wisely, in accord with reason, treating others fairly and with kindness and exercising the virtues of self-discipline and endurance where necessary. (You can think of this as a fork in the road before you, consisting of two opposing paths, like the Choice of Hercules.)

Throughout the day

1   *The Discipline of Desire and Aversion.* Exercise courage and self-discipline ("endure and renounce") by facing your fears and moderating your desires, in accord with wisdom, making decisions that are healthy and prudent in order to live wisely. Remember that only your own actions are up to you and other things are not. Accept circumstances beyond your direct control

without complaint. Contemplate the transience of material things and their place within the whole.

2   *The Discipline of Action.* Exercise the social virtues of justice, fairness, and kindness. Try to dedicate each action to the fundamental goal of developing wisdom and virtue, and to act in the service of humankind by trying to genuinely understand others and treating them as if they were your brothers and sisters. Ask yourself what Socrates, Zeno, or an ideal sage would do if faced with the same situations you encounter and try to emulate them. Apply the "reserve clause" to your actions by accepting that they may not turn out as you would prefer.

3   *The Discipline of Assent.* Exercise wisdom and Stoic mindfulness (*prosoche*) by transferring any strong, emotional value you place on external things onto your faculty of judgement itself. Continually bring your attention back to the use you are making of your mind, your mental activity in the here and now, during any given situation, particularly the value judgements that influence your desires and emotions. Separate your *thoughts* from the real *facts* ("cognitive distancing"). Stick to the facts and avoid using rhetoric to distort your own emotions. Question each impression that enters your mind, especially those that are accompanied by distress, asking yourself whether it is objectively true or not, i.e., an emotive distortion of things. Remember what is under your control and what is not.

Evenings

1   Mentally review the main events of the day three times from beginning to end.
2   Ask yourself what mistakes you made in relation to living wisely, in accord with your core values (the virtues).
3   Ask yourself what virtue, that is, what strength or wisdom you showed, and sincerely praise yourself for what you did well.
4   Ask yourself what you omitted or what could be done better, that is, what you should do instead next time if a similar situation occurs.

CONTINUE TO REPEAT THIS PROCESS EVERY DAY

The "View from Above" script

This is a transcript of an exercise that I have used with thousands of people, individually and in a variety of group settings. I, and my colleagues and students, have been surprised how much people seemed to enjoy and feel a sense of benefit from merely listening to the script. It is loosely modelled on similar processes used in mediation and self-hypnosis. It helps to provide a practical illustration of how a modern audience might be guided through a contemplative exercise based upon the "View from Above" section in this book. This kind of guided imagery contrasts with the use of semantic and cognitive techniques from Stoicism within the context of Socratic disputation in CBT. We have also found it useful to provide people with recordings of this script on CD or MP3.

The script

Take a moment to settle into your posture and make yourself comfortable. . . . Close your eyes and relax . . . [Pause.] Be aware of your breathing . . . Notice the rhythm and pattern of the breath . . .

Do nothing for while, just be contented to contemplate your breathing more deeply . . . [Pause.] Now, begin by paying attention to the whole of your body as one . . . From the top of your head, all the way down into your fingers and down into your toes . . . Be aware of your body as one . . . every nerve, muscle, and fibre . . . Don't try to change anything. Don't try to stop anything from changing . . . Some things can change just by being observed . . .

Just be content to notice whatever you notice, and feel whatever you feel . . . Be a passive, detached observer . . . As you continue to relax, turn your attention deeper within, and become more aware of your body . . . until you can almost imagine how you look right now . . . Begin to picture yourself as if seen from the outside . . .

Now just imagine that you are taking a step back and looking at yourself. It really doesn't matter how vividly you can picture yourself, it is just the intention, just the idea that matters. Imagine your body posture . . . your facial expression . . . the colour and style of your clothing . . .

Now keep looking at the image of yourself resting there, and imagine your own feet are gently leaving the ground. You begin floating serenely upwards, slowly and continuously, rising upwards. All the while your gaze keeps returning to your own body, now seated there below you as you rise above it. Keep looking down toward your body as you float higher and higher . . . The roof and ceiling disappear, allowing you to float freely upward. Gazing down you see yourself seated comfortably below in the building, looking contented and contemplative. You see all the rooms, and any other people around.

As you continue to float gently higher and higher, your perspective widens more and more until you see the whole surrounding area. You see all the buildings nearby from above. You see the people in buildings and in the streets and roads. You observe people far below working, or walking along the pavement, people cycling or driving their cars, and those travelling on buses and trains. You begin to contemplate the whole network of human lives and how people everywhere are interacting with each other, influencing each other, encountering each other in different ways . . .

Floating higher, people become as small as ants below. Rising up into the clouds, you see the whole of the surrounding region beneath you. You see both towns and countryside, and gradually the coastline comes into view as your perspective becomes more and more expansive . . . You float gently up above the clouds, above the weather, and through the upper atmosphere of the planet Earth . . .

So high that you eventually rise beyond the sphere of the planet itself, and into outer space . . . You look toward planet Earth and see it suspended in space before you, silently turning . . . resplendent in all its majesty and beauty . . .

You see the whole of your home planet . . . the blue of the great oceans . . . and the brown and green of the continental land masses . . .

You see the white of the polar ice caps, north and south . . . You see the grey wisps of cloud that pass silently across the surface of the Earth . . . Though you can no longer see yourself from so far above, you know and feel that you are down there on Earth below, and that your life is important, and what you make of your life is important. Your change in perspective changes your view of things, your values and priorities . . .

You contemplate all the countless living beings upon the Earth. The population of the planet is over six billion people . . . You realize that your life is one among many, one person among the total population of the Earth . . . You think of the rich diversity of human life on Earth. The many languages spoken by people of different races, in different countries . . . people of all different ages . . . newborn infants, elderly people, people in the prime of life . . . You think of the enormous variety of human experiences . . . some people right now are unhappy, some people are happy . . . and you realize how richly varied the tapestry of human life before you seems.

And yet. as you gaze upon the planet Earth, you are also aware of its position within the rest of the universe . . . a tiny speck of stardust, adrift in the immeasurable vastness of cosmic space . . . This world of ours is merely a single planet, a tiny grain of sand by comparison with the endless tracts of cosmic space . . . a tiny rock in space, revolving around our Sun . . . the Sun itself just one of countless billions of stars which punctuate the velvet blackness of our galaxy . . .

You think about the present moment on Earth and see it within the broader context of your life as a whole. You think of your lifespan as a whole, in its totality . . . You think of your own life as one moment in the enormous lifespan of mankind . . . Hundreds of generations have lived and died before you . . . many more will live and die in the future, long after you yourself are gone . . . Civilizations, too, have a lifespan; you think of the many great cities which have arisen and been destroyed throughout the ages, . . . and your own civilization as one in a series . . . perhaps in the future to be followed by new cities, peoples, languages, cultures, and ways of life . . .

You think of the lifespan of humanity itself . . . Just one of countless billions of species living upon the planet . . . Mankind arose as a race roughly two hundred thousand years ago . . . animal life itself first appeared on Earth over four *billion* years ago . . . Contemplate time as follows . . . Realize that if the history of life on Earth filled an encyclopaedia a thousand pages long . . . the life of the entire human race could be represented by a single sentence somewhere in that book . . . just one sentence. . .

And yet you think of the lifespan of the planet itself . . . Countless billions of years old . . . the life of the planet Earth too has a beginning, middle, and end . . . Formed from the debris of an exploding star, unimaginably long ago . . . one day in the distant future its destiny is to be swallowed up and consumed by the fires of our own Sun . . . You think of the great lifespan of the universe itself . . . the almost incomprehensible vastness of universal time . . .

Starting with a cosmic explosion, a big bang they say, immeasurable ages ago in the past . . . Perhaps one day, at the end of time, this whole universe will implode upon itself and disappear once again . . . Who can imagine what, if anything, might follow, at the end of time, in the wake of our own universe's demise . . .

Contemplating the vast lifespan of the universe, remember that the present moment is but the briefest of instants . . . the mere blink of an eye . . . the turn of a screw . . . a fleeting second in the mighty river of cosmic time . . . Yet the "here and now" is important . . .

Standing as the centre point of all human experience . . . Here and now you find yourself at the centre of living time . . . Though your body may be small in the grand scheme of things, your imagination, the human imagination, is as big as the universe . . . bigger than the universe . . . enveloping everything that can be conceived . . .

From the cosmic point of view, your body seems small, but your imagination seems utterly vast . . .

You contemplate all things, past, present, and future . . . You see your life within the bigger picture . . . the total context of cosmic time and space . . . The totality is absolute reality . . . You see yourself as an integral part of something much bigger, something truly vast, the "All" itself . . . Just as the cells of your own body work together to form a greater unity, a living being, so your body as a whole is like a single cell in the organism of the universe . . . Along with every atom in the universe you necessarily contribute your role to the unfolding of its grand design . . .

As your consciousness expands, and your mind stretches out to reach and touch the vastness of eternity . . . Things change greatly in perspective . . . and shifts occur in their relative importance . . .

Trivial things *seem* trivial to you . . . Indifferent things *seem* indifferent . . . The significance of your own attitude toward life becomes more apparent . . . you realize that life is what you make of it . . .

You learn to put things in perspective, and focus on your true values and priorities in life . . . One stage at a time, you develop the serenity to accept the things you cannot change, the courage to change the things you can, and the wisdom to know the difference . . .

You follow nature . . . your own true nature as a rational, truth-seeking human being . . . and the one great nature of the universe as a whole . . .

Now in a moment you are beginning to sink back down to Earth, toward your place in the here and now . . . Part of you can remain aware of the View from Above, and always return to and remember that sense of serenity and perspective.

Now you begin your descent back down to Earth, to face the future with renewed strength and serenity . . . You sink back down through the sky . . . down . . . down . . . down . . . toward the local area . . . down . . . down . . . down . . . into this building . . . down . . .

Down . . . down . . . You sink back gently into your body . . . all the way now . . . as your feet slowly come to rest upon the floor once again . . .

Now think about the room around you . . . Think about action . . . movement . . . think about looking around and getting your orientation . . . raising your head a little . . . Begin to breathe a little bit more deeply . . . a little bit more energetically . . . let your body feel more alive and ready for action . . . breathe energy and vitality into your body . . . breathe a little deeper and deeper again . . . until you're ready to take a deep breath, open your eyes, and emerge from meditation . . . taking your mindfulness and self-awareness forward into life . . . beginning now . . . take a deep breath . . . and open your eyes now . . . when you're ready . . . entering the here and now with deep calm and serenity.

Index

religion: Buddhism/ist 18, 42, 54, 101,
    135–136, 139, 219, 221, 225, 233;
    Christianity 47; Islam; Taoism 18
Robertson, D. viii, 3, 7
Ruddell, P. 186
Rufus, M. 57, 79–80
Rush, A. J. 8, 16, 18–19, 61, 72, 128,
    136, 183
Russell, B. 4, 101, 189–190, 213
Rusticus 50, 76
Ryle, G. 195

sage(s): -hypnosis 34, 156, 245;
    -improvement 45; -interest 76–78,
    96, 108, 112, 138, 207, 211–212;
    -knowledge 39; -mastery 48, 64, 90,
    129, 163, 168; -monitoring 30, 139,
    149–151; -preservation 77–78
Scipio Africanus the Younger 47
Segal, Z. 135
self: -analysis 175–178; -aware(ness)
    20, 23, 77, 89, 134–135, 138–139,
    142–143, 148, 248; -blame 42, 204;
    conscious(ness); -control 21, 23, 67, 74,
    89, 106, 132, 148; -discipline 17, 40, 42,
    170–171, 222, 229, 237, 243; -evaluation
    128; -help 1–4, 6, 8, 10, 17, 21, 35,
    37–40, 43, 48, 51, 54–55, 65, 77, 96,
    101, 104, 109, 123–124, 147, 152–153,
    155, 178, 189, 200, 235, 237, 243
Sellars, J. 4, 51, 79, 125, 153, 169,
    172, 212
Seneca 1, 10, 16–18, 29, 31–33, 49–51,
    56, 76, 79, 83–84, 90, 92–93, 98,
    124–125, 127–129, 136–138, 146,
    148, 150, 168, 172, 175, 181, 183, 187,
    190–191, 199, 201, 212, 232, 235–237
Serenity 107: Prayer 20–21, 24, 61, 85,
    202, 221

Sextius 175
Shakespeare, W.: *Hamlet* 17
Shaw, B. F. 8, 16, 18–19, 61, 72, 128,
    136, 184
Skinner, B. 1–2, 67, 82, 159, 162, 198
Socrates 1–2, 4, 17, 29, 33, 44–48,
    52–53, 58–59, 67, 69, 79, 89, 106–108,
    115, 118, 123–132, 134, 138, 143,
    145–149, 158–160, 163–164, 171, 180,
    183, 196, 201, 206, 214, 229, 233, 236
Solon 210
Sorabji, R. 93–94
Spinoza, B. de 4, 18–19, 25, 36, 98,
    187–189, 193, 198, 213, 236
St Ignatius of Loyola 4, 123
Still, A. 7, 17, 72–73, 75, 100, 115
Stockdale, J. 5–7, 29, 34, 50, 60, 74, 113,
    140, 200, 208, 211, 236
Stoic(ism) 1, 4–11, 16–129, 132–133,
    135–237

Teasdale, J. 135

Williams, M. 135
wisdom 1–2, 21–23, 36, 40–41, 51–53,
    55, 58, 60, 62, 64, 66, 69, 79, 81, 86,
    88–90, 98, 106–108, 111–112, 114,
    129, 131–132, 138, 144, 160, 168, 202,
    221–222, 225, 229, 232, 236
Wolpe, J. 2, 24, 184, 186, 203–204, 219

Xanthippe 128, 206
Xenophon 44, 46, 67, 107, 130–131, 158,
    163–165, 170–171

Zeno 16–18, 21, 46–47, 49, 54, 56–57,
    98, 115–116, 124, 126–127, 129, 134,
    202, 233, 244
Zeus 23, 55, 57, 107, 201, 212, 214, 233